Dedication

For Geraldine MacNeill

Mary Rose Liverani

SICILY, A CAPTIVE LAND

AUSTIN MACAULEY
PUBLISHERS LTD.

Copyright © Mary Rose Liverani

The right of Mary Rose Liverani to be identified as author of this work has been asserted by her in accordance with section 77 and 78 of the Copyright, Designs and Patents Act 1988.

All rights reserved. No part of this publication may be reproduced, stored in a retrieval system, or transmitted in any form or by any means, electronic, mechanical, photocopying, recording, or otherwise, without the prior permission of the publishers.

Any person who commits any unauthorized act in relation to this publication may be liable to criminal prosecution and civil claims for damages.

A CIP catalogue record for this title is available from the British Library.

ISBN 978 184963 980 4

www.austinmacauley.com

First Published (2014)
Austin Macauley Publishers Ltd.
25 Canada Square
Canary Wharf
London
E14 5LB

Printed and bound in Great Britain

Acknowledgments

Hundreds of newspaper features and an autobiography are no preparation for writing a book on Sicily. Rather like attempting to prepare a formal banquet when picnic sandwiches have hitherto marked the limits of your culinary experience and organizational skills. I needed a lot of help with this book.

While Sicilians in general talk surprisingly freely, contrary to myth and were happy to direct me to diverse sources of information, the kind that may be disclosed in an empty crypt or on a marine promenade late at night with bodyguards scanning the surrounds, my greatest good fortune was to learn of the fascinating research performed by the English language staff at Catania University into the work of 18th century diplomats and artists, Europeans and British, who had travelled in Sicily and written up reports for their respective governments.

What a treasure trove, opened wide by the ebullient and generous Professor Rosario Portale, whose own publications as well as those of his staff and postgraduate students, both local and from universities in the Anglosphere, must invoke not only my gratitude but that of all Sicilians seeking to understand the idiosyncrasies of their environment.

My very good friend Rita Piana, a Catanese whom I met on an Internet house-swapping service before arriving in Sicily and her husband Grzegorz were treasures of another, vital kind. They welcomed me into their home and introduced me to a quiet community of cultured Sicilians through whom I gained access to a wider range of writers and artists outside the canon. Our friendship has deepened over the years as has my gratitude to Rita and Grezorz.

Writing up the material, however, required a very special kind of assistance, especially at the beginning and the persons who helped me in Sydney so very generously at no gain to themselves, and despite some religious qualms, know their own immense value even if they prefer to remain nameless.

Sydney based Michael Visontay and his wife Aviva Lowy, have both exercised their outstanding journalistic and editorial skills on my behalf and have been great morale boosters.

I very much appreciate the labours and positive response of Professor Rosario Portale, a very busy academic, who read the mss not once but twice through, and corrected its errors in Italian.

However, it is no exaggeration to say that Sicily A Captive land would never have been written without the hard labour and invaluable insights of my friend, mentor and former lecturer in English at the University of New South Wales, Geraldine MacNeill who in the first instance drove me to write The Winter Sparrows, and then never gave up nagging me to write another book, though this one has made far greater demands on her than the autobiography.

Not many editors work on a complex draft while spending thirteen weeks in a hospital bed.
"It keeps me sane," she would assure me, dismissing my pleas to wait until her release.
I can't swear that wrestling with Sicily has kept me sane, but I wouldn't have missed the experience for worlds.

Sicily, the second largest region in Italy

Part I

Introduction

Sicily, A Captive Land is a travelogue based on fifteen months I spent in Sicily encompassing the winter, spring and autumn of 2006 and the autumn/ winter of 2008. Going to Sicily was triggered by the recent death of my beloved husband, Ermete, a Florentine himself, but one who always spoke of the South of Italy and its people with affection. After Ermete died I felt desperate to get way from Australia but, on the advice of friends, held off for a year before resigning my position as senior writer on a Sydney legal journal.

Sicily, I had occasionally imagined, must surely have a lot more to offer than the mafia, a bunch of criminal romantics running around on the loose, and even they themselves might have interests beyond their regular business preoccupations with high volume murder, torture and other pathologies. Now I would be in a position to explore the region in a leisurely manner and perhaps write a few articles on its various archipelagos. Ultimately, however, it became apparent to me that the interest, complexity and importance of what I was finding in Sicily called for a book.

My friends cautioned me against that decision, assuring me a book would be time wasted, 'umpteen books have already been written on the place'. This was news to me. Thousands of books have possibly been written on the Mediterranean and Italy, wherein a short chapter might be allocated to Sicily, but of non-academic books dedicated to the region, there are many fewer, while the most impressive among them like those of Norman Lewis and Gavin Maxwell, though graphic, dramatic and compassionate, shy away from examining the Church's significant contribution to Sicily's wretched condition.

Maxwell's family are from the Scottish aristocracy, devoutly Catholic, their support for the Church reaching back to the Reformation. Lewis married into the Sicilian aristocracy, his brother-in-law reportedly a member of the mafia. Even the famous historian Denis Mack Smith whose impressively researched and illuminating histories of Italy have won him well-deserved plaudits and medals from the Italian government, merely alludes to the Church, abandoning the close scrutiny and analysis normally characteristic of his Italian scholarship.

Some readers may think it odd to focus on politics and history in a travel book, but my experience of reading travelogues is that one can be prepared for anything between their covers. For myself, I hope to learn something about a place even if I might never have an opportunity to visit it. I'm not looking for a plot or a powerful narrative, or thinking of a structure other than what's involved in moving around a chosen terrain and chatting with people who have something significant to say about themselves and their homeland.

I look for entertaining meanders and meaningful maunders, lots of novelty, interesting anecdotes with bizarre details, the scotching of a few stereotypes, further development of issues familiar to me and a clear exposition of new ones I should know about. But I found more than I ever imagined in Sicily.

Few people realise – I had no inkling of this myself – that Sicilians are actually Greek, so deeply rooted in their Greek heritage it's a wonder they don't still think of themselves as Greek, having had Greek thoughts and values embedded in their DNA for 1500 years.

For five hundred years they were part of Magna Graecia, Great Greece, for seven hundred years Greek-speaking members of Rome's first overseas province (upper-class Roman colonists chose to speak in Greek) for another three hundred years Greek again, during the re-Hellenisation of former Roman territories by the Byzantines, and for two more centuries, Greek-speaking beneficiaries of an enlightened Arab administration that allowed them to continue practising the rites of Greek Christendom.

So for seventeen centuries Sicilians spoke and thought as Greeks. On the scales of history seventeen centuries outweigh just over ten. The Church of Rome when it moved in on Sicily was very much the new boy on the block, not entering Palermo till the 11th century, behind the banners of Norman warriors, and intent on indoctrinating Sicilians in Latin Christianity, mass conversions from the Byzantine church promising irresistibly huge economic and political gains.

Since Sicily's absorption into Western Christendom and after a short brilliant renaissance of its own under the Normans, subsequent centuries of relentless oppression by the Church of Rome have almost obliterated the real value of Sicily's Greek heritage – joy in thinking, the passion to explore and understand the cosmos and the will to discover a socio-political system that brings the greatest good to all.

All that is gone. Iron curtains have screened from Sicilian purview the Renaissance, the Reformation, the Enlightenment, the development of the secular state, the Industrial Revolution, the teaching of Physics and Chemistry in schools. Today Sicilians endure a miserable present with little memory of their past, or any hope of a better future.

However, some are becoming more aware of having been shunted into a siding of history. They want their region to get back on track. Their heritage warrants it. And the advance of international human rights law now offers the perfect opportunity to make a case for rethinking the Church's temporal power in their land.

1

I didn't land in Palermo like most other tourists, but in Catania instead, to link up with the Catanese couple who were renting me their holiday cottage on Favignana, one of Sicily's westernmost islands, and who had promised to take me there and see me settled.

Those few days before we left were more significant than I appreciated at the time: I began a wiry friendship with Rita Piana and her Polish husband, Grzegorz Kaczynski, skidded on ice near the top of Mount Etna, legs flaying, and was engulfed by Catania's biggest religious festival of the year.

Rita Piana and I had made contact on the Homelink International website where, for a hefty subscription, I was given an opportunity to induce a Sicilian (or anyone else in the catalogue) to make a year-long house swap with me. Ha! How could I ever have imagined such a thing of an Italian? A year or a week, it made no difference, not one was rushing to relocate in Wollongong – such a long flight, you understand – as if I might not, and impossible without a collective of friends in tow. They're like flocks of budgies, Italians. Just the suggestion of going anywhere alone has them mopping their brows in panic.

I was about to give up on the idea of an exchange when I received my first email from Rita. No nudges and winks. No coded language. None of the allegedly secret Sicilian communings. Straight off she announced she had friends in Australia but no desire whatever to visit there. Instead she wanted to rent out a little holiday house she had not long ago purchased in Favignana.

'I can offer you a good price,' she said. 'Homelink only accepts renters who will do that.'

At the beginning of February, late winter, what would be a 'good price' for a holiday cottage in Favignana? Oddly, I couldn't bring myself to ask the Catania woman. I felt I had to take her offer on trust. And what would I do on a minuscule island unfamiliar even to many Sicilians?

Favignana, barely a dot on the map, dominates the Egadi archipelago. An island offshoot of an island. Shaped like a butterfly, the Greeks had confidently declared. Where had they gotten their bird's eye view of the place? You can't always see everything from the top of a mountain. Finally I wrote to the woman and told her that my husband had died a year past, after a long illness, and that I would be glad to spend a quiet month in an isolated spot, to recoup my strength.

She responded immediately.

Dear Mary Rose,

As a travelling adventurous heroine, you want to know, to understand and to discover. A journey has many aspects – destination, means of transport, companions and so on, but surely travelling is an adventure which leads you to build a new awareness. So although the main goal, or better, the practical goal of your journey is writing a book on Sicily, eventually your adventure here will lead you to a deeper self-knowledge.

I mean, you wanted to test or maybe discover, your strengths and your limits, after you lost your husband. Every person has their own weaknesses, however strong they may feel. The point is that they find it hard to show them. That is what happens to me when I don't feel well.

Now I have to go because Donald, my cleaner, is arriving.

Though never having met Rita, after six months of receiving her vigorous and thoughtful letters I felt a great affection for her. She was a 'Catanese, Catanese' she had informed me, proudly. A Sicilian through and through.

'Try to come to Catania before February 3, the first day of our three-day festival of Santa Agata,' she wrote me. 'It's our biggest religious carnival of the year and you will definitely want to be there.'

Despite my determination to avoid prejudging Sicily, I was 'rigid as a fish' according to Rita when she met me at the airport. Little wonder. It was late at night. The arrivals section was emptying alarmingly fast as if the place were strewn with 'no loitering' notices and I suddenly found myself conspicuously alone, while the males hanging about outside, unsmiling to start with, were turning grimmer by the minute. They were not the friendly teddy bear Italians that compere cooking shows or joke with customers in the bars. Much more like the types who bury people in concrete. What if someone snatched my bags before Rita came? Or snatched me?

I'd never seen a picture of her, but I recognized her immediately, a little acorn figure, russet brown all over, making everyone else look grey and dismal. Her shoulder length dark hair that alternately radiates out around a small, neat head, or coils on top of it – whatever her busy hands find to do with it while she's talking – was up under her beanie and seeing her in her tan cords and matching overcoat, drawn in to show off her waist, leaning forward, with her eyes popping out behind jazzy tortoiseshell spectacle frames, my panic began to recede.

'You're...?' Her eyes were bulging with inquiry. I remembered George Bernard Shaw's observation that protuberant eyes bespeak a vivid imagination. 'Yes, yes,' I said, thankfully.

She put her arms round me, releasing a torrent of apologies in perfect English and drawing me towards the exit. 'Grzegorz is parking the car. Let's get your luggage outside.'

I was pretty weary that first night in Sicily, after two weeks in Ermete's village where temperatures had stuck on 14 degrees below zero and I, fleeing Australia's extended hot summer, had arrived deliberately and desperately underclad, wanting to feel cool, but now shivering in my deepest core, trying to hug myself still, ravenously hungry every hour of the day and night, and watching with doleful fascination the fat melting off my bones.

But a glass of wine and a light supper, eaten en famille in the kitchen with my new friends banished sleep for most of the night which we spent animatedly exchanging condensed versions of our biographies. They had met in London where both were advancing their academic studies, she an undergraduate and Grzegorz a doctoral candidate from Warsaw University. A year's correspondence turned a brief romance into a courtship, at the end of which Grzegorz invited Rita to come to Warsaw to meet his family. Then it was his turn to visit Sicily to plead his suit with her mother and grandparents, her father having died when she was fifteen.

This was to be a marriage between a Polish intellectual and a member of Sicily's landed gentry, a social class not especially attached to schooling, Rita being the first among the women of her family to attend university and to have a job.

'I must tell you my grandfather squandered our family estates in gambling. Big landowners often do that in Sicily. But he did it because he was depressed. His labour force just walked off the land in the 1950s. Farm workers were rebelling all over Sicily. They had wanted higher wages, paid in money too, not in kind. About twenty per cent of farms ended up without labour then but Grandfather wouldn't give in to the peasants' demands. Communists, he thought them. So they literally dropped their tools and walked away. Up North.'

Well, the Italians were still paying their farm workers in kind, not with wages, in the 1950s? No wonder so many Southern Italians came pouring into Australia then. Mainly Calabrese rather than Sicilians, though two hundred thousand Sicilians alone are said to have quit their region in 1950-51. Paying in kind makes it easier to keep wages down. That Rita's grandfather knew absolutely nothing about farming was not itself a real problem. Absentee landlords are no strangers to the rural sector. More to the point, Grandfather knew nothing about management and industrial relations. And then to turn to gambling in a crisis. Tsk. This is not the stuff of good capitalism.

Rita went on: 'Grandfather couldn't find labourers to replace those who had abandoned him. The place started to fall apart. You don't know how sickening it is, to have been wealthy, with no money worries of any kind, and then to lose it all. My mother had grown up rich. Then my father died. We had no income and no property. My mother had to raise three of us. I don't know how she got us the apartment in this building. I just hate to think of it.'

Rita said she and Grzegorz had recently celebrated his appointment as associate professor in the sociology department of Catania University, a position, she lamented, an academic might normally have expected to gain in his mid-thirties. Grzegorz, unfortunately was already in his thirties when, with their daughter and son, six years into their marriage, they had left communist Poland and returned to Sicily. Since a Polish Pope had just been elected at the time, opportunities for Poles were forecast to open up all over Italy. Grzegorz, unfortunately, would have to begin his Italian academic career from scratch. Learn to read and write in Italian. Now, twenty years on, he was in the happy position of commuting regularly between Catania University and the University of Warsaw, having managed to integrate the Italian and Polish strands of his research and writing.

I congratulated myself when I retired to my room about three in the morning, that in all of Sicily I could hardly have met another couple who would be more fascinating or lively.

2

Rising early to find my room suffused with light, I breathed aloud to the apartments opposite, 'I'm here, I'm in Sicily', and eased the white transparent curtains aside, to open the French windows leading onto the balcony.

'Turn your head to the left', Rita had instructed me, 'and you will see Etna.'

Can a people fall in love with a volcano? If it's Mount Etna, they can be bewitched, not for moments but for millennia. And it's the best kind of love, filled with gratitude, blended with awe, fond but not familiar, intimate but respectful and never taking the loved one for granted, aware that fiery depths underlie the bounty lavished on those who welcome its largesse. In my brief stopover at Catania before crossing to the west of Sicily I loved Etna from the moment I saw it.

There it was, snow covered and bleaching the sky, the greatest, most active, most studied volcano in Europe. A mountain nearly two miles high, estimated age 700,000 years. It is reportedly piled on a soft base of rocks formed of clay and silt, thought to be tilting slightly to the east, with Etna itself sliding eastways on the base. If some part or all of Etna should collapse in a giant landslide to the sea, US geologist Richard Cowen has speculated, it will be followed by a tsunami, and the two events become a catastrophe of unspeakable dimensions. And just up the road from me! I should have felt terrified, but beauty, however deadly, is irresistible. I beamed at the volcano, drawing in copious draughts of its sulphurous air.

'How can I get to it?' I asked Rita. 'Today.'

She walked me to a street near her flat. It led directly to the bus interchange at Catania station. A bus left for Etna about eight thirty a.m.

'There'll be nothing to see but snow,' she warned me as I was hurrying off. 'The lava will be completely covered and probably all the side craters too.'

'Don't worry. I'll visit it in spring or summer to see the lava.'

Had I known what was in store I would have been less chirpy hurrying to the interchange – that once deposited at the 'Refuge', the highest village on Etna, I would have a long wait for evening when the bus returned, and every comfort – warmth, shelter, food and coffee – I would pay for over and over again.

But happily ignorant, I rejoiced to think that nothing is ever so clear and sharp as on a bright winter's day, when my glasses seem to have been properly cleaned for the first time, with the outlines of every object large and small seeming newly incised and the air chilled blue. I was shivering with excitement in the bus, breathing the beauty of the landscape into my soul, pinching myself to remind me that soon I would be stepping onto a living volcano.

Up close as you are allowed to go in winter, that is, 800 metres from the summit, at the funavia terminal, altitude 2500 metres, Etna was looking like Big Momma, with all the baby craters she had delivered from her flanks tucked around her under their snowy blanket, and she, a veteran smoker, taking it easy, emitting little wisps barely visible in the absorbent whiteness, to reassure everyone that she was still undertaking her major regional responsibility – to keep Sicily rich.

The softness of the snow and its purity and the flowing curves of the craters underneath it made winter Etna 'la' montagna. All woman. In summer, I would discover, she underwent a radical gender change. No longer white, but every shade of black across an infinity of lava fields, booming to deafen you from depths estimated at twenty-five kilometres into the earth, tossing molten lava and glowing scoriae out of multiple furnaces, she would become 'il' volcano, macho mountain.

That winter day, I felt euphoric stepping out from the cable car onto Etna's snowy southern slopes. Hot air drifted across my cheeks and drops of condensation were forming on my chin. I examined my wet fingertips and shook my head wonderingly. It was romantic to be a little flustered when skiers or snowboarders pushed past, tenaciously followed by hardy miniatures of themselves shoving just a little less vigorously. After all, getting pushed about on Etna is different from being hustled at the local supermarket.

In fact, anything that happens to you on Etna is different, practically and more so potentially. When my foot slid away from me on a patch of ice and I thudded onto my back, legs skewed, I had every thought for the potential. Not mere injury. Broken bones or paraplegia. No, Nothing like that. There were things going on under that ice that I could not see, the parturition of more baby craters, for one, crumbling edges, the earth transmogrifying under the soles of my boots. So close to my upper half, my precious brain and all its little bits and pieces, my hair, which could easily catch fire from sparks.

And I suddenly recalled something I'd read. In 1979 a small crack distant from the erupting crater became a gaping trench. Lava flowing along a subterranean tube, as it is wont to do, had found an obstacle and rearing up, broken the surface, right under nine tourists who toppled into the searing magma. Oh, my God! What agony. What an end.

But useless to call on God in this inferno. It's not His territory. Best suck up to Satan, the glorious but fallen archangel. Far more dynamic a character than God in Milton's long poem, as everyone concedes. I can't remember a thing about God in Milton's poem but I'll never forget Satan on that burning lake, so beautiful. And fallen from such heights.

From morn
To noon he fell, from noon to dewy eve,
A summer's day.

Made me swoon. And that great palace he and his marvellously named devilish mates built. Pandemonium. St Peter's is a poor copy, I can tell you. And the Mafra Palace? Hah! Not all the gold in Brazil can outgleam Pandemonium.

Believe me, you need no reminder of where you are in supernatural terms, on Etna. There are posters all about showing a horned devil rising out of a crater, clenching a pitchfork between his teeth.

An hour was enough for me up there. I suddenly felt in a panic to get back to the Refuge. Elbowing skiers aside to clamber aboard a 'going down' cable car, my mind was racing: snowy Etna is a fantasy land that would look good in Disney comics, but it's grounded – oh, what made me say that – on a substratum of reality so gothic in its horrors I can't continue with the thought. People have had to get into their cars and drive like the hammers of hell for Catania, down those specially long, specially straight streets designed to chute fleeing cars and trucks to the coast – before the lava hits the sea. Eighty kilometres an hour might, might just, *just* beat the lava. I can hardly breathe. I think my lungs are caking. That's what happens when the heat from the lava hits the moisture in your lungs. They cake and stop flexing. And I'm going to be here all day. No bloody buses to take me away.

I dig into my bag for the crumpled piece of paper I'd printed out in an internet café at the Refuge. It is headed, 'What to do if a volcano erupts near you,' and begins, 'If possible, immediately leave the area.'

Can you believe that people actually need to be told that? Yet they do. There's a spellbinding factor to consider, the fascination an eruption can exert over people. Empedocles is said to have thrown himself into Etna to prove he was a god, but I'm certain he just got closer than he intended and tipped over the edge, probably overcome by the fumes.

Skiers, snowboarders or hikers apart, no sane person has reason to hang about on the Etna snowfields all day, hugging themselves, rocking backwards and forwards, stamping their feet and blowing on their hands in the sub-zero temperatures. Had I known about the enforced stay, I would have hired a one-person tent, a sleeping bag and picked up some army rations to while away the hours without having to dig into my wallet every half hour for 'refuge': a roof, heating and coffee.

****

Fortunately I had Patrick Brydone's Journal to read – for hours – passed on to Rita for me, by her friend Rosario Portale, Professor of English at Catania University. Brydone is Saro's great passion, a Scottish scientist who visited Sicily in the 1770s. His journal was the 18th century's best-selling travel book, having gone through twenty-five printings and been translated into five languages.

He writes brilliantly as a scientist. Observed all the different levels of climate and vegetation on Etna, not visible to me of course in winter, and cited the view of some French academics that the various zones effectively represent a climatic progression covering eighteen to twenty degrees of latitude. This accounts for the wonderful variety of fruit and vegetables grown on the volcano. He said the first region was much too hot to support a great deal of vegetation, but the second, known as 'La Regione Sylvosa', the woody region, was one grand forest wrapping the mountain round.

He also described passing through beautiful woods of cork and evergreen oaks that he said must grow entirely out of the lava, because the soil covering was so very thin. But he got a real surprise to discover how long it might have taken for even that scant cover to form.

His guide, the ecclesiastic, Recupero, a keen amateur scientist, told him that the area he was querying had been referred to by Diodorus Siculus who said it had burst from Etna in the time of the Second Punic War when Syracuse was under siege by the Romans. That's almost two thousand years ago. Given that the soil under the chestnut trees was five or six feet deep and the surface covering so thin, Brydone concluded that the earth was much older than had been thought. He put that to Recupero who squirmed and said he was 'exceedingly embarrassed by these discoveries when writing a history of the mountain, that Moses hangs upon him like a dead weight and blunts all his zeal for inquiry, for that really he has not the conscience to make his mountain so young.'

'What do you think of these sentiments from a Roman Catholic divine?' Brydone wrote his friends. 'The Bishop, who is strenuously orthodox – for it is an excellent See – has already warned him to be upon his guard; and not pretend to be a better natural theologian than Moses; nor to presume to urge anything that may in the smallest degree be deemed contradictory to his sacred authority.'

Basing his description on interviews with locals Brydone describes the titanic clash between the volcano and the ocean when lava hits the sea.

'Conceive, if you will, the front of a torrent of fire, ten miles wide and heaped up to an enormous height, rolling down the mountain and at once pouring its flames into the ocean. The noise, they assure us, is infinitely more dreadful than the loudest thunder and is heard throughout the whole country to an immense distance, the water seems to retire and diminish before the fire and to confess its superiority, yielding up its possessions and contracting its banks to make room for its imperious master. The clouds of salt vapour darken the face of the sun, covering up the scene, under a veil of horror and of night; and laying waste every field and vineyard in these regions of the island. The entire body of fish on the coast are destroyed, the colour of the sea itself is changed and the transparency of its waters lost for many months.'

I had already spent an hour or so walking along the coast for three kilometres to see the impact of the lava. It had turned the sands into black and grey pebbly beaches, the stones smooth to the touch, therapeutic to walk on in bare feet. It had reared up, the lava, hissing at the sea, before cooling and setting spasmodically in massy forms, some craggy and sharp, others smooth and rounded, some smaller, some as tall as towers, a priceless sculpture park casually thrown together by elemental forces at work in Etna's core.

Platforms occurring naturally in these lava monuments are seized on by the Sicilians who cut steps out of the sides reaching up to them. When I returned from Favignana in mid-spring, everywhere I saw the young, single figures or couples or small groups, sprawled every which way on the outcrops, white on black in the sun, like jellyfish, toasting slowly and drying out over the days and weeks of spring and summer.

That afternoon on Etna I put away Brydone's book at five o'clock and deposited myself at the bus stop for the first transport out, feeling very cold and poorer than I'd budgeted for. I was shortly joined by a married couple from Chicago, retired and on a regular visit to their village which they had left in their early twenties. This was their first visit to Catania and to Etna. Catania was a bit of a dump, the husband opined in a lordly fashion. Nothing like Palermo. The drivers were appalling. If they drove like that in Chicago, the police would be on their tail. 'Like that', snapping his fingers.

Chicago police. 'I've heard of them,' I said, drily, remembering press pictures of their crowd control methods.

Both had thick, work-worn hands. Life obviously hadn't been easy for them in the States. They were probably illiterate when they arrived. And neither was as well groomed as the older men and women I saw in Catania's streets. But they had bought a house and a small piece of land in the village, left it in the care of relatives and made it readily available to friends and members of the American family whenever any chose to holiday there. 'How lucky they are,' I said. 'Sicily is a beautiful place.'

'Yes,' they nodded complacently, momentarily forgiving the traffic.

3

Over the next day or so I wandered the city trying to feel hospitable to the idea of an extended religious festival calling for thousands of people to be continually in the streets, day and night, for three days, every mind and impulse concentrated on one person, Agatha, the martyred virgin, and on one emotion – 'adoration'.

Such festivals are older than the Church of Rome, having been inherited from the Greeks or the Romans. Their enormous economic value would have been difficult for any new religion to ignore, and just as Sicily's Islamic and Christian churches recycled old temples, mosques and churches for their purposes, so too the Church of Rome has obviously recycled ancient gods and festivals: the panoply of Catholic saints is a professedly monotheistic religion's answer to its subjects' need for many gods.

In the Christian heaven, however, the passive nature of the saints and the narrow scope of their duties make them less distinctive than the gods of Olympus and it's a common practice to replace one with another, should any fail to notch up the number of successes required in controlling natural disasters or the other vicissitudes of life that their cult members choose to attribute to God. Agatha is said to have saved Catania a number of times by holding back onrushes of lava, and is well placed in the city's affections.

Rita pointed out to me that Catania is only one of many, many cities that have adopted Agatha as their patron saint. I imagine that might have something to do with the fact that there were very few other martyrs to choose from at the time. Indeed there seems to have been a shortage of saints in recent decades, as John Paul II, the Polish Pope, canonized over 200 personages during his pontificate – 100 of them Korean martyrs exalted at one wave of the censer.

Mass devotion to St Agatha turned out to be so muted and quiet I was gobsmacked. Catania's population hovers around 500,000 and most of them in the festival period were out in the streets every spare minute. Discomfiting for a person like me. I avoid crowds like the plague, especially sporting mobs or any other assemblies of fanatics. Yet in Catania the atmosphere was never at any time threatening or aggressive. Men, women and children packed the pavements and the roads, infants and ancients, all dressed in their Sunday best. Where were the yobbos? The drunks? The loudmouths? The fights? Not a one to be seen, or even better – heard. Vast numbers of people flowed steadily and silently along streets and avenues, diffusing through the city squares like a warm current over a delta.

At one point, standing in a narrow street coming off a square, I became aware a man close to me was trying to signal someone on the far side. In his fifties or early sixties, neatly suited and wearing a hat, he was stretching up and raising his hand aloft above the press of people, waving vigorously but not calling out. Eventually someone observed him and began nudging people, directing their attention to the waving hand, the man in the meantime having pushed forward to the edge of the pavement. He was spotted, his wave returned, then beckoned to cross over. Everything in dumbshow. Respect for Agatha.

In the small shops the proprietors and assistants were taking intermittent breaks: the owner of a jewellery store, an assistant from a children's wear shop, others from travel bags or toys had abandoned their counters and were standing in their doorways, sometimes leaning against a doorpost, arms folded, keenly interested in the street scene like everyone else. The bars were offering special delicacies based on marzipan, in Agatha's favourite bright green. Freshly squeezed fruit juices were on hand to boost a temporary flagging of spirit.

This festival was no funfair. Forget Rio. There was no music or dancing and very little in the way of a parade, except for a line of artisans representing about eleven different occupations, filing past proudly, holding high the guild signs representing their skills. I recognised the most obvious: fishmongers, butchers, pasta makers and bakers.

Agatha's innumerable male devotees were dressed in white knee-length tunics belted at the waist, trousers or jeans and running shoes or the like showing below. A much smaller number of females signalled their adherence with similar tunics coloured green. Even little babies were clad in tiny tunics. Entire families clung together in the crowds, straining forwards to see what was coming, little oases of devotion, in their 'I'm for Agatha' garb.

Sometimes they became part of the moving scene, making their way up the pathways left free in the middle of the streets. Another phenomenon. The pathways appeared and people standing made no effort to block them. I could see no policemen or anyone else to keep order. Nor anyone presiding over the program. The majority of people waited patiently while others in small groups were passing to and fro, carrying props of some description, obviously involved in the action. Very long candles, some a metre and others even longer were pushed in handcarts or transported in open-sided vans that stopped to allow devotees to distribute candles to those meant to have them. Presumably they were being dispensed for night activities. I was told that the practice of offering candles to divinities in the winter months goes back to the Greeks and Romans, an act of expiation to bring comfort and peace to ancestors.

What was to be made of this weirdly calm demeanour exhibited by these myriad Sicilians I observed exalting the patron saint of their city?

I was not the first person to pose the question. Dominique Vivant, Baron Di Denone, a thirty-one-year-old 18th century French aristocrat and career diplomat who wrote enthusiastically of the club life enjoyed by the Palermo gentry concluded his article on that city with a comment on the five-day festival of Santa Rosalia, patron saint of Palermo. 'It is proper to say on this occasion that one can note the seriousness of the Sicilian people, that their joy is without any external manifestation of enthusiasm. They would revolt, if the senate tried to suppress this festival, but they participate in it, in a very composed way, without laughing, without outbursts of joy, in perfect order, without there ever having to be recourse to the police.'

He too was astounded that without any apparently conscious effort, the crowds divided to let people pass through. 'Likewise, at midnight, (though I never was in a position to observe such a practice), every man went off with his own woman who had remained constantly by his side, and peacefully ceded his place to the nobility who entered the scene in the same orderly fashion and showed off with that marvellous Italian pomp, their splendid carriages and gala livery.'

I had trouble making up my mind whether I admired such docility and impassivity in crowds. Was it a good thing? Shouldn't crowds act like crowds? Some kind of invisible control must be at work here and the likeliest agency, given the social context, would have to be the Church. What a labour to create such a phenomenon – and make it look natural.

I made a mental note to start having a look at the theology and teachings of the Catholic Church, of which I knew practically nothing.

Since there was a surfeit of literature for sale on Agatha, I bought one of the slimmer volumes to peruse the story of her life and canonisation. Focusing on her travails offered little to cheer about. Far from it. The young Catanese girl had declared her desire to share the sufferings of Jesus, but martyrdom in late adolescence was not necessarily what she had in mind. Unlike Jesus she was not fulfilling a prophecy or acting out a manifest destiny meant to cause rejoicing among believers. Rather, as the author of the book conceded, she was unlucky. She might well have consecrated her life to God without losing it.

From a noble family of independent means, the possessor of farms and property, beautiful and chaste, she had refused the importuning of Quinziano, the Roman governor of Sicily, said to be 'mad' about her. In revenge, Quinziano demanded she produce a document certifying that she had properly performed the stipulated winter sacrifices to Roman divinities. To perform them inadequately would have the gods visit their wrath on the people. This certificate was meant to flush out covert Christians, widely known to worship only Jehovah. Agatha refused. She did not have such a document.

At this point Agatha begins her metamorphosis from an unlucky teenager to a heroic martyr. She could easily have wriggled out of her predicament. She could have procured a false certificate. Her friends could have arranged an escape from prison. But like Socrates many centuries earlier, she chose to do the honest thing. The strength of her belief was manifest in her withstanding grisly tortures that culminated in the slashing and severing of her breasts.

What intrigued me most, though, was the conscious attempt to convert a myth into a historical fact. Recent theology, popularized by Canada's Tom Harper in his *Pagan Christ,* has argued that until Augustine's time people ranked Christianity as only one among the world's great myths. To make it unique and enhance the authority of the Church of Rome, the Papacy undertook a massive propaganda campaign to convert the myth to historical fact, even slaughtering those 'pagans' who rejected the religion's change in status.

The author of my booklet concentrates on seemingly historical details claimed to have preceded Agatha's incarceration. He cites documents: 'Agatha,' Quinziano is said to have cautioned her. 'Sacrifice to the gods, or I will be obliged to torture you horribly.' Then he sweeps within this 'factual' compass what amounts to sheer invention over centuries by artists and hagiographers seeking to add their gloss to the tale. Everything merges in the mind, strengthening the faith necessary to dispense with reason, and make the leap into an unbridled fantasy: that during Agatha's first night in prison, Saint Peter, accompanied by an angel, visited her and in the morning her horrific wounds were cured, and the breasts restored.

'Clearly,' the author says in a remarkable understatement, 'a life event of this nature requires faith to render it comprehensible.' But is he saying that he himself finds it comprehensible? He affects to take a detached view of the situation. 'Some say that Saint Peter was more likely one of the missionaries who were allowed to visit the imprisoned and offer them a minimum of comfort, but saint or whoever, it is certain' –'certain' this author says, when it was impossible – 'that Agatha did not die during the night and appeared to be completely cured in the morning.'

Quinziano, the governor, was allegedly dumbfounded at Agatha's transformation as well he might be, and promptly had her dispatched with maximal pain, 'arsa viva', that is, burned alive.

One might ask why it was necessary to include the apocryphal element of the visit by Saint Peter and the magic healing of Agatha's tortures, when she could have been even more of a martyr had the story been wholly grounded in the plausible. But the blending of fantasy with what might possibly be historical fact, repeated many times over, in a closed and substantially illiterate society, makes the Church's 'subjects' readier to believe in magic, to relinquish the need to be reasonable, and to accept whatever the Church says as authoritative.

At an internet café I consulted *The New Advent Catholic Encyclopaedia*, which describes Agatha as 'one of the most venerated virgin martyrs of Christian antiquity, put to death for her steadfast profession of faith in Catania, Sicily. Historic certitude attaches merely to the fact of her martyrdom and the public veneration paid her in the Church since primitive times.'

The detail relating to Peter's visit was cosmetic, the kind that will, however, lodge in the imagination of both the credulous and the incredulous.

Thus informed, I returned to the streets to see if anything were happening. There was a sense of subdued excitement. Something was coming. Every head turned to one end of the street in eager anticipation. A massive tower lurched towards us, carried like a sedan chair on the shoulders of eight men who were finding it a heavy labour, half-trotting, which would have been easier than walking. They were men in their middle age, not callow youths, 'bulls' with thick necks and broad heavy torsos under their white tunics. By chance the construction was carefully lowered almost in front of me and I could see the men perspiring and breathing hard. One reached into his pocket for a packet of cigarettes and lit up, drawing the tobacco deep into his lungs. Two more men followed his example. A boy of about twelve appeared, having carried a cappuccino from a bar, the cup seized gratefully by a man who might have been his father or even his grandfather. Sicilian males reportedly marry young.

'Excuse me,' I said to a woman standing beside me, 'what are these men carrying.'

'You're a foreigner,' she said immediately, smiling, happy to enlighten me. 'That's the big candle. Are you a believer?'

I shook my head.

'German?' she asked.

'No. I'm from Australia.'

'Perhaps you don't understand that the light of the candle signifies the light of God and the heat from its flame, the purification of fire? It's made of solid wood, and is very, very heavy. But it's a privilege to carry it. You see that it has three tiers, the base, then above it, one tier with a number of stage settings each depicting an aspect of the saint's martyrdom: Agatha on trial, the Roman soldiers abusing her, cutting off her breasts and Agatha in prison.'

I followed the woman's pointing finger first at the horrors, and then at the happy denouement in the top tier where Agatha, reincarnated, reigns, beautiful and serene, cherubic figurines, angels and other personages, winding round her, together with masses of flowers and an infinity of embellishments, conveying the mood and matter of her ascent into heaven. A large and heavy crown surmounted the whole.

'The museum of the Comune has a magnificent silver big candle, donated by a local family,' the woman said. 'The silver one appears at the close of the festivities.'

'And how far do the men carry this big candle?'

They travelled around the city, taking a different route on each of three days. On the last day they carried the big candle non-stop for twenty-four hours, eventually arriving at the cathedral about three in the morning. This was starting to sound like whacking your bare chest with iron nail brushes.

'And will people be in the streets at that time when they arrive?' I asked.

'Oh yes,' my kindly informant answered. 'Many many people will be there to welcome Agatha back.'

I pressed a bit further. 'And what is it all for?'

She blinked, surprised by my obtuseness. 'We love her. We admire her bravery, her enormous faith. She wanted to share the sufferings of Jesus. And as a saint, she has protected us from terrible eruptions, held the lava back more than once. We like to see again the pictures on the big candle to remember her, and to show her our devotion, that we haven't forgotten what she did or how she suffered. The men who carry the big candle are also sharing a little in her suffering.'

Indeed. I wondered if there had been any heart attacks recorded en route, or if anyone had tripped and fallen, bringing the candle down.

The candle had been the idea of Pope Gelasio I, who, at the end of the fifth century, decided that the parade of artisans with their representative occupations should be joined to the Agatha celebrations and a big candle carried as her symbol. It was conceived as a work of art, constructed largely of polished wood coloured to suggest gold plating. By Gelasio's time, I imagine, the utility of these ceremonial devotions in maintaining the faith and offering distractions to the populace, not to mention boosting the economy, would have been well evident.

Later in the day I met up with the big candle again, this time carried at a run on the last lap to the Cathedral, where the crowds welcomed the bearers with muted clapping before they entered the church, the city's great beacon of salvation borne aloft in loving hands.

4

The next morning was a quiet time. I told Rita I would spend a few hours walking about Catania. Piazza Galatea, where the couple had their spacious apartment, though very quiet at night, was only ten minutes from the centre of the city but the window displays in the shops were so intriguingly different and eye-catching, dramatic and eccentric rather than glossy, that my walking slowed to intermittent spurts, and a 'little hour' passed before I found myself at a very large intersection with seven streets feeding into it.

Standing at the kerb, I took time to observe the streams of traffic flowing smoothly. Three sets of light changes were required to move every line of cars. So far as I could tell, not a single car went through a red light, nor even a motorino, whose drivers are notoriously casual about road rules. And when pedestrians were crossing at the green lights? Every last one made it to the other side. Drivers observed the walk signal. I plunged ahead myself at the next one, squinting in every direction to catch an errant motorcyclist, but nothing untoward happened.

So much for the wild and lawless Catanese drivers. That they ignored standard traffic rules was not true in all circumstances, I decided, even forcing myself to cross the intersection a number of times to confirm survival was not a chance occurrence.

But later, at two or three pedestrian crossings, I saw some reports vindicated. No one would stop. I had to wait for a gap in the traffic and on the big marine drive that could take an hour. Then a stratagem suggested itself. Though Italians are arguably not acculturated to obey a red light at an empty intersection in the middle of the night, their institutions, private and public, accustom them to respond to authoritative airs and tones of command. And they enjoy theatrics. Waiting till a car was a few metres off, demonstrating the usual intention to speed up at the sight of a pedestrian, I stepped boldly on to the crossing, advanced purposefully and then held up my hand like a traffic policeman, signalling the driver to stop. He braked immediately. That was fun. I repeated the exercise at different crossings. Not one driver resisted. Some smiled and saluted. I smiled back. We understood each other. From that moment I embraced the Catanese. I felt safe and comfortable in their city.

The following morning Rita greeted me approvingly when we sat down to breakfast. 'You look very happy this morning. Transformed.'

Grzegorz didn't rise till later unless he had early classes at the university.

'So we can have a lovely chat, together.'

I watched astonished while she poured leaf tea from a pot that she had previously warmed.

Noting my surprise, she said: 'Ha! Teabags, you thought. You haven't landed in a typical Sicilian household, you know. I must confess that my friend, Pinelda's sister, Adriana, a lovely person who teaches biology at the university has a much more typical situation and she did ask me if you might like to stay with her – she has teenagers whose English she'd like to see improve. But I thought the house might be too noisy and distracting for you if you wanted to write. So many young people coming and going and loud music.'

Adriana's was a scenario with certain attractions for me, but I was more than happy to stay with Rita and Grzegorz, especially since we had only another day or so before I left for Favignana.

At the second cup of tea, I asked Rita, 'Well, are you going to enlarge on the atypical character of your family?'

Glancing at her watch, she made a face. 'Nearly ten o'clock. I want to be at the market by noon to get some fish for lunch'.

Then off on a tangent, it seemed, she began to tell me that 'the other day' she had been to the Catania Hospital for tests relating to her Graves' Disease – the reason for her protuberant eyes – and in the waiting room her attention had been drawn to a woman aged about forty, *lutto stretto* – in deep mourning – standing quite still, her hands clasped in front of her. A couple, similarly dressed, were seated close to the woman.

'I was a little shocked,' she said. 'I hadn't seen a woman like that for ages. She had black hair parted down the middle and pulled back very tightly in a bun. She was buttoned up to the chin in a black blouse that covered her arms to the elbows, and down to the ankles in a black skirt, with black stockings. Around her neck, suspended from a gold chain, a cameo displayed a picture of her husband.

'Since we were waiting and she was standing, I said to her: "You look tired. Why don't you sit down?" And she said, "Thank you, no, I've been sitting in the car for five hours."

'"Your husband looked very young," I said.

'"Yes. He was only thirty-six when he died."

'"Oh, what happened?"

'"High blood pressure."

'"Do you have children?"

'"Yes, I have four."

'Then the woman seated near her said, "I'm the sister-in-law." The man in the group had nothing to add. He looked very simple.'

I waited, unsure where this was leading.

'It shows the solidarity of the family,' Rita said, sensing my query. 'Her two in-laws had come with her for support.'

While I was mulling this over, Rita went on: 'Grzegorz came with me to the hospital only the first time. Women of my generation and our social class are used to going on our own. Grzegorz comes only in an emergency or something serious, like when I was getting nuclear medicine.'

At that moment Grzegorz, almost conjured up by his name, appeared in the kitchen doorway, smiling broadly. 'Ah, you've been talking since dawn?'

He kissed Rita affectionately on the brow, patted her hair and moved to the stove where he checked the Mokka. The coffee was too cold. He lit the gas under it directly from the gas tap, I noticed: no matches needed. That was a relief.

'We're going to the market, Grzegorz,' Rita said. 'So we'll have to leave you to eat alone. *Va bene?*'

Her husband had an extraordinarily amiable expression that sometimes deepened into gravitas, and a pleasant voice, calm and quiet.

With an ironic flick of the hand to register that our departure was of no moment to him, he said: 'Carissima, you are perfectly free to go to the market. There are no chains on you. I will survive my lonely meal. I will wipe my tears in secret. No one will know that you left me to go the market.'

Rita gave him a push, signalled to me to follow her, and half an hour later we were standing at a fish stall in Catania's big central market, which filled and spilled out of a great square dominated by a church with Ave Maria scrolled in high relief above the doors. Rita immediately engaged in conversation with the owner of the stall, running an expert eye over the display before settling on some sardines whose freshness she lauded at length. In fact, quite a number of creatures in their boxes or on trays were showing signs of being still alive. If only I had the gumption to be a vegan.

Within the hour, Rita's sardines, panfried, became the basis of a light lunch accompanied by a mix of Polish and Mediterranean fare. Grzegorz made the coffee afterwards, I assisted Rita to put the kitchen to rights, and then, shutters drawn, everything quiet, the couple went off to perform what I duly learned was a long established routine, withdrawing for a rest from two p.m. till four thirty p.m. I too was gently nudged in the direction of my room, where I sat in a rocker, reading, but thereafter began an entirely new routine of my own that I maintained for the duration of my stay in Sicily: waiting for siesta to take a walk, when most other people were home eating, or resting, and the traffic was lighter.

Part II

The West

Sicily's west coast is almost in rowing distance of North Africa. A spray of dotted lines can be imagined radiating from Tunis across the Sicilian Channel to several Western Sicilian towns, Trapani, Marsala, Mazara del Vallo and further south, to Sciacca and Agrigento, the last a cultural aberration, a Greek, not a Phoenician prize.

Palermo, a jewel of a port with a lavish hinterland, though not on a line of sight from Tunis, was encountered swiftly by the Phoenicians and promptly made their own. So steady and constant has been the to and froing of traffic across the Sicilian Channel that refugees heading for the European mainland now enter daily by that route, their numbers swelled by people from the south of Africa also seeking entry to Europe via north-west ports.

Northern Italians are well aware of the Sicilian connection with North Africa, commenting on it so often and pejoratively that many Sicilians in the north are careful to conceal their origins. Tim Parks, the English writer now resident in Verona has related how busloads of doped-to-the eyeballs soccer fans from the North following their teams south to matches in Bari, Catania or Palermo routinely hurl 'Africani' at the home team players, accompanying their chants with appropriate monkey pantomimes.

On the same latitude as Tunis and only thirty-two miles straight across the open sea is the island of Pantelleria (a corruption of the Arabic Bent-el-Rhion, Daughter of the Wind), host to an American military base. The three small Pelagian Islands further south, while administratively part of the province of Agrigento, geographically belong to the African continent. One of these islands, Lampedusa, now a holding camp for refugees, became Sicilian after Phillip II of Spain gave it to the Lampedusa family, minor nobility and ancestors of the famous novelist and critic, Tomasi di Lampedusa. His family, happy to luxuriate in their Palermo estates, relinquished the distant paradise in 1860 to the Kingdom of Italy.

Place names suggest that the Greeks and the North Africans moved towards one another in a crablike fashion, the latter curving round the islands in a north and east direction and the Greeks meeting up with them by a south-west route. It took a century of gradual encroachment by both parties before the Greeks made a huge westward lunge and established Agrigento, intending thereby to block any further advance east by the North Africans.

Palermo, long a great capital of Europe, its current population just under 900,000, dominates the west of Sicily, but many of the small towns imprint themselves on the imagination. Marsala, Trapani, Erice, Mazara del Vallo, Alcamo, Palermo, Monreale, Castellamare del Golfo, Cefalu, and the Egadi Isles, all pull on the heartstrings. Castellamare del Golfo may be well known to the FBI as the birthplace of some notorious American mafia who continued their shootouts after relocating in the States, but its beauty rivals that of the Amalfi coast. No one quits such a place without a heavy heart.

Trapani, at the very tip of the west coast, its salt pans aglitter in the sun, was, I'd guess, the location for the closing scene of Leni Wertmuller's hilarious film, *Mimi the Metalworker*, the story of a Sicilian labourer, a communist who, in fleeing to the North to resist the mafia's code of 'honour', finds the organisation every bit as vigorous in Turin and all of a muddle begins to shed his own integrity in various ways that include marital infidelities. The women he betrays eventually abandon him, leaving him a lone figure lamenting on the blazing white and arid salt plains by Trapani's shores.

Trapani has a marvelous cable car. On the stomach-turning ride up to Erice, its eight-seater compartments, glassed all round, afford, with a bit of a swivel, 360-degree views of mountain, sea and salt. Erice, an ancient town with a great

Norman fort and an ecclesiastical museum that displays an eye-popping jewelled chasuble guaranteed to humble any peasant population, is a picture postcard place seemingly more suited to a book of fairy tales than the real world.

Nonetheless, the ambitions and entrepreneurship of an Erice scientist from an old ruling family with ties to the Church have made the town host to an outpost of CERN, The European Council for Nuclear Research. Erice is probably the only town in Sicily to have briefcase-carrying scientists from all over the world regularly jostle with tourists in local shops. The Erice scientist's ambitions extended to his demanding the presidency of CERN, the Italian government voicing threats should he not be elected. His failure to secure the appointment restores my confidence in the limits of clientilism.

Many Western Sicilians, liberated from destitution, have carved out US reputations in every field of the arts. Frank Sinatra, his family name filling pages in the Trapani phone directory, was only the brightest star in an entire galaxy of impressive entertainers and artists of Western Sicilian origins, their names still household words.

Of equal stature was Frankie Laine, a singer who enjoyed immense popularity over a seventy-year-long career. Al Pacino, whose grandparents came from Corleone, the heartland of the Sicilian mafia, is a highly-regarded actor and coincidentally played the role of Michael Corleone in *The Godfather*. *It's a Wonderful Life* and *Mr Smith Goes to Washington*, award-winning films made in the 1930s and 1940s by the director Frank Capra are still loved and prized today. Partinico, the desolate mafia precinct I visit in Palermo is the birthplace of Frank Zappa's father.

But everywhere I go in the West, in some wise or another, the mafia are reflected. They have a pervasive presence. It emerges even when I'm seeking a beauty salon to have a facial. Following up the role of the Church in what it refers to as a 'Catholic state' whose members are its 'subjects', I spend nearly six weeks in a 'closed' Palermo monastery to enhance my understanding. It's in Palermo I encounter a billboard advertising that people will be meeting in the piazza for prayer during an industrial strike. Twice in the interior, famed for its silence – which has a lot to do with the almost total extinction of birds on the Italian peninsula – I feel threatened by violence, though I've written of only one instance, largely because of its comic overtones.

Some of my time in the West is spent with a young Sicilian woman I know from Sydney, the rebel of a family I eventually decide must have mafia connections. Invigorated by her lively personality and activist goals, I see Western Sicily through her eyes as well as my own.

My stay in the West begins on a very, very tiny island.

Favignana

Favignana dominates the Egadi archipelago whose population hardly exceeds four thousand. The entire archipelago, comprising Levanzo, Marettima and Favignana, is a city. The city of Favignana, so named since the Middle Ages, before which Favignana itself was known as Aegusa, Goat Island.

'Favignana' the modern name comes from a wind locally known as the Favonio, which, when I have it described to me, seems to be the very same that east coast Scots recognise as the wind bringing 'Indian summers' to Aberdeen in the middle of January, when temperatures can suddenly rise fifteen degrees and hover there for up to three days. Plants and trees, allured from their winter sleep, hurriedly send out new growth, only to retreat in panic, too late for some, when stricken by a new freeze. That happens on Favignana too, so a local tells me.

The archipelago's odd urban status is recognition, perhaps, of its self-sufficiency before the ferry service started operating in the early 1960s, and a tribute to its extreme age, maybe to its membership of both Great Greece and the Roman Empire, to its fortitude, to its combat experience – seven hundred ships sunk in one of its bays, in the last mighty battle between the Romans and the Carthaginians in 241 BCE – and to its enterprise, its inhabitants reputed to have salvaged the stores from shipwrecks before hastily dispatching survivors to a watery grave: even the mafia leave them alone – 'if they try anything here they have to get off the island – alive,' one local assured me. A savvy population, the islanders, on the margins of civilisation, but for long delineating the constantly disputed boundaries of several imperial powers and therefore, like new and previously sidelined entrants to the European Union, of a certain interest to the powers at the centre.

5

At the end of what turned out to be a bit more than a week in Catania, Rita and Grzegorz decided they would have to chance the weather and get me to Favignana. They squeezed our luggage into the boot and back seat of their little Fiat, and we took off, moving up north and then westward, right across Trinacria, as the locals call 'Sicily,' bypassing Palermo till we reach Trapani on the west coast, a four and a half hour trip. Then down to the sea to board the hydrofoil.

It was a scary crossing. A few minutes after we left Trapani docks, in calm waters but with the clouds felting, I paused in my survey of the life jackets slotted below each seat to register a black rock that seemed suddenly to be peering in the porthole at me from about ten metres away. Grzegorz was bowling my suitcase into one of those niches boats abound in, where I could keep my eye on it from all angles.

Suddenly, to my consternation, the hydrofoil started acting like the big dipper in a funfair, rising up and throwing me backwards, then plunging down and toppling me forward out of my seat. Had we hit the rock? I'd concluded that every moulded chair did have its appointed life jacket, but what use would one be to me when I can't swim? I've even emerged a 'sinker' rather than a 'floater' in the lessons my friend Helen Gapps was persevering with before I left Wollongong.

Besides, the life jackets might well have perished from disuse and no one picked up on it. That is always happening with safety equipment. Ancient fire extinguishers are found rusted rotten when flames rampage through heavily populated apartments or hotels.

'Did we hit that rock?' I asked Rita, whose eyes were slewing about, straining with the effort to see in the gathering dusk.

'What rock? Where?'

I pointed to the porthole.

'That's not a rock,' Rita said, patiently. 'It's a big dark cloud. Did you really think it was a rock?'

I nodded, my attention now focused on the turbulence outside.

Tactfully, in the way that Italians often try to save you from your own idiocies, she murmured, 'Yes, it's not a good light.'

The sea had turned midnight blue. How could it, so early in the evening? Rita was worrying that I might get seasick. Was it really pertinent whether I became seasick or not on a twenty-five minute ferry trip? Then I remembered sliding about in my bunk at three in the morning on the all-night boat trip from Aberdeen to Lerwick in the Shetlands and, relieved, I told her, no, I don't get seasick. Thinking, it'll be a transient discomfort in any case if we die drowning.

'Have you ever heard of a ferry go down in these waters?'

A good question, easing the tension.

She shook her head. 'Of course not. Are you serious? Don't you know the Sicilians have been fishing these waters for more than two thousand years? They know every wave. I'm sure of it. Besides they *never* let a ferry go out if the seas are rough.'

'They weren't rough when we left,' I pointed out.

'But they would know conditions were going to become a little rough later. I'm sure. They're expert weather observers.'

Grzegorz had opted out of conversation, partly because he was sitting across the aisle, out of easy earshot and partly because he was still catching his breath after an enforced sprint with the luggage.

There was hardly time for him to recover completely before we were merging with the commuters disembarking at Favignana. It was now dark, and the little port was floodlit, as were one or two fishing boats lying at anchor, their crews visibly hard at work on board, swilling and scouring, preparing for the next day's fishing.

Almost opposite the gangway, no further than ten metres or so, outside a bar next to the shipping offices, stood a huddle of men, some in caps, others in beanies, bulked out in duffle jackets and up to their ears in scarfs, drinks in hand, with two or three seated at little tables randomly placed by the doorway, all aglow in the bar's amber light. Car doors were opening to receive the smiling homecomers, or slamming shut on privileged wage earners returning from their jobs in Trapani. Taking a last look at the ferry as it did a U-turn to get out, I noted the dark ragged outline of a mountain rising behind it. The harbour was well protected, nestling in an inlet running between the mountain and the seawalls. At the far end of the harbour on the left, I spotted a network of massy buildings squatting around some kind of tall tower.

Immediately Grzegorz set foot on the quay, he thrust himself between me and my monster suitcase, refusing to surrender it, hauling it behind him over the cobbles on two wheels, ignoring its supermarket trolley design which allows it to be pushed with one finger. I gave up protesting. In a country where women are madonnas or whores and everyone, gender notwithstanding, either an infant or a parent – adulthood not commonly a permitted aspiration – what use to say, hey, I go to the gym?

So we lumbered on, through a boundless maze of narrow streets, the city centre much further away from the port than I've been led to believe. With the sun down, a real chill had entered the air. My cheeks and nose were cooling fast. The temperature must be close to freezing, I surmised, only to find myself smartly reproached by an electronic weatherboard fixed high up on a palazzo wall, flagging time, temperature and barometric pressure, and showing eleven degrees above zero, a positive, almost benign figure during a European winter. This was the lowest night temperature I observed during my five weeks' stay at Favignana. Nothing to compare with minus fourteen in Ermete's Tuscan village.

Abruptly, with no preparation, we stepped into a square. Let's see – would it be the Piazza del Duomo? I look around for the inevitable cathedral resonating the inescapable power of the Church. The church was indeed present but much too modest for a cathedral. And off-centre, easy to overlook. On pillars? None that I could see. The Greeks had left Western Sicily to the Phoenicians. We crossed the square diagonally and turned into a side street that sloped up a gentle rise. Grzegorz, still dragging my thirty kilos, finally stopped before a narrow uncovered passageway on our left, a few metres long, leading to the front door of Rita's holiday house – mine alone for the coming weeks.

****

That first night on Favignana was the closest I ever got to being miserable in Sicily. I had been completely unaware that labelling a house a 'holiday' home implies traditional comforts are of secondary interest to location and to the hours of sunshine the latitude can boast. Proximity to the sea is alone sufficient to call a holiday house 'perfection'.

The front door, its upper half a pane of glass draped to let in light but maintain privacy, opened directly into a small rectangular dining room where we dropped our luggage in front of a kitchen table and stood, bunched together, breathing, momentarily silent, trying to relax into the cold, clammy atmosphere. Then Rita crossed to a door on the right, inviting me to follow her. When she switched on the light inside, I was startled to see a mezzanine platform a bit more than two metres high dominating the room. A ladder in the middle of the structure gave access to the top.

Eyeing the rungs upwards I could see the edges of two mattresses lying end to end. Underneath the platform was a single bed. A second's thought decided me that the creature was actually a magnified double bunk bed, save that there were three beds and you had to crawl about on top to get into two of them and to change the linen.

In the middle of the far wall at right angles to this dramatic structure, a third door stood open, and beyond it, in the dim light from the bed lamps that Rita switched on, the traditional matrimonial bed loomed abnormally wide – twin beds inside a wooden frame, the furrow up the middle no encourager of matrimonial closeness, but rather an inducement to abstinence, especially after Augustine's macabre ruling that sex served to transmit original sin to succeeding generations, instigating the practice of post-coitus prayers among the devout.

Rita proudly showed me the en-suite bathroom coming off the matrimonial bedroom. It was surprisingly modern, with a good sized shower, washbasin and lavatory. 'You can move into this room tomorrow,' she said. She and Grzegorz were returning to Catania late the next afternoon. I had talked them out of staying longer. Grzegorz was preoccupied with finishing a book and the three days they had spoken of in the winter here without the comforts of home would have been a trial for him, even if, as a pious Catholic with a proud boast of marital fidelity, he wanted to do the right thing by me.

So tonight I would have to go up in this little world. Climb the ladder. I gulped. Still, I shouldn't like them to see me in the morning if they were passing through to the kitchen. I loathed the idea of a mezzanine with a ladder parked right in the middle of it. But, with two beds end to end, I could see there was no alternative. Gloom suddenly enveloped me.

'Have you thought what might happen if you get a bunch of heavy Americans here?' I said, 'Or old people with arthritis? They could have a problem climbing that ladder. And I don't think there's standing room at the top.'

'Don't be silly. It's designed for children,' Rita said.

I forbore to say the obvious. It was shameful to be so negative, but the cold, the dampness in the air, the idea of climbing up a ladder less than rocklike, even for one night, and if I didn't remember to empty my bladder last thing, the fear that I might have to grope my way on to the rungs and feel my way down in the middle of the night depressed me.

As if reading my mood, Grzegorz said, 'We'll buy a heater tomorrow morning. The house is usually shut for the winter. It will feel better after a day open to the sun. For now, let's put our suitcases in place and we'll go and find something to eat.'

Stretched out that night on my elevated bed, I mentally sketched the layout of the cottage. It was a single-storeyed rectangle, whose ceilings were high enough to accommodate the mezzanine sleeping platform. The former owner, a woman architect from Palermo had renovated it, the interior conforming with the traditional Italian domicile that spurns internal hallways and has one room opening into another so that doors are everywhere. The little dining room and the kitchen each had three doors. Maybe when opened they channelled cool breezes through the cottage in the summer months, but in the winter, apart from raising security fears in me, there was a question of draughts.

I couldn't sleep, unable to determine whether I felt hot or cold in the bed. Flopping and flapping my arms about as I tossed and turned, I suddenly became conscious my skin was sliding over soft dust rising in piles up the walls. When I turned on the light for a closer look I saw it was no ordinary dust but a fine yellow powder.

Very early, before Grzegorz and Rita were awake, I got up on to my knees and wriggled somehow backwards onto the ladder to go down in search of the second bathroom leading off the kitchen on the right. Its walls I soon discovered were distempered in the same buttery yellow as the dust above the bed, not an unattractive colour in artificial light. A big tank containing the hot water system had obviously usurped shower space and I could hardly wash or turn around without brushing against the walls. Each time, some of the dust rubbed off on me and I thought, 'Hell, I'm turning into a stigma.' One syllable short of a miracle.

After dressing and taking a brisk walk outside, I returned to find Rita sitting on a chair in the courtyard left of the kitchen, enjoying her breakfast coffee and warming herself in the sun near a small barbecue obviously well used for outdoor eating. Overhead a clothes line was strung out with pegs still attached.

Another courtyard, perhaps marginally bigger, was visible through a window on the right side of the street passage to the house. Rita and Grzegorz shared this courtyard with an unruly looking assemblage of sturdy males.

'That courtyard could be a really lovely place to withdraw to when the sun shifts,' Rita lamented, 'if the family would only desist from using it as a dump for broken machinery and boxes of junk. They treat the space as if it's entirely theirs. I've asked them to tidy it, but they just look at me and say nothing. They ignore me.'

'Mightn't it affect the re-sale value of the house?'

Rita shrugged. 'Houses aren't so plentiful in Sicily. And it's a holiday house. Tourists come for weekends, rarely longer. We bring friends occasionally. It could be more of a nuisance if one lived here permanently but that's highly unlikely to happen. So let's sit down and think of lovely things. Like being here in the courtyard till the sun shifts. You can warm yourself like a lizard. Grzegorz has gone out to get some croissants. And there's coffee in the pot. Wait and I'll bring you some.'

She made to rise but I stopped her. 'Don't wait on me, Rita. I can see the Mokka on the stove and the cups hanging above the sink.'

'Can you?' she said, smiling. 'And tell me, have you seen the floor tiles?'

I looked down at my feet. If my eyes had lit on the tiles, my brain had failed to register the fact. I could see nothing remarkable in them. They must have been blue and yellow at some stage but now they were old and faded. Nothing like the tiles I'd seen in the annual catalogues of a major Sassuolo tile manufacturer.

'Antiques,' Rita informed me, proudly. 'Majolica. Very expensive. The Palermitana architect put them there. So we've left them. Grzegorz and I had a problem trying to determine whether we should risk leaving valuable furniture in here, but so far, people seem to appreciate it. There's an eighteenth century pasta-making trough in your room.'

I would have preferred to see an early twenty-first century mezzanine floor with an electronically operated chair that went up and down, and proper beds, not mattresses; also ducted heating under the floorboards, but I forbore to say a word, mainly because I knew I was in a bad temper and I'd better not let it escape me. Besides, the sun was shining. And I had succeeded in crawling about on the mezzanine platform, like man in his pre-biped state, removing the dust.

A cleaner had been hired to air the house and clean it thoroughly, but obviously she had not bothered to climb the ladder. Sensible woman. However, the thick ropes of yellow tufa dust around the mattresses gave me the horrors and I had gotten rid of them as soon as the sun rose, creeping into the kitchen for a bucket and disinfectant.

Grzegorz returned sooner than expected, carrying a new heater, and some long rolls, *panelle* filled with deep-fried slices of chickpea dough, the flour having been soaked all night in water. They were warm, tasty and filling. I felt my spirits rise as I savoured the last crumbs and Grzegorz revealed that the *forno* was only about twenty metres down the street. I would become a regular customer there for breakfast.

Another *panelle* straight off would have been a joy, but by now I had resigned myself to the small portions Italians eat. Normal ones, to be truthful, as I remembered them in the halcyon days when weight was an abstruse multifaceted concept shared with dimensions of length and breadth on the back of a school exercise book. Italians have not yet been forced to wise up on American obesity linguistics, Kiddies, Regular and Tall, meaning normal, bigger and gluttonous-sized coffee mugs, thrust at customers in those authoritarian American coffee house chains whose bland sludge insinuates the gospel that quantity can replace quality.

Grzegorz, whippet thin, was now preoccupied with examining the heater. Electricity being hugely expensive in Italy I held little hope that this heater would make much of a dent in the cold. It had no fan. Even so, I would have to use it as little as possible. Rita had offered me the house for a hundred euros a week, and at that rent I couldn't expect her to meet the electricity costs. But in case she and Grzegorz proved resistant to my paying, I would have to make sure the electricity account was minimal.

Breakfast over, we dawdled off to meet with Mimmo, the factor. He welcomed new holiday tenants, collected rents, organized repairs, arranged for the laundry, for between-tenants cleaning and informed Rita of any new developments in Favignana he thought she ought to know about. He lived in

Trapani but came to Favignana for two or three hours most weekday mornings, returning home before lunch. His brother owned a bar which functioned as Mimmo's office. Clients met him there.

A few minutes before we left I nipped down the passageway into the street to get a feeling for the temperature. It was brisk but pleasant out. Warmer than the night before. No need for the cashmere coat I had bought in Bologna when I was visiting Ermete's relatives. The black Paddy Palin's jacket, a new design in outdoor gear, tailored at the waist and shoulders for women, would keep out even the strongest breezes that blew up.

Rita was wearing a smart oatmeal-coloured woollen suit with classic brown Italian walking shoes, and her wintry trinity, beanie, scarf and gloves, as when she met me at Catania airport. Grzegorz had a black leather jacket over heavy drills with a blue shirt collar rimming the neck of an Aran knit they had bought in Ireland.

In the Piazza Madrice, the Square of the Mother Church, old men, pink-cheeked and shining clean, capped heads tilting close in to the sunlit walls of their favourite bar, pored over the newspapers, solitary and rigid with concentration, or sitting back, expansive and benevolent, chatted to this one and another, done up in fisherfolk style, denims, polo necks, duffle coats or windcheaters, Adidas or leather boots on their feet.

I doubt tourists, especially other Europeans, would have found the piazza in any way remarkable. Modest in size, it had a no-frills ambiance, with a string of shops on three sides. The church straddled the fork of two streets leading from the square. A post office, two or three ATM outlets, the pharmacy, the bakery where Grzegorz had bought the rolls with the fried chickpeas filling, a pizzeria, and two bars took up the rest of the piazza. Other businesses, bars, hardware shops, a newsagency which recharged phone cards, a white goods store selling washing machines and cellphones, fruit and vegetable shops, were in adjacent side streets.

6

Mimmo was waiting for us in a bar off the square. From farming stock, a sturdy figure of a man dressed in a well worn suit and tie, he presented himself with an air of quiet confidence, reaching out promptly, when Grzegorz introduced us, to take my hand in a warm grip, '*Un piacere, signora.*' A pleasure.

Then tilting his head, parrot-like, a little to the side to take us all in and gesturing towards the bar, he added, 'Let me offer you a coffee with something.'

He led us into the back room, where we squeezed together at a very small round table, noting briefly a television high up on the wall showing a soccer match, with the sound switched off. His niece, a quiet, composed girl of about eighteen, entered promptly to take our order.

A fixer depends entirely on his reputation for honesty and reliability and according to Rita Mimmo's reputation was gilt-edged. He displayed none of the salesman's usual bonhomie at the table, listening carefully while Rita put a few questions to him, and responding in the same quiet tones I had observed in so many Sicilians when they were talking, inside their homes or on the streets. I have never known other Italians speak so quietly and was keeping my ear out for the first yells of abuse.

Mimmo's family were long established in Favignana. He knew the island intimately, its every nook and cranny, thousands of which ruffle the twelve and a half mile coastline. Many nooks are the result of quarrying for tufa, the local building rock that produced the yellow pollen I had encountered in ropes around my mattress, and in the shower. It's very similar to Rome's famous travertine but harder, a porous limestone formed by the evaporation of water.

Mimmo knew the genealogy of most families, understood the many changes of mood and season in the Egadi Isles, what made the islanders prosper and what diminished them. In the season of the Arabs who broke up the great estates established by the Romans, many locals were given a smallholding and learned from the invaders how to capture tuna in huge numbers. But the Normans, new converts to Christianity, dispensed with the smallholdings, giving much of the land to the Church and the small farmers became landless labourers. After the Unification in 1860 came terrible times, with the peasants in constant revolt. The Church railed against the state from the pulpit, threatening excommunication for any who voted in elections or engaged in any other political activity.

And then there was the flowering of the Florio family's entrepreneurship when Ignazio Florio decided to start canning tuna and sensibly set up his factory in Favignana, near where the tuna were landed from the boats: one of the Florio's many instances of vertical expansion. Italians, I've observed, greatly favour expansion of the vertical rather than the horizontal kind, keen, apparently, to control all the levels of production and distribution.

It came as a surprise to me to learn that Sicilians, though islanders, are not seafarers like, say, the Shetland Islanders. They have been scared, not without reason, of what can emerge from the sea: raiders seeking to carry off their women and children, mercenaries and warlords bent on adventure, imperial powers in search of colonies, foreign armies, most recently the Allies during the Second World War, and hostile acts from the sea itself in the form of intermittent tsunamis. Moreover, since their volcanic soils deliver easefully a wide range of fruit, vegetables and grains, the islanders turned naturally to the soil rather than the sea.

Nonetheless, foodwise, the sea till now has pampered them. Not for them the hard life of whalers in the North leaving home for months at a time hunting and haunting the whale in southern oceans. The region's famed tuna for centuries have journeyed annually over oceans to reach the Mediterranean. They move on dedicated routes so consistently and so close to shore, their arrival can be anticipated by what was formerly an armada of rowboats whose crews firmly shepherded the doomed creatures through a specially designed undersea fortress to a chamber of death. There they were slaughtered pitilessly with hook and gaffe.

'We're losing our traditional skills,' Mimmo told me after Rita and Grzegorz had departed for the market. 'The European Union's production standards are so strict, private individuals can no longer bring their garden surpluses to the market. Even middle-size commercial farmers don't have the capital to reorganize their farms in accord with EU regulations. Only agribusiness. My grandmother, who makes better salted ricotta than anyone else on these islands, can't sell it in the market any more. So people who used to buy the best from her have to eat the supermarket product now. But you must come and visit Nonna and taste her salted ricotta at home.'

Agribusiness and its destructiveness is nothing new to Sicily. The Romans cleared thousands of hectares of tree cover to have grain planted on the huge landholdings the Senate allocated to the warrior class and its scions, cultivation being on such a scale that Sicily became renowned as 'the granary of Rome'. But Sicily has long since become a grain importer. Very soon, with only one of seven tuna factories remaining to handle – in Trapani – what was once an enormous catch, Sicilians may also be importing tuna.

Before leaving Mimmo I asked if there were an Internet service point somewhere on Favignana. 'Where I can check my emails?'

He shook his head, apologizing: 'This is winter. No tourists. Quite a few people have the Internet service at home but the women who operate the service for tourists nowadays turn up only occasionally at their premises. I don't know when.'

He took my arm and led me outside the bar. Pointing towards a cathedral: 'See there, the street on the right of the Chiesa Madrice? The Internet service premises are a few doors up on the left. And Antonio, the owner of the white goods shop is a little further, on the opposite side, on a corner. He knows the women and he will tell you when they are likely to come to their office.'

By this time, two of Mimmo's associates had arrived at the bar, ready for their morning coffee and a chat. 'Call on me any time you have a problem,' he said, shaking hands again. 'If I'm not in the bar, ask my niece to phone me.'

On arriving back at the house, I found Grzegorz and Rita sitting in the courtyard in the sun, and the table set for lunch. Rita had promised she would show me how to make pasta with *bottarga*, the tuna roe she found among the basic groceries Mimmo had stocked in the cupboards for our arrival. I opened the packet, not much bigger than a 10gm packet of dried mushrooms, and examined the pinkish brown blob that costs a fortune per kilo, but is feasible if you buy only an *etto*– one hundred grams.

Rita told me the roe is worked at the *tonnara*, the tuna factory, in Trapani, where it is massaged by hand to eliminate air pockets, then cured in sea salt for a few weeks, pressed and hung to air dry for a month. Semi-dried *bottarga* is less tasty. Trapani's vast pans of sea salt are at hand for the process. The end product is a hard dry slab, not unlike the salted ricotta, and you grate it or slice it in the same way.

'*Bottarga* is something like anchovies,' Rita said. 'It will disappear when you fry it a little. Some people serve it as antipasto, with a squeeze of lemon.'

She had bought fresh tagliatelle, and when it was ready, tossed it in the frypan with the *bottarga* and the faintest gleam of oil. 'I'll leave the rest of the packet for you,' she said.

We had scallopini and vegetables to follow. And then blood oranges. Rita had brought them from Catania. 'From Etna, of course,' she said, in a tone implying 'all good things come from Etna.'

She wanted to know what I thought of Favignana. 'Can you really be happy here for several weeks?'

This was a question heavy with negative implications but knowing that I would have the matrimonial bed and its furrow to myself for the entire period, and a pollen-free bathroom, I felt positive.

'Yes, of course,' I assured her. 'I have a little house with a sunny courtyard. I'm in a friendly place of which I have a lot to learn. The air is lovely. Everything's clean and bright. And there's that tasty breakfast of fried chickpeas to get me leaping out of bed every morning. Not to mention Mimmo the fixer, ready to unravel any knots in the fabric of my existence. What else can I need? I'm in paradise, Rita.'

She and Grzegorz regarded me doubtfully. Grzegorz said: 'If you want to leave and return to Catania, you can take the ferry to Trapani and catch a coach from there to Palermo. From there another coach will bring you to Catania.'

I nodded, relieved now that I would be in one place for a few weeks. 'No worries. I'll be here until the end of March.'

The only negative was that it would be freezing cold as soon as the sun set in the afternoon. The heater Grzegorz had bought barely took the edge off the chill in the kitchen. Still, I could wrap myself in blankets or take a book to a bar.

Suddenly remembering, I asked them, 'Did you tell Mimmo the house will be empty from Saturday? When I go away for a few days with Gaby?'

'There's no need to worry about its being empty,' Rita said. 'There's very little crime on this island. Some, maybe, in the tourist season, when delinquents come over on the ferry looking for opportunities. But people keep an eye on strangers here.'

'So the Sicilian girl you knew in Sydney is not coming here?' Grzegorz interposed.

'No. Not at present,' I told him. 'She says she's too ill.'

Rita and Grzegorz had expressed a readiness to meet Gaby di Santis on Favignana after hearing my selective account of the lively Sicilian girl I had met almost on the eve of my departure from Sydney. I had emphasised her intelligence, her education and culture and sense of fun, omitting her religious shortcomings and political activism, the Catanese couple being devout Catholics and Grzegorz a theologian as well as a sociologist.

We'd arranged that once Gaby's English fiancé, a graphic artist then visiting her family in Alcamo, returned to Australia, Gaby should come and spend a few days on Favignana while Rita and Grzegorz were still there, but the day that we were expecting to meet her at the wharf in Trapani, she had rung me to say she wouldn't be able to make it, wailing in the voice of a child seeking petting, that she wasn't feeling well, she had had to go to Trapani hospital for tests and no one in the family would accompany her or even lend her a car. She had had to make her way by coach and wait hours alone, sick, by herself. I could hear tears starting in her voice.

Her family had been vile to her. Simon, her fiancé, had rushed off in a rage, without goodbyes to her parents, telling them their behaviour to their daughter was appalling and he wouldn't tolerate it. Between clenched teeth her parents had promised her they would never forgive his discourtesy.

I had listened in silence, trying to make sense of this extraordinary new world. Saying nothing seemed safest. At the end, when Gaby had talked herself out, she informed me she was waiting for her parents to depart the following Wednesday on a three weeks' cruise. They had refused to let her have any money but her mother had relented sufficiently to leave her the little car.

'So I can come to Favignana in the middle of next week,' she finished up, 'and spend a few days. Then I'll go home to see what's stirring, and you can come to Alcamo whenever you like, but preferably while my parents are on their cruise.'

Thinking of the way Rita and Grzegorz related to their daughter, Rossana, and their adored son, Giordano, of the respect and affection each of them showed one another, and their friends, equally gentle and loving with their children, I wondered what kind of family Gaby de Santis belonged to. In Sydney, a laughing, brilliant girl, full of energy, ambition and plans for the future, including reading for a Master's degree at the University of New South Wales, and negotiating work as a researcher with an academic there: in Alcamo, from where she rang me the day we arrived in Favignana, unrecognisable as a little girl, quavery and petulant, a victim, but not for a moment deflected from the need to hang on to her inheritance; and determined not to let her return to Australia deprive her of her share.

I had never had any experience of someone in this situation. Nor was I certain that I wanted to be better informed. Well, we would see. I would be meeting up with Gaby again in a few days.

After lunch we went for a walk along a bitumen road skirting the seashore. There was no beach to speak of, but the water shone like cut glass, clear and green. Active too. Rips clearly visible, the currents splitting round the ever present rocks weathering into sculpture gardens. Rita exulted over the beauty. I nodded. A lovely long flat walk lay ahead for another day. At four o'clock I waved them good-bye at the quay and when the ferry had turned about, headed back to Piazza Europa.

7

Cold was often a clammy presence in the holiday house, like being inside low cloud. I had hung my overcoat in the bedroom determined not to wear it inside or to put it across my knees. But I couldn't do without my woollen scarf and my beret. At night I waited till seven sharp, before switching on the little heater Grzegorz had bought. What was I doing here, I asked myself, sitting in this bleak little kitchen on a tiny island in Western Sicily, with nothing but my curiosity to warm my toes?

No point in conjecturing . None of the reasons would have meant a thing. But at some stage I would find out why. In the meantime, I lived as if I were running a low-grade fever of excitement.

Early in my stay, Rita's agent, Mimmo, invited me to watch a 1958 prize-winning documentary Radio Audizioni Italiane (RAI) had made of the blue-fin tuna trapping at Favignana. In 1954 RAI had become Italy's first public broadcaster, at that time educative in function, like the BBC. The film was in black and white, a marvellous evocation of the labyrinthine technique and associated ritual said to have been taught Sicilians by the Arabs.

Once, as a member of a Glasgow children's cinema club, I saw an outstanding film on the North Sea herring fleet, made by the documentary film pioneer, John Grierson. His take on the herring boats emphasised the dangers and privations endured by the fishermen, and their valour in netting food for Britain while grappling with mountainous seas.

Fishing in early summer for tuna in the Mediterranean is, instead, 'fair weather' fishing, where the sun shines, the sea is calm, the fishermen quiet and intense, and the tuna swimming close to the surface, readying to spawn, totally unaware of the horrendous slaughter awaiting them.

Creatures of habit, these magnificent animals, their warm blood giving them the muscular strength to swim at up to fifty kilometres an hour, roam the Atlantic, moving as far north as Greenland, and spawn either in the Gulf of Mexico or on the littorals of Greece, Turkey and other Mediterranean countries. Sicily's fisheries once numbered close to forty. Now there are only two, one based in Favignana. The tuna pass close to the Egadi Isles more or less annually but not always at full strength. Historically, when they failed to arrive or their numbers were down, Sicilians had to import grain from the North, brought by fleets that also carried salted cod, thus adding cod and dried stockfish – unsalted fish – to the Sicilian diet, something now considered integral to the traditional cuisine, and utterly delicious. I can vouch for it.

In every Sicilian primary industry, agriculture, sulphur mining, salt production and fishing, workers have traditionally been paid appalling wages. When the tuna slaughter was over, and a celebratory dinner held, no fisherman felt rich enough to eat tuna steak: he and his fellow labourers confined themselves to using every part of the tuna except the meat. The fish's gills and innards were braised in a rich stew. Bones were ground for fertilizer to grow vegetables and the tail of the fish was nailed over doorways for good luck.

I have to acknowledge, however, that while the volume of tuna taken can spell out a dazzling gross income – a single big tuna today reportedly bringing the price of a new car – a fishery also represents a substantial capital investment. The Florios and other owners in Favignana generally favoured collaborative ventures to meet the costs of capital and labour and also to spread the risks.

In tuna fishing, a prime capital item was the *tonnara*, a portmanteau word signifying both fishery and trap, the latter a famously complex system of nets once heavy as chain mail, downloaded on the seabed in such wise as to lie across the migratory path of the tuna which, sometimes in their thousands, would be thus diverted into narrow channels kilometres long and functioning like entrances to a freeway. Once funnelled into the main passage the animals would advance until reaching a chamber about fifty metres square, where a portcullis-like gate would be raised to allow them entry and lowered to block any attempted retreat. They would pass through six more chambers in similar fashion, till finally, the doomed creatures were impelled into the *camera della morte*, the chamber of death.

This shepherding process through the fortress could take several days, tuna backing up behind and on top of one another in the various chambers till every inch of space was occupied.

Seated on a hard chair beside Mimmo in a back room of his brother's bar, I waited impatiently till his niece's boyfriend and two other youths, clearly with no pressing employment to occupy them, arrived to make up the audience. The youths, like me, would be seeing the film for the first time.

It's late April, I think, when the film opens and still cold. Everyone is wrapped up. The women are all in black, with black scarves over their heads. Barely fifty years ago! It's a rare event to see this type of dress in Favignana today, even among very old ladies. People dress smartly, their bones are better covered, and their faces less wrinkled, partly because tourism has enabled some to eat protein and to pay for dental care or dentures.

The RAI commentator was saying that a poor tuna harvest would portend a wretched winter for the people on Favignana. Every year they waited anxiously, praying that the tuna would come. It was a vital part of their economy and they were terrified of the misery which followed the creatures' non-arrival. In 1958, after several such disappointments, the Favignanini are poor again.

The Rais has come into view, a big man of about seventy, very well fed, unlike the others, fit and strong, striding through the streets. Rais, an Arab word meaning 'leader' or 'chief', is a title given the master of the tuna hunt, so to speak, a title originally handed down from one generation to another. He is the high priest, the reader of signs and portents, wind, currents, bird movements, matter hauled up from the sea in buckets: only he can intuit exactly where off the coast the tuna are likely to pass on their way to spawn.

The villagers watch the Rais make his way through the streets. A small group of fishermen accompanies him. The men taking part in this ritual slaughter that has been ongoing for many centuries look surprisingly old to engage in a feat calling for brute strength and stamina of an awesome order unknown in most other regimes of manual labour. One of them tells the RAI interviewer that he has done forty-six seasons.

Most look older than their age, with narrow, bony foreheads and few teeth. Their cheeks are sunken, and their chins protrude from under their noses. But when I see them later in the chamber of death, hoisting up the incredibly heavy net filled with threshing, panic-stricken creatures, some weighing up to 400 kilos, bending precariously over the edge of the boats to lift the tuna out of the water with the hooks on their three-metre long gaffes, I'm speechless with admiration and pity, for the men, and the tuna.

The Rais and his small group spend several days walking the beaches looking for intimations of their quarry's prospective arrival. Eventually they return to the harbour and launch the boats. When the men leave, the women gather on a headland to see them off. There is no ceremony and almost no talk among the men, then or during the hours of waiting in the boats, except for occasional consultations from boat to boat about the material floating around them. They continually dip buckets into the sea to read the contents. Finally the Rais tells them to raise a cross on a buoy to mark the spot where they will download and install the *tonnara*. It is four kilometres off the coast.

Now we see them waiting for the tuna to arrive. But a swordfish enters the *tonnara* first. They grow even larger than the tuna and can swim faster, up to sixty kilometres an hour. The daring, drama and technological achievement of the underwater photography is astonishingly modern, rendering commentary almost superfluous. We follow the fish's dark shape with the characteristic bill, a young one it seems, swimming along, turning about, playfully, unperturbed, innocent and ignorant.

So painful to watch. 'You're done for,' I think. 'There's no escape. It'll be on and on, crammed in, more and more of you, fish above you, fish below, such crushing weights, no room to move, to breathe, and that horrible *camera della morte* waiting for you.'

Tuna have started entering the *tonnara*. The Rais will be happy: his reputation is enhanced by yet another correct decision and the catch promises to be a heavy one.

The camera shifts to the beach. A man on a white horse is galloping along at full pelt, carrying the good news from the *tonnara* to town. The tuna have arrived. Church bells ring out. Back at the nets, the men are encouraging the tuna.

'Tuna, tuna, rise. Rise, tuna, rise.'

It's an incantation. Not Italian and probably Arabic in origin. Mimmo had no idea if the translation were accurate. It was just what one says to the tuna at this point.

In the town, all the men are pulling on their jackets and caps and running to the port to launch their boats. Those back with the nets are counting the fish as they enter. They're moving fast, the tuna, confidently, not knowing they've been seriously deflected from the path leading to the spawning grounds. While the corralling process goes on, the men spend their time maintaining the nets, and shepherding the tuna from one chamber to the next, raising and lowering the gates as necessary. When the entire system is filled with tuna, the Rais will call for the *mattanza*, the slaughter of the tuna that are imprisoned in the chamber of death.

At the quadrilateral bounding the chamber of death, the men's reflections can be seen in the water. The Rais, his black outfit discarded for a workaday smock, is wearing a headband. He and one of his team are standing in the middle of a rowboat gently bobbing on the waves. They are both effortlessly erect, totally focused on the activity surrounding them. No problems maintaining their balance. It strikes me this is quite a dangerous place to be, with scores of tuna starting to mill about in this last room of the dungeon they have entered without a care, devoid of any warning instinct.

A sound operator in the RAI boat anchored just outside the quadrilateral is pointing a long microphone over the top of it. There's a tremendous racket underwater. Triangular fins keep breaking the surface, packing increasingly close together, looking like a fleet of toy boats crowding a pond. The slaughtermen, urged on by a colleague at their back leading the chant and conducting the tempo of movement, are heaving and hauling with all their might, drawing the net up under the fish. The Rais is thumping on the prow of his boat with a hammer, adding to the din.

At last a show of sense from the fish: they don't want to come up. They're resisting, trying to push down below the surface. But as more and more enter the quadrilateral, sheer numbers force them to pile on top of each other, and finally one rises almost vertically out of the water. I can see the upper half of his body, his eyes slewing about in panic, mouth gaping. Whistles are blowing. More and more tuna are breaking the surface and the slaughtermen have their sharpened gaffes poised. The confusion is dizzying, the water roiling with fish, but nobody moves. The Rais keeps blowing on his whistle. He has put on a sou'wester. Then he raises his right hand.

Eight men lean over the side of their boat and in unison plunge their gaffes into the first fish, then hoist it up and over the side on their hooks. Once started, action is speedy and rhythmic. Cut, twist and hoist. Sometimes when the tuna is a real giant, there's a break in the rhythm. Assessing its weight, the men lean so far over the side I marvel they don't fall in. The victim, cut in numerous places, seems exhausted as it is heaved up, but not yet over, the edge of the boat; it's so heavy the men are straining with every muscle. Suddenly the tuna starts snapping feverishly, trying to bite hold of an arm or whatever is in reach. This galvanises the men to give one more tug, and the fish topples over among them still flailing blindly, the men jumping back, dodging its blows, before the stricken creature subsides, and sinks below the frame. If the film weren't in black and white, the foaming water in the chamber of death would be rose pink like Red Bay when the Romans slaughtered thousands of Carthaginians and 700 ships went down.

Hours later, the nets are emptied, the Rais signals the *mattanza* is at an end, and the men raise a cheer. Depending on how many tuna enter the *tonnara*, there will be more *mattanzas*, as the Rais determines, until the season comes to an end, some time in the middle of June.

Mimmo signals his niece and tells her to bring us a cappuccino. I address myself to the youths. 'None of you has participated in a *mattanza*, I take it? I believe that nowadays you're only putting on mini-*tonnare* for tourists.'

One gives a shudder. 'I never wanted to be a fisherman.'

A commercial fishery using purse seine nets now has a base in Trapani. The *tonnara* is substantially finished in Favignana. Mimmo told me tuna numbers are rapidly dwindling in the Mediterranean because of the astronomical numbers of tuna being taken up in the purse seine nets. The nets are so big they can clean out an entire lakeful of fish. And the tuna farms are actually increasing the numbers of fish being taken from the water, because the farming does not start from scratch. Fishing companies take smaller tuna as well as the larger ones to fatten them up. And tuna have to be several years old before they spawn. So fewer tuna are being spawned.

I thanked Mimmo for organising the viewing. His niece's boyfriend laid a hand on my arm.

'Signora, would you like a copy of the film?'

I told him I would be delighted to have a copy if it were at all possible. 'But only if you let me pay for it.'

'Of course, signora,' he said, indulgently. 'I will bring it to the bar in a week's time.' He brought me the copy within the week, but resolutely refused to accept payment from me, insisting as usual, 'I've done nothing.'

Such a gesture of kindness and generosity was one among many that Sicilians extended to me throughout the year and I never ceased to feel discomfited by their refusal to accept payment. After all I was a stranger. They had no accrued obligations to me. But it was useless to protest.

I did notice early in my marriage that Italians placed enormous emphasis on being kind. Their reputation for warmth is vested in that kindness. But time passing, I began to wonder if constant exhortations to be kind can force conformity and passivity on people, and dissuade them from exercising the critical analysis that in other societies may spotlight and generate resistance to dishonesty, corruption and the abuse of power.

Ultimately I found in the writings of the Nobel Prize winning playwright Luigi Pirandello, famed for dramatising psychoanalytic themes, an illuminating exposition of the Italian dedication to kindness: "Where there is no active mastery of the situation there is passive suffering and effort to compose matters through affection. When all else is blasted away, kindness, like joy is the pearl of great price. In this situation man is isolated not only from others, but from himself.'

8

Since I was planning to stay at least a month in Favignana I decided there was no point dashing about the way I might were I a weekend tourist. By the same reasoning – that I was to have an extended stay in a place where the population seemed to be in semi-hibernation – I thought I should buy a small radio. That gave me an excuse to visit the white goods shop Mimmo Sparta had mentioned.

I found it in a street growing out of Piazza Madrice, with two energetically dressed display windows exploiting a corner block position. Inside the shop everything looked new and spruce, light and airy, the appliances dazzling bright, but modestly sized, fridges reduced in bulk, tall and slim, one in black, one Chinese red, but none yet with a television set built into the door like the one my Wollongong house cleaner, blushing, recently confessed to having bought herself.

On hearing my muted footsteps, Antonio, the owner, rose from his computer to greet me with an 'at last a customer' eagerness in his expression, thinking perhaps that I was moving on to the island, and in the market to buy a fridge, a stove and a pop-up toaster.

Good looking, I thought, but then who isn't in Italy, in Sicily? Some of the youths and young girls I'd already seen in the region were so compellingly beautiful, it was difficult to avoid gaping at their perfectly oval faces and glossy dark eyes, the very same physiognomies that inspire so many of those religious portraits on view everywhere, aides memoire when piety falters. Those near black eyes are less common on the streets, however, than they are in paintings. Antonio's eyes were hazel, their flecked amber shot through with a hint of green. Of middling height, with his head of thick dark hair and clear complexion, trim and neat, in jeans, topped by a shirt under a sweater, he hardly met with Guy de Maupassant's description of Sicilian males as 'fiery and swarthy'.

Within a few minutes he was confiding that he had opened his shop for business only at the start of the last tourist season. But sales had been disappointing. In fact no other customer appeared during the half-hour we spent chatting, while my own purchase was very modest: the second cheapest radio in stock. Still, Antonio was obviously pleased by the sale and I, an ABC classics FM devotee, trotted off, beaming at strangers I met on the street, giddy with delight at the thought of stretching out on Rita's matrimonial bed and listening to music again.

The radio was about the same size as the one I had in the kitchen at home in Wollongong but this one in Favignana had no pull. I directed the tuning cursor backwards and forwards, across the country, I imagined. Across Europe. I could hear foreign languages being transmitted from some stations. Finally – something local.

A male voice was now resonating in the kitchen. Talking. Talking. Not a pause for breath. He had the same velvety tone as the radio opinion shapers in Australia, his speech similarly soothing, mellow and meaningless. From time to time I thought I heard someone offer up a prayer. But no music worthy of the name. Antonio's radio was useless. Eventually I went to see him again. He nodded sympathetically.

'Yes, signora, you're right. We don't have programmes of your ABC kind. And what you tuned into was Radio Maria, from the Vatican. Only the Church can transmit its signal all over Italy.'

'You mean you don't even have RAI here in Favignana – the national broadcaster?'

He shook his head. 'No.'

So the Church, whose major benefactor and funder is the State can afford to transmit all over Italy while the State broadcaster cannot? No wonder the Italians are recorded as being so miserable. I can feel my Protestant passions starting to darken. Later I tried out the radio in Palermo, Syracuse and Florence. Radio Maria had at least some competition in Florence, but classical music seemed to have been banished from the Italian airwaves. Too subversive, perhaps, in a country with so much public utterance given over to pap.

****

Only a few days after buying Antonio's radio I was sent a copy of an email received by the Danilo Dolci centre in Partinico, a district of Palermo, that cast an interesting light on Vatican Radio and its controlling power over who broadcasts and who does not.

The email had been sent to the Centre by a Neapolitan, the President of Radio Azzurra, a community broadcasting cooperative formed by people with disabilities in Campania, the region that includes Naples. Since 1985 until 2005 when Vatican Radio bludgeoned the group off their frequency, it had been transmitting on 105.500 from Vesuvius.

The broadcaster said: *'I am writing to you because some time ago the quintessentially political Radio Maria* [Vatican radio station] *installed and began using a powerful new system transmitting from 105.550. This is dominating our frequency and has silenced us since March 2005. Our frequency is our heart and without it we are completely closed off. Ought not a Christian radio to be full of love for its neighbour?*

'The Minister has been taking an interest in the matter, especially in the area of crammed frequencies and broadcasting from outside the licensed zone. Here in Naples we have had a small victory over other malefactors... but Radio Maria, the politician, is STRONG against the weak – those whom it is supposed to defend. Just think that in Naples it has five transmission stations, in contravention of the legislation. But then, Radio Maria has so many saints in paradise to speak for her.'

Curious to know what might have eventuated I discovered from material posted subsequently on the Web by the leader of Radio Azzurra that*: 'Now the pious and powerful Radio Maria who has so much help from her connections has laid an array of charges against me personally in court. I needn't describe the psychological and physical condition of some in our* *cooperative, and how many people in authority we have written to, but when we deal with Radio Maria which is a religious persona, it's as if we are in touch with bandits, pure and simple, men who believe they can do anything they want and that no one dare oppose them.*

'What am I asking? To help us regain possession of the station that has been operating since 1985 in via Osservatorio n.10, Vesuvio and to give us back the voice that we have lost to the most holy and most political Radio Maria. If people would write or fax protests to Radio Maria and to [A list of various communications authorities follows] *this would help us not to feel ourselves abandoned by those who should be supporting us'.*

Antonio had attributed Vatican Radio's monopoly of the airwaves in the Egadi Isles to the fact that the Vatican was the only broadcaster able to afford the equipment necessary to transmit a signal. But the Neapolitan's experience was suggesting that by squeezing Radio Azzurra off the airwaves, removing a unique opportunity for disabled people to voice their interests, the Church was pressing on with its historic goal of suppressing diversity of opinion, wherever possible, even to the extent of breaching secular law.

Aside from neglecting to love a neighbour in special need of love – a community of people with disabilities – the Church was exercising the principle of Dual Sovereignty to advance its dominion over Italian radio. Putting aside normal feelings of outrage against what would widely be seen in a secular society as an abuse of power and callous indifference to justice from an agency purporting to be Christian, I discovered that the Church's behaviour in this matter is entirely consistent with its mission statement as published in the *New Advent Catholic Encyclopaedia*, a document that bears close reading by anyone trying to understand Sicily's wretched condition.

'The State exists to help man to temporal happiness, the Church to eternal. Of these two purposes the latter is the more ultimate, greater good, while the former is not necessary for the acquisition of the latter. The dominating proximate purpose of man must be to earn his title to eternal salvation: for that, if

needs be, he must rationally sacrifice his temporal happiness. It is clear, therefore, that the purpose of the Church is higher in the order of Divine Providence and of righteous human endeavour than that of the State. Hence, in case of direct collision of the two, God's will and man's need require that the guardian of the lower purpose should yield. Likewise the argument for the extension of the powers of the higher society in a measure into the domain of the lower will not hold for such extension from the lower into the higher.'

Considering the plight of the disabled Neapolitans and their community radio station we see from the above that the Church can justify any action it takes to achieve its single purpose. The end justifies the means – normally an unsavoury proposition associated with totalitarian states. The Neapolitans' loss of happiness is not the Church's affair. On the other hand if the State in performing its God-given obligation to make the disabled community happy, passes a law permitting them a radio channel that the Church thinks would better serve its purpose then the Church will simply ignore that law. It is above temporal law. In order to 'earn' their salvation, the Neapolitans must sacrifice their community radio station, presumably so that the Church can better ensure that every Catholic is of the same mind. The more avenues of communication it controls, the better to secure that result.

As the President of Radio Azzurra reveals, the Church began running a legal case against him, in Church terms a perfectly reasonable use of State law to fulfil its divine purpose. Punishing the President would discourage others from obstructing the Church.

The legitimacy of the Church's power base having been successfully challenged over the centuries by liberal philosophers and scientists, and constraints imposed on the temporal powers of all religious institutions, the Roman Catholic Church has been forced to recognise that in the liberal democracies where it is simply one of many churches and where 'revealed' truth has no scientific standing, its relationship with its congregations differs in character from that which it enjoys in 'Catholic States'. In liberal democracies, Catholics are 'subject' to the State and only 'members' of the Church – a significant distinction.

Sicily, as I soon learned, is a prime example of a 'Catholic State'.

****

To thaw out in the mornings, I quickly established a routine of walking up to the top of the street, out of the shade and into full sun, sometimes to the phone box where I could ring Australia with a phone card. Eleven thirty local time was just right to catch my beloved brother Jack at home.

At the top a trattoria curved endlessly round a wide corner into a street with a few shops and some terrace houses. It had a folksy, woody look about it, with a multi-paned door under a fascia, multi-paned casement windows and outside, heavy wooden tables with bench seats. On my first day alone I stood looking through the windows till I realised with embarrassment that I was staring directly at what might have been the proprietor and his extended family seated at a long table, eating early before the main lunchtime diners arrived. They got their eyes on me. I moved away and stood in the sun, feeling myself melt joint by joint. Later, I entered the trattoria and ordered lunch. The first and last time because everything in that place was too pricey. I chose spaghetti marinara and a steak with salad. The proprietor offered the wine menu. The bottles were not cheap. I asked for a house wine.

'We have a bottle of white wine already opened,' he said. 'We can let you have a glass of that.'

'No red?'

He shook his head. I asked for water. Not far from me was a table where five workmen were already into their second plate. By the time my pasta arrived they were finishing up on the fruit and cheese, and the proprietor was preparing to settle the bill. The men began pushing their chairs back, rising and reaching for their jackets and scarves on a rack nearby. When the proprietor returned with their change one handed him a bottle of red wine, still a good two thirds full, and directed him to bring it to me, raising his voice to let me know,

'We're not drinking any more, signora. Enjoy it.'

It was Nero d'Avola, a popular Sicilian wine I'd been introduced to in Catania, and the men's thoughtfulness was yet another expression of the spontaneous generosity Sicilians so readily demonstrate.

On leaving the trattoria I walked to the end of the street where I had seen the laundry/dry-cleaner. It was shut – again. A pamphlet advertising some event was stuck to the door, and reading it, I suddenly noticed that for further information readers were invited to contact the shop owner on the phone number listed. I copied this precious item into my filofax and headed to the phone box beside the trattoria. The number responded immediately.

'Are you the owner of the dry-cleaning shop?' I asked.

'Yes. I am.'

'And do you ever open your shop?'

'Of course. Six days a week.'

I couldn't believe it. 'Is it open today?'

'At four o'clock.'

'Fine. I'm a visitor from overseas. Been here several days but I have not yet found your shop open.'

'I can assure you, signora, we are open. And we are very busy. Come and you will see all our work.'

What a relief. Keeping on into the sun I started following a street that circled round in a crescent and came up against what looked like a huge grey battleship. Some kind of government building. I walked around it twice. A very odd shape, hexagonal, not rectangular. Not a single window opening onto the streets. A woman wheeling a stroller suddenly rounded a corner and I took the opportunity to ask her, 'What's this building, signora?'

It was a prison. Good heavens. So massive for such a small village. Perhaps a variation of Jeremy Bentham's panopticon, the prison shaped like a hubbed wheel where every prisoner at the rim could be isolated from every other and from the guard at the centre, who could see inside every cell without himself being seen. I stopped at various places along the wall, pressing an ear close to it, straining to hear something. Not a whisper. I looked up. Nothing like the US prisons featured in movies, with huge spotlights and a bridge where the guards march up and down like sentries on watch muttering things like, 'Five bells and all's well.'

Most likely it was out of commission. Probably built in the Fascist era to house all the political prisoners that hadn't been murdered. It would have aided the island economy, employing caterers, cleaners, guards, office staff, medicos and nurses and the like. But now? While puzzling over this, I was drawing closer to the prison entrance, thinking to go right up and peer through the gate, when a car with two carabinieri inside passed me and came to a halt at the gate. Quickening my pace, I managed to reach them as they exited the car and went to the boot, raising the lid to remove their leather attaché cases.

I greeted the driver while he was straightening up. He turned slowly, looking me up and down in a very professional manner, returning the '*Buon giorno*' with a faint hint of impatience in his voice, but waiting, nonetheless. I waited too. Then. 'Can I help you?' he said.

'Is this prison in active service?'

He and his colleague, both now facing me, exchanged looks. 'Of course? Why else would we be here?'

I ignored that. 'Are there any prisoners inside at the moment?'

'Why do you ask?' This time a clear note of authority was present in his voice. And suspicion.

'I've just arrived here,' I said. 'I'm living in a little house down the street,' pointing in the general direction. 'I couldn't figure out what kind of building this is. It's an odd shape. Then I learned that it is a prison. So I'm wondering why a little village should have such a big prison. Are there many criminals inside?'

They both relaxed. 'Quite a number,' the driver said. 'But they come from all over Italy. It's rare to have a local in custody but it can happen occasionally. The prison is designed so that its activities do not disturb the villagers.'

His colleague spoke up for the first time. 'Up on Santa Catarina, the mountain above the harbour, you can see a fort. That was the prison used by the monarch, before the Unification.'

'Have the crimes changed?'

'Not entirely,' he said. 'Many of the convicted are still murderers, but their crimes are sometimes related to drugs trafficking. That is different.'

Here was an excuse to visit Antonio for a little chat. I would ask him to tell me more about the prison. Had there ever been an escape, I wondered, with a manhunt? But when I reached the shop I discovered his wife in attendance. I introduced myself. 'Angela', she said in return, proffering her hand.

She was a few years younger than Antonio. In her mid-thirties, I guessed. Bright and attractive. More diffident than Antonio, but making no secret of the fact that she was curious to meet the Australian her husband must have described to her. She explained that Antonio, an electrician by trade, was having to continue his house-call service until his business grew, when he might be able to devolve it onto an employee, 'if we should ever have need of one,' she added, just a trace of doubt in her tone.

She did not know how many inmates were incarcerated in the prison. Or who they were. Apology in her tone, she professed to know nothing about the prison. People who worked there or supplied services to it were reluctant to speak about it.

Then obviously trying to be helpful, she asked me, 'Have you been up to the fort at the top of Santa Catarina? It has dungeons underground. The King used to put prisoners there even after the Unification.'

It was a terrible place, she recalled, but not nearly so bad as the prison on Marettimo, at the foot of the castle of Punta Troia. Not a prison. A pit. It had used to be a water tank. The Spanish would put so many people, mainly political prisoners, into it that there was room only to stand up. People were half suffocated. And they could be left for years. Some went raving mad.

During the Risorgimento many of the prisoners were middle-class people and minor nobility. Some wrote accounts of conditions so horrific they moved Ferdinand II to write in his will that the pit had to be closed on his death, a last minute apprehension, perhaps, that having maintained such an inhumane lockup mightn't go down well for the Bourbons in the Book of Judgment. Fortunately, his successor complied with the instruction.

Exile to island prisons or to a village in a distant part of the country is a sentencing staple of the Italian justice system, generally employed for terrorists, subversives or mafiosi who might be sprung in an escape, or killed by former mates to block any leakage of information. Napoleon, first on Elba, then St Helena, and the mafia imprisoned by Mussolini on islands represent the kind of persons best confined offshore, far distant from admirers, vengeful enemies or treacherous friends.

I wanted to visit Marettimo, the Sea of Thyme, but never made it, partly because I spent more than a week roaming the west with Gaby de Santis, and within the time left in the Egadi, whenever I thought of venturing onto the smaller isles – so small, one of them is called Formica – ant – the weather was too grim for boats to go out.

****

But no matter what the weather, and it was often fine, every day that I spent on Favignana I was out and about. My first excursion was along an endless bitumen road with ragged edges, leading away from the port in a south-east direction, running parallel to the sea on its left. On the right, set way back from the road, were newish looking flats in a pale sandstone colour, bereft of shade and radiating waves of heat, the land around them dry and bone bare. In the same area I noticed a bus stop and a little depot where on another occasion I was to find a bus parked and a driver more than happy to take me around the island, then, having gotten to know me, to offer me a lift whenever he found me out on a walk.

The black road wound along for kilometres and though over time I followed it for increasing distances, I never came in sight of the end, for the landscape started to unnerve me with its heavy pall of solitude and silence.

Australians would marvel at the paucity of sandy beaches. One or two only. They're not a feature of volcanic littorals. I stayed well back on the rocks, noticing several rips, the currents rearing and tumbling over one another.

Hanging out of fissures and crevices in rocks along the foreshores were caper bushes. Rita had pointed them out to me on our first day.

Quite small shrubs, not much more than a metre in height, capers are as hardy and robust as the olive, Rita told me, and they actually love to grow near the sea. They're all over Favignana. I noticed them on my walks, close to the water, but also on the hills, a major feature of the cover vegetation. Thorny things, I learned, when I tried to use them as handholds, clambering up Santa Catarina.

Like the tufa and the tuna, the sulphur and the salt, capers are a wonderful gift of nature, of inestimable value in older times, and even today to landowners who cultivate them big time on Salina, the most important of the Aeolian Isles.

Rita had already pointed out to me the tufa in the sea, the rock that shed the pesty yellow pollen in the bathroom. The tufa is not always pollen-coloured but starts off with a high concentration of calcium, glowing with a wonderful iridescent blue like moonstone. It's born of the sea, since it's formed from shells, and is said to have emerged towards the end of the last ice age, deposited over an area of about twenty square kilometres of Favignana, one mass conveniently covering four square kilometres at a single point. Gradually oxidisation darkens the tufa to a blonde ochre that gives way to various shades of bronze.

Quarrying tufa was once Favignana's second biggest industry after tuna fishing, great blocks being exported to other parts of Sicily and to North Africa, but the introduction of the ferry service allowed other building materials to be imported at competitive prices.

The tufa blocks had to be cut perfectly square, hard labour, especially because some blocks were misleadingly soft on the surface only to prove diamond hard inside. Quarrymen were paid the highest fees for cubic perfection. More than any other structures I encountered in Sicily, including the temples, quarries made me want to linger, and after discovering the stunning 'latomie' park in Syracuse, I decided a quarry is my favourite form of 'found' art. Something about the labour that has gone into a quarry moves the emotions. Like being inside the pyramids or ancient tombs. In Favignana some tall shapes left standing after the extraction look like an artist's prevision of skyscrapers.

One afternoon I caught the bus to Cala Rossa, Red Bay, where the Romans defeated the Carthaginians in 241BCE. A place of desolate beauty and watchful silence, it reminded me of Port Arthur in Tasmania, a bottomless well of grief and horror that keeps bubbling up in the collective memory. Seven hundred ships had sunk in the almighty battle between the two rival powers and the blood spilled had bloodied the waters, giving the bay its name.

Reflecting on the slaughter I recalled that the Phoenicians had come here from Tunisia at a time when the Greeks too had been content with visitor status on the opposite coast. Both had enjoyed happy relations with the indigenous Sicilians, arriving and departing as welcomed traders, or settling down beside them in a friendly way. But the fierce competition for wealth eventually set them all, Carthaginians, Greeks and, worst of all, the Romans, at one another's throats.

I wondered if T. S. Eliot's *Death by Water* in *The Waste Land* had been inspired by a visit to the bay.

Phlebas the Phoenician, a fortnight dead,
Forgot the cry of gulls, and the deep sea swell
And the profit and loss.
A current under sea
Picked his bones in whispers. As he rose and fell

He passed the stages of his age and youth
Entering the whirlpool.
Gentile or Jew
O you who turn the wheel and look to windward,
Consider Phlebas, who was once handsome and tall as you.

Letting my eye drift over the quarry patterns I became aware of a lone man standing motionless but on a lower rock shelf, about a hundred metres away, his gaze fixed on a sailing boat out in the bay. After a moment's hesitation I decided to pick my way down to him. He gave no sign of noticing my presence until I was standing right beside him.

Then he returned my '*Buon giorno, signore,*' with a smile, his face and demeanour a picture of serenity. On discovering that I was a foreigner, with no further ado, he began to recount quietly the history of the battle of Red Bay, almost as if he had been an eyewitness. Then he led me over the quarries, up and down steps hewn out of the rocks, pointing out differences in the colour and texture of the tufa, and drawing my attention to the long, deep chutes that had been gouged like slippery dips out of the high banks to allow blocks of tufa a rapid descent into the ships. He had worked in the quarries at Cala Rossa all his life, since he was eight.

Finally he pressed me to accompany him to his little cottage close by to fetch some implements he kept inside, waxed and shining, one for hewing the rock and the other for shaping it. For two hours he had me enthralled. Clasping his hand to say goodbye, I tried to press some notes into his palm, but he refused to accept them.

'I have done nothing,' he said.

I protested. 'You've done a great deal, lived a hard amazing life, on this melancholy bay, to tell me your story.'

He was very happy, he assured me, and had everything he needed.

A few days later I passed him in the Piazza Madrice, standing with a little group of men outside a bar, chatting. His eyes lit up when he saw me and he raised his cap.

Away from the sea, the land on Favignana very quickly rises steeply in most parts, though more on the scale of hills than mountains. Before 1637 when the Pallavicini purchased the Egadi Isles, the islanders were plagued by pirates, mercenary soldiers and any riffraff with a boat, looking for plunder.

Turkish raiding parties were a menace, constantly on the lookout for slaves of both genders, or bright young boys to turn into Janissaries, the Sultan's personal troops, substantially manned by Christians raised in the Islamic faith. So frightening were the Turks to Sicilians that mothers still warn recalcitrant children to behave, or the 'Turchi' will get them. Caves were the islanders' favourite habitats because cave entrances were much easier to camouflage than little cottages. However, after the Genoese arrived and taught the locals the principles of agriculture, the cattle went into the caves and the people moved into tufa dwellings.

9

Favignana was not where I had expected to find a riveting monument. But there it was in Piazza Europa which hosts the town hall, a bronze statue, easier to associate with a British industrial city than a very small town in Sicily: a male in distinctly Victorian garb, obviously from the upper middle class, a portly, prosperous-looking businessman, hoisted high on a magnificent pedestal decorated with symbols denoting his business interests, conspicuously shipping. Radiating a florid optimism, his demeanour pointed up the threadbare vitality of the sculptured sages I had noted outside Catania's numerous churches, somewhat enervating old men with long beards, wrapped in an approximation of Middle Eastern robes and bowed over in postures of perfect obedience.

Who then was this unpriestly burgher in the long overcoat, wide open and thrown back on the shoulders to display a double-breasted waistcoat, left hand bunched casually in his trouser pocket, a picture of calm confidence and serenity? The inscription on the pedestal read, *To Ignazio Florio, Favignana, in 1896, a civic tribute: with spontaneous offerings from workers and an official contribution from City Hall, this monument was raised to the benefactor of Favignana, demonstrating that there need be no discord between capital and labour, between riches and poverty, where justice, piety and love preside.*

I noted the date. Two years after one of the most momentous periods in Italian modern history, when the entire peninsula had been swept by a movement dedicated to the ideals of social democracy. Amazingly, the greatest influence on reformers in the North came from the '*Fasci Siciliani*', *fasci* loosely translating as rods bound together in sheaves, the idea being that the sheaf is stronger than its individual stalks.

Initially the Fasci were led by the salt and sulphur miners, the bulk of whom began work when aged nine. In the very low and narrow seams children could produce as much as an adult. And were prey to abuse. Their wages were so trivial that when the Americans came into the market late in the nineteenth century, the mine owners, Ignazio Florio among the largest, could not compete by cutting labour costs. A centuries-long monopoly of the world's sulphur output came to an end for Sicily's regime.

Women and children, reputedly the most combative members of every Sicilian uprising, joined the Fasci from the beginning. But what drew even educated middle-class people from both North and south to the movement was that its leaders had come up with an efficient structure and a coherent program designed to radically transform the economy and implement democratic rights.

So speedily did the Fasci grow that the Church and the nobility panicked, especially those nobles sufficiently foresighted to have formed partnerships with the Florios and other capitalists, liberal elitists convinced that they alone, not the masses, were capable of turning Italy into an industrial economy.

But the Sicilians were seeking a lot more than wage increases. They wanted social democracy. They maintained pressure on the regime, wearing insignia, forming bands to sing inspiring songs, and organising study groups to learn how to develop a socialist party aimed at assuming government.

In 1893 the miners confronted proprietors with claims for improvements in wages and conditions. The nobility refused even to talk to Fasci representatives and pressed the parliament to urge stronger action on the government. A state of emergency was declared and in the name of anti-anarchism troops and police did a massive sweep of the region, arresting people for such offences as calling out 'Down with the King' or 'Long live anarchy'. Every leader, actual and putative, was committed for trial, their custodial sentences ultimately stretching from six to eighteen years. Ordinary members were badly abused and beaten by troops and the movement collapsed.

I concluded this Favignana monument must have been projected very quickly after the demise of the Fasci. There had been 'an official contribution' from City Hall, the plaque said. An attempt to calm people harbouring feelings of resentment and thwarted political ambitions? And how voluntary or spontaneous was a contribution from destitute Sicilians who had not long since been physically abused and imprisoned by the class of whom Ignazio Florio was a representative, he being the first of the family to reinvent himself as an aristocrat? How did they contribute? As we read in Giovanni Verga's stories, penance among the poor often took the form of free labour, skilled and unskilled, on church holdings.

The speaking voice in the inscription irked me. It is clearly that of the shepherd talking to his grown-up sheep, gently admonishing them. The people are to remember their benefactor, the man who set up a fish canning factory in Favignana and gave jobs to locals. They are not to believe all the rubbish socialists go on with about conflict between capital and labour, or even between rich and poor. *'There need be no discord between capital and labour, between riches and poverty, where justice, piety and love preside.'*

Justice can't, as the inscription romances, do away with discord, only regulate it, because conflict is inherent in the right to private property. Justice systems develop to deal with conflict between often socially and economically unequal parties, and the famous scales are never in equilibrium. As for love? On the work scene, fairness is the only apt expression of love. The Fasci Siciliani had been driven to revolt by desperate poverty with no prospects of improvement in their lives. Justice and love were the very things denied them.

Piety may be another matter: artificially and in the short term, it can suppress discord, involving as it does, the collective and public expression of conforming thought and action, of subjugation to the reigning orthodoxy on pain of otherwise being deemed a heretic or subversive bound for the stake or the gulag. But history, Sicilian history at that, has shown the absence of discord in totalitarian regimes to be an illusion.

So much for a monumental piece of propaganda. A whopping big lie. But looking up once more at the solid, almost four-sided figure on the pedestal, I could see he knew his contribution to economic growth had far exceeded that made by any king of Sicily since the Normans or any of the aristocratic idlers who hung off the monarchy. On the other hand, as the biggest mine owner paying wages that bought very little more than a loaf of bread a day, he too must have regarded the peasantry working in his enterprises as beings with whom captains of industry had no common humanity. Buber's I-It, not I-Thou.

Still, he was a brilliant entrepreneur as I learned from Salvatore Requirez's brief, dense and admirably researched *A History of the Florios,* released in 2007 to commemorate 200 years of the Florio presence in Sicily. Given what I now know of the Sicilian regime's long enduring and continuing hostility to capitalism, that the five Florios, Calabrian innovators and entrepreneurs of genius extending across four generations from the late eighteenth to the early twentieth century, actually used Sicily not only as a starting point, but the base for what became a mammoth industrial empire, is a powerful reminder that Sicily has resources and opportunities to offer the talented. Its riches are natural but its poverty man-made.

Writers tend to regard the Florios as money-making cartoon figures. A comprehensive biography remains to be written about the family. Ignazio, the man on the monument was clearly an entrepreneur with few equals, then or now. But notwithstanding their dynastic genius, by the 1920s the Florios were history, most likely because the *latifondisti*, the big landowners were basically rentiers, unwilling to risk their capital in Florio-style enterprises like foundries, ships and *tonnaras*, especially if they were also required to work, themselves.

In modern Sicily, with its twenty-five per cent chronic unemployment rate, ruthless, stingy, greedy, lying, big-thinking entrepreneurs need to be embraced so long as they can be made to share a fairer portion of the enormous surplus value Sicilian workers have historically delivered to the regime. I couldn't forbear to smile on Ignazio Florio every time I passed his statue, his radiant expression and obvious enjoyment of his wealth and status, offering one contradiction at least, of the pernicious Sicilian ideology that there is no connection between work and reward.

10

On one of my visits to Antonio, I asked him what he knew of the Florios. Of the statue in the Piazza Europa:

'That's Ignazio.'

'I could read that on the plaque, I would like to know who decided to raise the monument?'

Parking his elbows on the counter, he rested his chin on his hands, concentrating. To no good effect. 'Probably the Comune. It was a long time ago.'

That made me laugh. 'How can a Sicilian say the mid-nineteenth century was a long time ago? A long time ago was when the Greeks first arrived.'

How could Sicilians live knowing so little of their social history!

'So what do you think of Favignana?' he asked, changing the subject.

By this stage I had worked out that unlike Florentines who never tire of declaiming the beauty and virtues of their beloved city, Sicilians are always tentative when seeking reactions to their region. They bear with shame their kinship with the mafia, the humiliation of involuntary indolence, the helplessness that goes with a wretched education, and the poverty that completes their disempowerment.

It was too soon yet for me to sort out my thoughts, I told him. And then, pondering a moment. 'Poets have a special name for that playful little breeze that is so delightful here. *Uno zefiro*. You have a word like that?' Antonio nodded. 'Compliments on your vocabulary, signora.'

'Well, it's an English word too, you know. We have borrowed many from you and the Greeks. But, Antonio, we have to determine if we're speaking of Favignana as a place to live in or a holiday spot. I have to say I need big city services, music, drama, and – practically tiptoeing over the words –

bookshops that are not mere propaganda centres for the Church.'

Had he understood the last part? Not a flicker in his expression. If he were unaware that pious booksellers in Sicily are slyly culling their stock of books that fail to promote 'Catholic values' he would wonder what I meant. I pressed on. 'I should find it very difficult to live in a society where there are obvious limits, not so much on my own freedom to read and think, but on the freedom of others, because I might feel that I'm living in a slave society. But give me time. Anyway, I'm thankful there are so few cars.'

He told me many of the locals park their cars more or less permanently over the water in Trapani, where they commute daily on the hydrofoil which is faster and more frequent than the ferry. Then they can drive to their work if it should be distant from the docks, or take off for Palermo or Messina. Some keep a pied-à-terre in Trapani so that they, or their high-school age children can stay overnight if need be, either by choice, or because bad weather has grounded the ferries.

That afternoon, after the siesta, I gathered my laundry together and set off to the drycleaner's. The shop was open. Big as a warehouse inside. And the manageress hadn't been fibbing. She and her assistant had enough work piled up to keep them going until their retirement.

'But where has it all come from?' I asked, casting an astonished eye over shelf after shelf lining the spacious walls, and crammed with neatly folded bedding and linen: sheets, blankets, counterpanes, towels, tablecloths, napkins. Elsewhere on racks hung the usual array of coats, jackets, dresses and trousers labelled and waiting to be picked up.

'Don't people wash their own bedding here? What do they do with their washing machines?'

The manageress, who had a thin papery look, as if she shunned daylight, and an angular body crunched with tension, held a cigarette clamped between her teeth, barely removing it to speak, while her skinny arm swept to and fro over an ironing board, expelling steam pumped up to the iron from a huge tank on the floor beside her. Between the smoke and the steam she was engulfed in a permanent fug. Different from most other women I had met in Sicily, certainly an oddity in Favignana. A slum sophisticate, I guessed. Who knew how to curse.

'You're not local,' I said to her. She didn't bother to raise her head, just her eyes.

'I'm Barese. I married a man from here.'

She paused in her ironing to draw on her cigarette, sucking deeply, all the way up from her toes, and, presumably strengthened, dug inside my laundry bag, withdrawing the sheets and towels that had been used by Grzegorz and Rita during their overnight stay.

'You see these sheets? You know how many people here live in *pensioni*? Not tourists, permanent residents? There are also the hotels and all their bedding and linen, and had you forgotten the prison? The inmates, the carabinieri and prison warders? The doctors at the Guardia Medica? We also do the laundry for people visiting Marettimo and Levanzo.'

No wonder the poor woman was thin and bony and smoking so fiercely.

'So will you be able to do mine at all?'

She reckoned she would have them ready in two days' time. She wanted to know when I would be leaving the island, adding, before I had time to wonder what business it was of hers, 'You'll have to leave the keys with me so that I can clean the house after you've gone. Before the next tenants arrive.'

So she was the cleaner Mimmo had engaged for Rita. I took the opportunity to enquire if she had climbed the ladder to dust the platform hosting the two mattresses. 'You know, it's not wise to have people turn over in bed and find themselves burying their nose in a heap of soft yellow dust. They won't like it.'

She sniffed and gave a slight toss of the head: 'There wouldn't be any tufa dust if they spent money on having it treated.'

Ah-ha. The tufa could indeed be sealed. I had thought it incredible that people so inventive as the Italians, even far back as the Romans, could not have come up with a solution to the tufa dust problem. Antonio had deliberately avoided revealing it to me, most likely, I decided, because he didn't want to speak badly of the Palermo architect, or perhaps of Rita, though Rita had only recently bought the house and probably knew nothing about the dust. She never used the shower off the kitchen and had no reason to scale the ladder and sleep on the top bunks. Nonetheless, the architect ought to have had the tufa treated because it was the right thing to do, aesthetically if nothing else. But perhaps since most people came to Favignana for only the weekend or a few days at most, she had considered the expense unnecessary.

'Still,' I said, to the Barese, 'it would be better to remove the dust when you clean. So that you have a perfect record. You can ask for extra money to climb the ladder.'

She stopped ironing and drew her head back, the better to focus on me: 'I should ask for extra money to climb the ladder?' And gave a little snort. 'In your country, maids get money for climbing a ladder?'

'The standard hourly rate doesn't usually include that,' I said. 'They're not supposed to have to climb ladders to dust.' I was sure a cleaner had once told me it cost more to do things above the head. The Barese resumed her ironing, pressing the iron forcefully onto a trouser placket, making the steam hiss loudly. Then with both hands she began patting the hot vapour into the cloth.

'How much would I ask for?'

I laughed. 'You're from a commercial culture. Say that it's negotiable.'

She stood up from the board, straightening her shoulders, the beginnings of a smile crinkling round her eyes. 'Come and see me when you can, signora. You really make me laugh.'

11

Gaby di Santis arrived in Favignana a week after Rita and Grzegorz departed. She had left her mother's car in Trapani, in the same parking lot Grzegorz had used, saying that since Favignana was a small place we would have no need of a car.

She reacted instantly to the cold in the house, and whenever we weren't out walking she would take herself off to a bar where, for the price of three cappuccinos as she put it, she could sit in a warm place all day reading. While she was out I either got on with my notes or went looking for someone to talk to. In early March I was the only tourist on the island, at least on weekdays, though I had noticed one or two outsiders bicycling about the previous weekend and caught a glimpse of them in a trattoria on the Saturday night. Gaby and I cooked very little. We both ate *panelle* for breakfast, pasta and fruit at lunch, and resorted to the trattoria at night.

One morning we woke up to a cloudless sky and a warmer sun than I'd felt for weeks. Gaby rushed into the courtyard and held her face up towards the heat, instantly declaring that now was the time to go up Santa Catarina which, let's be honest, might be a mountain to a Netherlander but is barely a hill to a Swiss, since it's only 310 metres high. Still, it calls for a certain level of fitness to make the ascent. The barista at the quay, when we asked how one got to the top swung an arm over the whole island conjuring up a mountain footpath so modern and inviting it appeared to have all the ease of a moving walkway. One could practically run up the ragged little rocks. 'A new road. You can't miss it,' he said. Eh, well, we did. And had to scramble on our hands and knees up an old goat track whose serpentine guile had deflected us from the wide and easy path. Still Gaby, resolute away from her family, managed the climb one-handed, texting a battery of fiery missives to Simon all the way to the summit.

It was a lovely day and having proved our worth to the gods we came upon the new road with inexplicable ease and made our descent almost at a trot, arriving home relaxed and peaceful, somnolent even. The next day, we decided, we would change our sport and turn to the sea in some fashion, try to find a fisherman whom we might hire to sail us gently through the grottos.

****

Next morning, alas, the weather was wild, fierce and noisy, full of bluster, with shutters in want of hinges banging against the walls outside. When I stepped into the small courtyard, the wind tugged so hard I imagined it might draw me up and hurl me out to sea. After breakfast Gaby departed for a bar. I put on practically my entire winter wardrobe, topping everything off with a big scarf and a beret, and went out into the winds looking for her, doubled over, head to knee, my arms wrapping me tightly, like others in passing. She was nowhere to be seen in any of the bars she favoured, but assured she would not be short of creature comforts, I decided a quiet read might be a consolation for missing out on Marettimo yet again, and never experiencing rolling in the thyme.

Back at the house I picked up a book Gaby had just begun reading, *Conversations in Sicily*, by Elio Vittorini and started flipping the pages. Promising. I would have to get through it quickly, though, otherwise we would end up hopping from one foot to the other, waiting impatiently to have our turn.

Vittorini's book was going to be something of a plod, however, having to be read with the Garzanti dictionary at my elbow. It opened on a grim note. I still haven't satisfied myself that the narrator, holding onto his bread and lump of cheese, and extolling remembered delights of eating the Sicilian product, was not trying to torture a wretched little couple of fellow travellers on the ferry, husband and wife, reduced to sharing an orange. After a long exile in the North, savouring his cheese in front of them and dreamily invoking memories of delicious Sicilian cuisine, had he forgotten his early poverty, thought their reliance on an orange just a momentary discomfort? If he were that insensitive, I shouldn't like him, I thought.

In fact, his character manifests a stumbling sensibility that emerges in an extended conversation, a kind of Socratic interchange between him, a son returning to Sicily after a fifteen-year absence, and his mother, a po-faced, taciturn, scratchy creature with no words of welcome for the prodigal who turns up unexpectedly on her threshold. Silent and resentful, she scrapes together some basic food and over the meal they begin to engage as adults in one of those conversations that are painfully wrung from heavy pauses and echoes, 'You thought that... but didn't you know...' 'How could I know that...?' A statement by one turned into a question by the other. Slow and mesmerising.

When the son enquires why Mamma is not eating *minestra* (thin soup) with him, he is shocked to learn that she gave up eating it in his childhood because there had not been enough to go round. That she never ate it had utterly escaped his notice. As had many other things: the almost total absence of meat in the family diet, and the fact that they were reduced to eating prickly pear and pasta in the last week of every month, because his father's salary could not stretch from one pay period to the next. They begin to speak about prickly pear in worshipful tones – it is the symbol of Sicily and grows freely everywhere.

For the first time I, too, felt an urge to eat the fruit, to think of it with affection. But without a brush and some dexterity in cleaning the 'pears' of their hairlike spines it is better to buy it from the shops. When it became available on my return to Catania, I started eating prickly pear regularly. In Wollongong, in rare moments, the fruit suddenly appears at my local Italian fruit and vegetable market and I purchase it by the box.

The son is surprised to discover that his mother, in his absence, has become some kind of community nurse. She invites him to accompany her on her rounds, beginning very late in the afternoon. These visits soon proceed in the dark, under the stars, in a hushed atmosphere, giving Vittorini ample opportunity to explore the personalities and plights of the aged, the young, men, women, sick and well, and to reveal different aspects of the mother's character.

'My son,' she explains briefly, when her patients shrewdly appraise her attractive young male companion.

The phrase gains weight by repetition. I sense a growing tenderness between the mother and son, and am surprised as well to observe her sly humour and sense of comedy. In a situation where she has to inject a semi-clad forty-year-old woman in the butt, and the woman, unabashedly lascivious, takes every opportunity to excite the son's attention, the mother, benignly complicit, enjoys his discomfiture.

Throughout the night, each carrying a torch, mother and son make their home visits; participating in a series of dimly lit, chiaroscuro domestic dramas; Vittorini's mother figure is slowly transforming into a peasant Madonna with the sturdy body and inner beauty of a Lucien Freud nude. The writing is very touching in parts, and the book impressed me as a loving tribute to Sicilian women. In the last section, however, the religious symbolism became too murky. By late afternoon, I put the book aside and got back to my laptop, wondering if the Internet point in town would ever open.

After dinner, Gaby and I went out for a stroll, heading in a direction almost opposite to our usual route. We walked and walked and had no idea where we were. Houses began to look much older and were set further apart. The land was uneven and raggedy, thinly covered with scraggy grass. Lights vanished to our rear, no more ahead, but there was a gibbous moon and we had no trouble keeping our footing on the unsealed road we were following and which began to slope gently upwards. Just as we decided to continue to the top, check what was on the other side and return home, a snappy wind blew up and we felt the sting of sea spray on our cheeks. So the sea must be over the rise. Yes, there it was, and with a jetty running far out into the water. Amazingly, a lone bar, solid as a rock, was located close to the jetty, its tufa walls covered by salt from gusting waves that must be continually ploughed up by the winds. Gaby immediately announced she was feeling desperately cold and we hurried to the entrance.

We pushed open a heavy door and entered a porch sufficiently warm compared with the cold outside to steam up my glasses. Then we were in a very large, barn-like room with tables markedly distant from each other, in an atmosphere overwhelmingly male and oddly nautical, some of the men wearing pea jackets, those short thick woollen coats, double breasted and in navy blue, that sailors often wear, or heavy Aran knits, polo necks in cream or dark grey. They looked a different breed of men from those I saw in the village streets, larger and heavier.

Cigarette smoke was making my eyes smart; it was so dense that it dimmed the light from the several oil lamps positioned around the room. At one table a card game was ongoing. And drinking was clearly of a serious un-Italian sort. Not much in the way of movement or conversation.

Glancing round the room before we took our seats at a table somewhat isolated from the male population, I felt a powerful tug on my memory, and by the time I was seated, had come up with the associative image: a scene from *Querelle de Brest*, the film based on Genet's gay novel. I'd seen it with Ermete in Sydney, at the old Paris cinema, probably thirty years before. Not that anyone in the room was hanging about lamp-posts flexing their biceps, but the pea jackets, the fug and the sobriety of the atmosphere, figuratively speaking, recalled the mood.

Later, we discovered the bar owner was a Genoese, a merchant seaman who had visited Favignana many times over the years and had decided to retire there and open a bar. Many of his clienti were old salts that he had sailed with.

'We have to go to the counter for service,' Gaby said, meaning I should go, since I would be paying. That was the deal we had made in Sydney. And Gaby would stick to it tenaciously. She wanted a *limoncello*. Fine. I was going to have a Drambuie. At the bar, I waited a few minutes for someone at the card table to spot me and nudge the owner, who was scrutinising his hand of cards, holding them close to his nose.

He turned round, saw me, called 'Subito, signora!' crossed the room swiftly, sought my order before arriving at the counter, and in one flowing movement had a liqueur glass brimming with *limoncello*. But when I asked him for a Drambuie, he stopped dead and stared at me transfixed.

'It's a whisky liqueur,' I prompted him.

Still he didn't respond. Was he having a petit mal? Then suddenly he dived below the counter and rummaged around for a bit before surfacing with a big bottle of Drambuie, its details buried under a thick felt of grey dust, holding it out to me for inspection. I nodded happily.

'Yes, thank you. That's it.'

Turning on a tap over an empty sink, he thrust the bottle under the water and quickly washed it clean of the dust. Then, to my stupefaction, he reached for a water glass and filled it with Drambuie to the top. Involuntarily I let out a yelp.

'No, no, no. Not a big glass like that. One drinks only a small amount.'

The Genoese sighed, reached across the counter and covered my hand with his big warm paw:

'Signora, you saw by the dust on the bottle that no one has asked for a Drambuie here these past ten years. It will be another ten years before anyone asks again. I pray you, take the glass, it is my present to you, drink it all and enjoy it.'

He gave my hand a little squeeze and leaving me still gaping, hurried back to his card game.

With my heart racing, anticipating the dreadful damage that might be done to it were I to drink such a huge quantity of Drambuie, I made my way back to the table where I handed Gaby her meagre little glass of *limoncello*, suggesting that she might have to finish off the Drambuie after her drink because I could not possibly drink more than two centimetres in a liqueur glass.

Drambuie was foreign to her but a few tentative sips decided her that the Scottish liqueur was *paradiso* and that we must take the remains of the tumbler home.

'I'll ask the owner to put it in a bottle for us.'

The night being early and copious draughts of liquor being put away at a disconcerting rate by the mariners, we decided after a half hour it might be prudent to leave. Just in case.

'Not without the Drambuie,' Gaby insisted, taking hold of the glass and carrying it carefully to the bar.

The owner was with her in a few minutes, leaning both hands on the counter, as before. He listened, frowned and ducked below again, emerging with the bottle. I watched him unscrew the top and pour the contents of the tumbler into it. Oh dear, he was taking the liquor back. But no. Smiling broadly again, he pushed the bottle towards Gaby, waving his hand in a 'don't mention it' gesture, and Gaby bounded back to me, her face wreathed in smiles.

'He gave us the lot,' she said, triumphantly.

'That would have cost close to $60 in Australia,' I told her, when we were at home, sitting at the kitchen table, with another little glass each in front of us. Marvelling.

'But if you can't sell it, it's not worth anything, is it? Gaby said, practically.

I thought he could easily have promoted the liqueur among his patrons and gotten rid of it in a few hours, but maybe he was just happy to be generous. The more amazing since Genoese are famous among Italians as misers.

'Yes, but living in Sicily all these years probably changed him,' was Gaby's complacent response.

The next day she caught the ferry to Trapani and we arranged to meet in Alcamo after a short break.

Part III Touring with Gaby

12

A few days later I made my way by ferry and coach to Gaby's *paese* Alcamo, the 'al' prefix on the name bespeaking its Arab origins. She met me punctually at the bus interchange and apparently concerned to postpone encountering her sister suggested we have lunch in a local trattoria. Over our meal we worked out the division of resources we would employ during our proposed ten days together in and around Alcamo: Gaby would drive, and I would cover all the expenses, food, accommodation, entertainment and petrol. We had barely finished eating when she began to lament that she had no money. Not a cent. She had come back from Australia, had a fight with her parents and was now stony broke. Indigence was not the family problem. Its members were enormously wealthy, something she had assured me of a number of times in Sydney.

Late in the afternoon we got into Signora di Santis's little Fiat and in ten minutes were pulling up outside two massive gates, each about three metres wide, big enough to guard a bus terminus. As the gates began to inch open, nothing I observed through the bars brought 'home' to mind. In fact, with a vaguely sinking heart, I realised we were in an industrial zone, if such a thing could be said to exist in pre-capitalist Sicily. Perhaps Gaby had changed her mind about going home.

'Is this just your dad's place of business?'

'No,' she said, taking my arm. 'Our residence too. You know Italians like to live above their business premises. Dad wanted something better than a few rooms over the office.'

I couldn't imagine that someone wealthy would be happy living off a noisy main road, within the smell and sight of great trucks, behind prison size gates, cheek by jowl with humdrum office buildings. Positioning the family home here broke a universal real estate rule: better to be the worst in a well regarded street than the best in a poor street.

Five brand new juggernauts were lodged on the premises. The little Fiat, parked before the three-storeyed palazzo, was like a gnat compared to them, their cabins so high up, it seemed the truckers would need a small crane to deposit them behind the wheel. Standing beside one, I felt it towering over me, its metallic bulk and the force within it awesome, even though it was perfectly motionless.

Gaby was amused by my little rave. 'Look, this is just a business. A truck is a big investment for an owner-driver. Dad buys these trucks up North and sells them to drivers down here. If they don't have the money he lends it to them.'

Borrowing money can be dangerous in some environments. 'Are they always able to meet their payments?' I asked her. 'What happens if they don't?'

Her reply surprised me. 'Dad's got an interest in the stuff they freight. He keeps a close eye on their businesses to make sure they're staying on track financially, so that there are no surprises and any trouble spots can be worked on together. He's very, very smart, my dad, and he advises the truckers because helping them helps him. He wants his money in.'

Despite the family squabbles she had been bemoaning I detected an edge of pride in her voice. 'You admire your dad?'

She shook her head. 'Not altogether. He's very bright. He's incredibly energetic. He came from nothing and he's now a multimillionaire. Like all the rich he wants power. Power helps him to hang on to his money and make more. It gives him freedom. That's where we clash. I'm like him. I don't want anyone to boss me. And he uses his money to try to control me. You get this if you do that. My sister and my brother are hoping Dad will cut me out of his will. He's always threatening it.'

'But you would know the Napoleonic code doesn't allow that,' I said. 'Not like British law which doesn't beep if you leave everything to the cat.'

'Ha! Who wants to become embroiled in a legal suit?' Gaby said, suddenly glum. 'Only the lawyers win out. Ariadne's partner's a lawyer.'

She had arranged for me to lodge in what was obviously her sister's bedroom. The palazzo was the classic dream home of every Italian family: three floors and big enough to house each generation on its own floor, keeping everyone close enough to continue the family cooperative where everyone had entitlements and obligations that allowed little opportunity for leisure or for making friends. Though the sister and her partner had an apartment in town, Ariadne's presence was everywhere in the room, silver-framed photographs of her and her lover in holiday mode, make-up on the dressing table, clothes filling the built-in wardrobes.

Noting my interest, Gaby said, 'Alessandro's often away on a case – he's a corporate counsel. On those occasions, Ria generally stays at home with our parents. She works late in the office and eats here. She's all het up at the moment about having breast implants done in Thailand and some liposuction on her belly.'

I deposited my things and we went back downstairs. Gaby frequently stayed at her parents' flat, but lodged in the tiny bedroom which she had sneaked back to, while they were away cruising. 'They couldn't very well invite you to stay without having me return,' she said.

In the small, eat-in kitchen she began rummaging around in the cupboards and delved into the fridge, stocked by her sister, for our arrival.

'One thing we must do is keep this place clean.' Ha! A rare spondee sentence. Almost every syllable hammered for emphasis. Very tense, Gaby. Yes, she was frowning again. In fact, she had smiled only rarely since my arrival. 'My mother goes on the rampage if she comes back and finds anything lying about. I can't stand it when she screams.'

'I've been trying to arrange for you to do an interview with Massimo Ferrara,' she informed me later before settling down on a sofa to text Simon in Australia. 'He's a retired neurosurgeon who became the Mayor of Alcamo. I've been trying to ring him again and again but no one ever seems to be at home.'

Her expression suddenly darkened and she heaved a sigh. 'It's so terrible not having any money. Not a cent.' She laid her phone down and took a wallet out of her bag, holding it upside down and shaking it. 'You can see around you how rich we are. My father knows I don't have any money. He's torturing me.'

'Why are you so desperate for money?' I asked her, impatiently. 'You have everything you need for the moment, do you not? You're not going to starve.'

'It's to buy my return ticket to Australia. My parents don't want me to go back.'

'Can't Simon pay? He's working. He could lend it to you.'

'He doesn't have any money. Only enough to live on.'

'So how much are we talking about?'

'Eight hundred euros. My brother has said he'll give me four hundred.'

She was watching me expectantly, hopefully. Bloody hell, I thought. I was taking a huge gamble coming here for a year. I had worked hard for the money. When it was gone, there would be nothing to replace it except more work. I sat teasing out the bits and pieces of the situation sifting through the moral, the financial and the humane. Then I decided in my Calvinistic fashion, 'Okay. I'm going to have to research the impact of the ferries on Sicily and its relations with the mainland, *et cetera*. If you'll do the work I'll let you have 500 euros. We can go and get the money this afternoon from the money machine.'

The sun came out. It was smiles and frolics again. Bouncing up from the sofa she swooped across and kissed me lightly on the cheek. 'Thanks so much. You can't imagine the relief. I'll try once more to get hold of Massimo Ferrara.'

I had little interest in meeting Gaby's mayor. Any mayor. Apart from London's legendary Dick Whittington, they're not officers that have rated highly in my league of impressive figures. And just to think about the post-War mayors of western Sicily chills my blood. From whatever other source a minority of mayors might be drawn today, the majority of these functionaries have for long been the political offspring of mafia handpicked by Lucky Luciano in an exchange of favours between the Sicilian-American gangster/convicted murderer and the US military.

Happily, Alcamo's ex-mayor was brought to office on a resurgence of elector hostility to the mafia. He certainly seemed a different prospect from the favourites that had for decades been filling mayoral office. At the least, he rated a question mark. I left Gaby to renew her phone calls, knowing she would wear out the handset before giving up, and went off to have a shower.

I returned to find her sitting on the floor, poker straight, fiercely focused on twisting her spine to the point of crickcrack.

'We've got lucky at last,' she announced, eventually rising to her feet. 'Massimo was there this time. He answered the phone himself and was very friendly. Says it will be fine to go to his place tomorrow about three thirty p.m.'

Arriving at the Ferraras' the next day, we turned into a driveway blocked by another massive gate made of strengthened steel. On Gaby's murmuring into the intercom, 'We're here,' the gate began to slide open. We had hardly cleared the threshold, when what seemed like a pack of huge, scary dogs rushed at us. After the first intake of breath, some rapid eye contact with the animals, and lots of billing and cooing with them, we were relieved to find that two were amiable Labradors and the third, an eager, if somewhat twitchy Rottweiler. So we took our time, distributing warm pats and hugs in every direction while the dogs licked our hands and tried to kiss us or bite us on the nose, as they do.

Ferrara came forward to greet us, tall, and broad and with that tightness across the back of the shoulders so common in even young Italian men. He was in mayoral rather than neurosurgeon mode, his face wreathed in smiles, kissing Gaby on both cheeks – 'You're looking so well' – and offering me a firm handshake, his hand the more remarkable for being warm on another day of near freezing temperatures.

Elegant in dark blue cords, with soft navy moccasins on his feet, he led us into the house across a large room that seemed to double as a foyer, and down a step connecting that room with another about the same size, where he had obviously been sitting waiting for us. A newspaper had slid to the floor beside the deep leather armchair he was now lowering himself into, after signalling us to sit in two other carefully positioned chairs.

Gaby had remarked more than once that she had found Ferrara surprisingly attractive for his age. At sixty-six, his thick hair, totally white and springy, capped a large leonine head. There was nothing classically Italian in his features which were somewhat smudged and knobbly rather than clean-cut. Cardinal Pappalardo whom I met later in Palermo had a similar physiognomy which by then, I had decided, was distinctly from northern Europe.

Ferrara, a natural story teller, needed little probing. He was a local, born in Alcamo, his mother Alcamese, his father Palermitano. He had gone to high school in Palermo then on to university in Milan to study medicine and later the practice of neurosurgery. But 'I am very much a Sicilian,' he assured me.

'Now that I am reaching the end of my medical career, and am old but' – a self-deprecatory shrug – 'still reasonably strong and active, I thought perhaps the time was right for me to return to Alcamo and try to bring about some improvement in the life of the people.'

He had held office between 1993 and 2001. If Parliament had not changed the law to have mayors elected directly by the people he would never have contemplated standing for the position. Those 1993 elections were an ebullient period for Italians generally but most particularly for Sicilians who, in twenty rural towns had elected women, a higher percentage than in any other region of Italy. So brave, he thought, the voters and the candidates. Many of the women and the anti-mafia males who were elected mayors endured death threats. Some had their tyres slashed.

'I had no experience of how to run an election campaign. Never done anything like it in my life before. But I felt I had to try. The city had many inadequacies. Lacked so much. I wanted to dignify the place. Clean it up. Make people proud to live in it.

'Nobody had any idea what I was talking about when I said planning had to be top of my agenda. In the end I became convinced that no one understood what was needed, that I had lost and I was preparing to return to Milan and continue with my teaching program. I was poised to renew my contracts when the election results came out and I found that I was in.

'No, I had no managerial experience whatever. Basically, I just brought people together to find out what they thought they needed and organised others to devise plans and put them into action.

'You understand how it is when you are a neurosurgeon, a highly specialised person, working in a constrained, closed environment, meeting only a few people of the same kind every day, solving the narrowest range of problems?

'As mayor, I was out and about the entire time, talking to community groups, to schoolchildren, to public works people. All kinds of projects had to be thought about and planned. New skills? How many I've learned! I can hardly list them all. But the entire experience has been overwhelmingly challenging and fun.

'Were there problems funding the projects? Oddly, enough, no problem at all. A number of works had already been approved by the national government before I came to office but they had not been implemented. I worked to set them in motion and have them completed. The people I worked were with me, heart, mind and balls.[!]

'Summer was a dead period, so we organised events, summer cinema, jazz concerts, plays. We built a theatre and a concert hall and provided premises for clubs for the aged. Public approval was running high.

'Yes, it's true that I introduced public transport to Alcamo. Ah, Gaby has been singing my praises, I see. Incredible, isn't it? Nearly two thousand years after Christ. Buses. Some of them now run on electricity. The community decided the first routes. They wanted buses to the cemetery, to the hospital and to schools.

'And yes, I set up a public library. Believe me I know and appreciate the importance of public libraries in the democracies. There's no debate that it's difficult for Italians to grow intellectually. They read very little and so many depend mainly on television and comics for information. I hope that some are now taking the opportunity to read books likely to give them the contextual understanding of their environment, which is difficult to gain by other means.'

With modern, comfortable buses plying the streets, a library, albeit shy and reserved as I discovered, to help grow the Alcamese intellect, and the delights offered by an absolutely stunning new swimming pool complex that was Gaby's favourite haunt, Ferrara considered he had gone a long way to meeting his goals for Alcamo.

'Here people try to get by on their own. Clientelism has taken the place of community spirit and expectations of the state. A sense of nationhood is developing only slowly. It's commonly said of us 'we live in a paradise inhabited by devils'.'

That Neapolitan proverb, originating in the works of the philosopher Benedetto Croce, is always being cited in reference to Sicily, Sicilians seeming to think it's theirs, never imagining other parts of Italy could share their condition. It would be more accurate to call Sicily a paradise *administered* by devils.

A good-humoured smile lit up Ferrara's face when I asked him if his projects had encountered any opposition. 'Signora, politics is by its nature opposition. One expects it. But it's true to say that the greatest opposition came from the mafia. Alcamo has always been mafia-ridden. It is, after all, halfway between two important ports, Trapani and Palermo, also plagued by mafia regimes. Oh, they warned me. The mafia, I mean. They got a message to me and then poisoned one of my dogs.

'Their objections are basically to change of any sort, anything that threatens their dominion over people. They just want to be left undisturbed to run things the way they are used to doing. I did have a rough idea of who they were, yes. And they're higher up the social and political ladder nowadays. The best thing to do is simply to go ahead with projects and resist their attempts to block change. It is becoming more difficult for them today now that popular feeling against them has intensified and extends to the grass roots level.

'Yes, of course it's possible to enjoy life in Sicily, even with a mafia presence. I love Palermo. I adore it. It's my very favourite city in the world.

'And I'm definitely hoping to win another term as mayor. One can apply for a third term after a break. Most of the people elected directly were subsequently re-elected. Many of us had two terms. When the conservatives were returned to national office, unfortunately they rescinded the municipal reforms allowing direct election of mayors. But I'm an experienced politician now, with a good record and I can organise to comply with the old laws.'

I asked him why the conservatives had been returned in Sicily when the reforming mayors seemed to have brought new services and new hope to the populace. He referred me back to what he had said about people being used to getting by on their own.

'We're talking here about the favour system. Recommendation. This is a system that is becoming the subject of growing contempt. People are saying things like, *my son got this job on his merit. No recommendation.* That's a way of saying, free of debts, of favours owed. If unemployment in Sicily could be reduced to a tolerable level in a more prosperous economy, recommendation would wither away. In the meantime... many, many favours will be called in to ensure the election of Salvatore Cuffaro over Rita Borsellino, in May.'

Gaby was pleased that I liked Ferrara. I thought he had a reassuring self-confidence based on a clear understanding of what he could achieve. He had judged the local mafia well, simply ignoring them and pushing ahead with his plans. And his linking of high unemployment to 'recommendation' implied that he knew unemployment was a desired political outcome vital to maintain the status quo.

In the car, Gaby took up again the subject of Rita Borsellino. She was involved with a support group for Borsellino and had been talking to me about her incessantly: Rita, the pharmacist sister of Paolo, a prominent judge in the mafia maxi-trials, car-bombed in July 1992, less than two months after a similar slaughter of his friend and colleague, Giovanni Falcone, was effectively railroaded by popular request into becoming an anti-mafia politician. The 'Rita Express' was bringing a trainload of young people from the North to campaign for her against Salvatore Cuffaro. But Massimo Ferrara had opined that it would be much harder to dislodge a Cuffaro from the Presidency than a local mayor from municipal office and that Borsellino would very likely lose the election.

As events turned out, his forecast proved accurate. Cuffaro was re-elected in May by favours and straight-out purchase of votes for an alleged 250 euros each – quite a rise on the standard fifty euros a vote the mafia has reportedly paid till now. While I write, the courts have found some of the charges (relating to association with mafiosi) proven against Salvatore Cuffaro and he has resigned as President of the Regional Parliament, a five-year sentence poised over his head, but unlikely to descend on it.

He remains buoyant and confident.

****

On the way home I asked Gaby if we could visit Ferrara's public library, an institution thoroughly alien to Italy, and especially Sicily, where free access to ideas is resisted ruthlessly, albeit with stealth.

'Sure,' she said. 'It's only a few minutes from here. Right in the centre of town.'

That impressed me. Not many public libraries can enjoy such a convenient position. I blinked when she stopped at a pathway leading up the side of a church, indicating with a tilt of her head, 'Up here.'

'Where?' I said. 'I don't see the sign. Where does it say *Biblioteca*?'

She shrugged. 'That's how it is with us.'

I stared at her incredulously. 'Not inside the Church? You don't say so.'

Then again, why not? If there just *has* to be a public library let it be lodged with the chief agent of illiteracy. As we pushed our way in through a heavy side door, I didn't know whether to laugh or cry.

No alterations had been made to the church's facade, and there was nothing to indicate to the public that the building was lodging a new institution, one might even say a rival institution. It could be the building was only on loan, in the hope that there may recur one of those periodic surges of religious fervour when books are burned in cathedral squares.

Inside I was struck first, not by the books but by the soaring height of the vaulted ceilings and the vast blankness of the walls. Stripped of their religious iconography, they looked bare and bereft. In this ambiance, any book collection would have appeared pathetically insignificant and since the books bays, about six shelves high, took up only one wall, the stock was in fact scanty, generating that air of futile struggle you find in some corner shops where you know nothing will keep the business going.

Two teenagers were the only members of the public in evidence. They were sitting at computers adjacent to one another, researching presumably, on the Internet. One of the librarians hovered at hand, whether to help or to monitor the images I don't know. Gaby counted aloud seven staff. 'What on earth can they be doing?' she said indignantly. 'There's absolutely no need for that many with so few books and so few people'.

The American literature section included a clutch of best sellers, no great poets or novelists, nothing on politics or economic theory, but the Italian collection of fiction and non-fiction was mainly quality writing so far as it went. Nothing, however, on modern philosophy, Kant or Nietzsche, or religious sociology. Every time I looked up from the books and gazed about me, I was conscious of the prayerful atmosphere in the place and the sepia faded print look. Gaby drew my attention to the periodicals display.

'All right-wing magazines.' Then, hopefully, 'Maybe the left-wing papers are out on loan'.

Three religious journals were prominently displayed on the periodicals shelves, one with an athletic-looking jolly priest on the front cover.

'Well,' I said, to Gaby, 'I don't quite know why the word "hijack" suddenly popped into my head. There'd be letters to the press if a journal like this appeared on the shelves of our local library.'

She nodded. 'Yes. Well, while we're in cheerful mood, let's go and look at the mafia development of Alcamo. It will help you understand what Massimo had in mind when he talked about the unplanned condition of our environment. We live on a beautiful bay, you know, Castellammare del Golfo, and a shanty town has recently gone up just metres from the foreshore. Can you imagine that on Sydney Harbour?'

Within a very short time we were entering on a long unsealed road, the foreshore on the right flanked for hundreds of metres by ugly dwellings sprung up with that grotesque higgledy-piggledyness of the Latin American favela. On the other side of the road, similar disgusting structures covered a range of steep hills, their ugliness secondary to what looked like a scary absence of stability.

'Just look at those beastly houses,' Gaby cried. 'I can't bear to think of everything they stand for. They're so incoherent, unharmonious, shoddy, cheap, with no sewerage, no septic, no services – just two small shops that have finally risked opening since it was realised this shanty town is here to stay. That's the mafia for you. Above the law. Literally spreading pestilence.'

One might also say it was anti-rationalism at its worst. Enlightenment throttled. Beauty and harmony vanquished as

Gaby had said. Squalid and depressing. A monument to ignorance, ill will and fanaticism.

Then my eyes were drawn to an old man carefully emptying some garden refuse into a bin at the side of the road. Noting the lush, lovingly terraced vegetable garden he had carved out down the side of his house, a steep, narrow, crooked construction put together from cement blocks that had probably never seen a spirit level at any stage of their thought-devoid assembly, I was pretty sure he could hardly believe his luck in having a cheap house with a view over the sea.

Possibly he had asked his local priest to come and bless the house, and render thanks to God for his good fortune, that in his old age, he had become the occupant of a tiny piece of land with an up-to-date shack, and might well have offered the priest something from his garden to celebrate his new status. Of course he would owe a few favours to the mafia who would call when necessary, not only on him but on his relatives, but then, some of the mafia *would be* his relatives. So everything was fine.

****

Ariadne had left a note at home for us to say she would be taking us out for dinner that night. It was only a short drive from Alcamo to the little seaside town where we were to eat. The marina and fishing port of Castellammare is like many picturesque towns on the Amalfi Coast, but less crowded – more boats than people – even if the hills rising from the bay, the Golfo di Castellammare, are covered with whitewashed houses, no doubt in their usual unplanned state, but to a distant eye, a cascade of rustic Mediterranean beauty.

At the dinner hour we could see only the great press of masts and sails curving round the harbour in waters sectioned off by jetties and pontoons, domestic lighting on the boats sufficient to show they were generally modest structures, and by inference, that Castellammare was not, like Capri, a haunt of the super-rich. It was very cold that night, the temperature not above eleven degrees. A large patch of water gleaming blackly through the huge glass frontage of the restaurant made me think of an ice hole, and I put my collar up, but hardly had done so when the waiter, with a little bow, relieved me of my coat so smoothly and deftly, I had no time to resist.

Then I noticed the vastness of the room, grand on a Chinese scale, equipped to seat well over 200 diners, though no more than twenty were present at the time. It was heated by mobile braziers, raised on high like medieval torches. The waiters quickly wheeled one closer to us. Ariadne, far too lightly dressed for the weather, greeted it with delight.

Gaby's older sister was obviously well known to the staff who bantered freely with her, treating her like a personage of some importance. For some years, when business took her lawyer partner out of town, she either ate at home with her parents after work or dined at this restaurant in the port, where, she told me, after eating she liked to go for a walk along the promenade, 'to breathe'. She loved the sea and always holidayed in seaside places. Phuket was a favourite, but she also liked the islands of the Caribbean. It seemed that short getaway holidays on a regular basis made up for long hours and a six-day working week.

Both Gaby and her sister were modest eaters, for which I was grateful. No menu was volunteered. Ariadne merely gave a brief nod when the waiter had queried, 'The usual?' Then, with her hand on the waiter's arm, lightly retaining him, she asked me: 'A spot of seafood antipasto and a salad? Does that sound satisfactory to you?

'Music in my ears,' I assured her, and suddenly feeling euphoric, quivering with pleasure, I asked the waiter to bring us a bottle of French champagne.

I sat back, relaxed, savouring the moment, outside, the rhythmic slapping of the waves against the jetties corralling the boats, and inside, the quiet murmur of conversation from other diners. I was pretty sure that the interaction between these two sisters would prove intriguing. Their sibling connection was in no way obvious in that they were very little alike in appearance, Gaby being taller, slender and very limber, Ariadne, short, curvaceous and seriously sexual in presentation. They each manifested a strong will, a real determination to get what they wanted – I wasn't sure at what cost – combined with a certain vulnerability that I'd already experienced in Gaby, and that the sister was now revealing in her plan to go to Thailand for procedures to alter one breast she felt was smaller than the other, and to 'get a bit of smoothing out' now that she was close to her 30th birthday.

'It's hard for a woman when her partner's good looking and five years younger,' she said to me, her tone inviting support.

'I wouldn't know about that,' I responded, smiling. 'I married a man eighteen years older than I. I doubt he would ever have entertained the idea of my undertaking plastic surgery to keep him enchanted. Do you think it really makes any difference in Sicily? My impression is that most Sicilian women, younger or older than their husbands, have to put up with men who think it a point of honour to have 'little escapes' as you call them in Italy. When I ask the women why they tolerate this, they say, 'But what can I do, signora?''

Ariadne groaned, 'Well what *can* we do?'

Before we could continue, the waiter arrived with a large platter of antipasto and briskly began transferring it to our plates. Then with quick deft movements he uncorked the champagne, filled the glasses and buried the bottle in an ice bucket, departing with a quick nod to each of us. 'Enjoy your meal.'

The two sisters were chatting quietly, Gaby enquiring about her niece, a three-year-old that her sister-in-law, a dentist, had engaged her to babysit for some weeks, paying quite generously. Gaby was very fond of the little girl, though she was a handful, never still for a minute. She had told me that with the demands of a busy dental practice, attending to her lively little daughter and the performance of domestic duties generally, her sister-in-law was in a state of collapse. Gaby had been a real help until she quarrelled with her brother, who had then sent her away. So she and the sister-in-law were now obliged to commiserate with each other on the phone and who knew when she would see the little girl again. I gathered from the tenor of the conversation, Gaby wanted Ariadne to act as an intermediary. Ariadne wasn't sure how effective her intercession might be. After all she and her brother weren't exactly sibling soul mates. He detested her partner, to begin with.

'And he didn't have any time for your Simon, either,' she added.

A shadow darkened Gaby's face. 'Oh, how terrible it was when Simon yelled at Mum and Dad.'

'They won't forget it,' Ariadne assured her comfortably.

I was becoming aware of something tough-minded in these two sisters, a kind of arrogance and awareness of power, no sense whatever of the humility and subjection I had noted in the mien of so many other Sicilians. Gaby's hassling me to give her money, her veiled implication that she was entitled to it, the implacability of their wills when wrestling over the transfer of a small sum of money to Gaby's account, had surprised me. And the fierceness of the family squabbles seemed completely at odds with the loving relations and gentle manners I had observed between family members in Catania. That an Englishman, a total stranger, could feel roused to yell at Gaby's parents in their own home and stamp off in a rage, surely signified an aberrant reaction to an unusual family culture.

By this time I am thinking that Ariadne is the family workhorse, loyal and reliable. Gaby is the bright one whose talents demanded a costly education, one whose value her father probably does not fully appreciate but it's what she wanted and he has given it to her. As a result of her Enlightenment studies, Gaby has become very anti-mafia and outspokenly so. She has joined the Borsellino Express. Her father and mother are now angry with her. They think she is out of control. How do I know that? The withholding of money. They hope this will prevent her going off to Australia.

Mr De Santis is obviously an entrepreneur, very confident of his abilities. He is rich. Therefore he interests the mafia. In a mafia-run town, in an industry that is the lifeblood of the mafia, at the very least he has to have cooperated with them.

There have been no torchings or Gaby would have mentioned them to me. There are no security guards anywhere in sight on the premises. Not even a guard dog. There were three at Massimo Ferrara's house. Gaby's father must be in good standing with the mafia.

Conversation between the sisters had paused. They were looking at me. I leaned forward and said, 'Tell me something about your father. I feel that you really admire him even if he frustrates you at times. I've noticed Sicily is not a socially mobile society for the most part and that wealthy people tend to come from wealthy backgrounds. Is that your father's case?'

This brought smiles and gurgles of laughter from each. Ariadne left Gaby to do the talking.

'My father finished school when he was eleven, but he never stopped learning. He wanted to know everything. He read anything he could lay his hands on. He felt he could be an artist, but that that wouldn't earn him any money. And he wanted to be rich. He told us that. He believed in fairy stories. He decided that tailoring was the best way to combine art and money. He would be a designer, and do his own tailoring. But he knew that to make money you have to have other people work for you. By the time he was twenty-three he had five tailors at work full time and an established clientele. When he married my mother, who was then eighteen and he about thirty, he set her up in a big house, luxuriously furnished. Fifteen years later, things had changed – even in Sicily. More and more people were buying clothes off the rack. And my uncle, who had been in transport for some years and was always plaguing Dad to join him in business, finally talked him into doing it. But Dad changed the nature of the business from haulage to finance, and buying and selling trucks. He also hired them out.'

'A smart move,' I said. 'Does he have property interests?'

Gaby shrugged: 'Is he Sicilian?'

She heaved a sigh and drummed her fingers on the table. Ariadne gave her a sidelong glance. It was full of understanding. Each of them had made their choice.

Gaby could no longer live in a mafia environment, especially since she was changing over to studies in environmental science, but she did not want to give up her family altogether. Ideally she hoped to escape to Australia, settle in a completely different society, but living in comfort, in the manner she was accustomed to, having already forewarned Simon that he was to find them an attractive apartment in Elizabeth Bay, one of Sydney's more salubrious suburbs. Achieving that on the Englishman's modest salary, with no contribution from her, could prove very difficult.

She knew her father could easily afford to make her an allowance. Her siblings would resist that. Nonetheless, for reasons not altogether obscure, Gaby's brother had given her the balance of her fare to Australia, and she was booked to depart in three weeks. In that short period she somehow had to conciliate her parents and persuade them to give her an allowance.

With my thoughts so neatly ordered and a scenario sketched out for the family meeting that I would be present at, I suddenly remembered where I was, picked up my fork and started eating, looking over at the two sisters, who, when they realised I had come out of my reverie, started laughing. 'So, you're with us again,' Gaby said. 'We thought you were dozing off.'

'It's so pleasant here,' I said, 'relaxing, I think I was dreaming.'

Ariadne reached over and patted my hand. 'Eat up, or there won't be any left for you. Gaby's been devouring everything. She can't find food like this in Australia. Can you, Cara?'

Gaby gave a little smile. 'Every place has its compensations.'

Yes, I thought. And one can't have only the benefits of alternative systems. She was loud for liberal democracy but was demanding the fruits of a quasi-totalitarian regime. In a democracy, her education, intelligence and good looks well equipped her to look after herself and make her own way. If she acted on that belief she would really have no problems with her family. Her problems were of her own making. The result of greed, really. Self-centredness at the least.

Ariadne took a few sips of her champagne, and replacing her glass on the table, sat back with her hands behind her head. She had something on her mind.

'I think you are a brave woman. Or mad. You have come here to write a book about a place, a very complex place, that you don't know. You may never know.'

She was challenging me.

'That depends on what you mean by "knowing" a place, Ariadne. Who determines what Sicilians can know in Sicily? Who has determined what I will know here? So far, I've discovered Sicilians generally know very little of their own history or even the geography of the region.'

'Do you mean they know less than the average Australian knows of *their* land?'

This was too easy.

'We-e-ll, if we talk about the resources available to ordinary Australians to know their land and their society if they want to know it and those available to ordinary Sicilians, Ariadne, the answer is self-evident. Ask Gaby.'

Gaby threw her arm round her sister and gave her a hug: 'Ria, I think we had better change the subject. Pay the bill and let's go for a walk around the port.'

****

Next day Gaby and I took off for Agrigento in the south west. Before leaving, however, we had appointed to tour the medieval fortress/castle that had given Castellammare del Golfo its name. The 'seacastle', erected on a convenient spit jutting into the bay almost from the centre of town, was modest in overall size, but a massy structure, suggesting that the town had probably been subject to incessant raids by marauding corsairs and Turks after the fall of the Roman Empire. Its incredibly thick-walled round tower with embrasures giving a 270-degree view of the coast signalled a will to resist.

Now the fort was a museum and a guide would be waiting for us at nine thirty a.m. Neither Gaby nor I had any inkling of the content of the museum and I was astonished when the guide, who also happened to be the manager of the Museum, told us that its focus was industrial archaeology – in a region that had never heard of the factory system. I was also surprised to find a woman holding what would have been widely viewed as a plum office. I figured she must have had a powerful patron. She was very attractive, the guide. About thirty, perhaps, simply and quietly dressed, in a sweater and straight skirt, flat walking shoes on her feet. The slant of her amber eyes, her olive skin and high cheekbones hinted at Asian ancestry. She wore her light brown hair in a neat bun at the back of her head. Her overall grace of movement suggested a ballet dancer, but in fact she turned out to be an actor manqué, and we were treated to a performance that held us entranced from the beginning to the end of the tour, more precisely a tour de force, that could have been successfully filmed as a television documentary.

Everything about this museum seemed perfect. The castle had been meticulously restored and it was a pleasure simply to walk through the rooms and climb the tower, looking out of every embrasure within reach and imagining a pirate ship approaching. But the implements and equipment were also fascinating, so old, so unthinkable outside the ancient world. Most intriguing of all, however, was the passion the guide brought to her work, placing each artefact in its social and economic context, conjuring up the people who made the equipment and those who used it, like a fast-working painter who dashes off a cartoon and rapidly fills in the details until in a few minutes there's a crowded scene, another world has come into being.

She knew her subjects through and through and making our way from room to room, we could almost see history developing in Sicily as a problem-solving experience, of manifest intelligence, of new ideas coming in with new invaders and sudden leaps in technology and art.

With one eye on a party of schoolchildren crowding into the reception area, I hurriedly explained to our guide why I was in Sicily, and asked if she could spare half an hour for a chat, whereupon she called her assistant to look after the children and we settled down in her office. There she outlined the means by which she had reached the heights of managing The Arts and Crafts Museum of Castellammare del Golfo.

She had clearly been a feisty girl, born and schooled in the north to a Sicilian farming couple that moved there in the 1960s, at the end of the boom, and at the beginning of two terrible decades for Italy when the country was poised for civil war. A high level of restive dropping in and dropping out was evident in the details of her vocational training and early work history. But it was her destiny (in Greek terms), she said, to become the manager of the Museum which had been established through a foundation set up by a wealthy local to commemorate the death of his daughter at age twenty-one. When the Manager's position became available, this youngest girl of a large family decided to apply, an extraordinarily bold decision for someone of her social background. However, the head of the foundation turned out to have been the girl's former teacher at a technical high school, a woman who was impressed by hearing:

'*Io non sono un uomo ma so fare più di un uomo. Mi metta alla prova.*' (I am not a man but I can do more than a man. Try me out.)

The Museum's function is to let schoolchildren understand what was not available in earlier times and the huge effort and serious labour that was required to live quite simply. Not a world-shaking enterprise. According to the Manager, in the early stages the service received scant attention. However, she herself was thrilled. At last she had found her niche.

'I poured myself into it heart and soul, and as a result, schools in particular, but also others began to come to the Museum and to look at how their ancestors lived and worked. The founder as well as local intellectuals appreciated what I was achieving. They gave me public credit and made more material available for the Museum. You can see how impressive it is now. You were very impressed, weren't you? I spend a lot of my time in summer making more contacts and promoting the Museum to sustain interest in it. Because of that, the Museum now receives the *concessione comunale* the municipal support and allowance.'

At thirty-seven, having lived and worked in Sicily much longer than she had done in the North, the Manager sees herself as a product of two cultures and someone who has succeeded in exploiting the best of both.

Asked for a recent highlight of her career, she described enthusiastically her involvement with the Touring Club of Italy when it filmed the Museum, following that with an outline of other projected developments for the institution. When we congratulated her and said she must find the future exciting, her confidence suddenly wavered and she confessed to certain apprehensions regarding her position at the Museum. Deprecating her shyness and her reluctance to gain a more public profile which would benefit the Museum, she told us she felt 'inhibited' by the mafia.

'I've seen the real mafia at work,' she said, 'and frankly, I am afraid when I shake hands with a rich man. The mafia don't interfere with the Museum itself but they block the cultural and educational development of the area. We are still in the grip of a ruling caste, the nobility and the politicians – whom we serve. They do not serve us.'

It was easy to appreciate her quandary: the more the Museum develops, the more attention it will attract, the more valuable and desirable her position will become and the more likely the mafia will see it as a source of patronage for them to dispense to their 'clients'.

13

Treks across Sicily are not without tensions even today. There's always an element of uneasiness once you start penetrating the interior where intensive farming is everywhere evident, yet a human rarely in sight. The ubiquitous silence, ever present and ever menacing, never fails to produce a shiver.

Angelo Palillo, a local journalist we were to meet in Agrigento, says in a fascinating but unpublished commentary on visits by travellers to Agrigento in the seventeenth and eighteenth centuries, that during the period of the Grand Tour, travellers tended to take the boat from Naples and go round the entire circumference of Trinacria by sea. So long as they could avoid the Strait of Messina, they preferred seasickness to the hazards of land travel, having to ride a horse or a mule because tracks were not wide enough to accommodate a cart. Only the intrepid risked crossing the Strait or, as we were about to do, venturing into the interior.

Travellers in those days were an elite, socially and temperamentally different from the modern tourist. Among them were scientists, geologists and astronomers hoping to expand their knowledge, make discoveries and enhance their fame, or artists seeking inspiration with the same goal in mind.

The period that Goethe spent in Sicily is said to have resolved his creative confusion and released all his latent genius. Guy De Maupassant, the famous short story writer, was another Sicilian enthusiast, along with the painters, Joshua Reynolds and Jean-Pierre Houel, and the celebrated theologian, Bishop Berkeley.

For these adventurous and doughty travellers, more challenging than riding over unknown and very rough terrain was to confront the terrors of the mind, conjured by tales of bloodthirsty bandits, highwaymen, wild animals and whatever monsters fired the imaginations of the local peasantry.

Gaby, who favoured criss-crossing in preference to straightforward linear advances, had no sooner pointed the car in the direction of Agrigento than she decided we must first go to Segesta, a town so small I had to open up my big Touring Club map again to find it. 'But this must be a one-horse town,' I complained. 'It's not on the other maps and it was pretty hard to find even on this big one.'

'It's not far,' she said. 'It's an abandoned town actually. So it doesn't have even one horse. But it has two or three important monuments. You haven't seen a temple yet, have you? Right. The temple at Segesta must be your introduction to our temples, keeping in mind also that this one was built by the indigenous people, helped by the Greeks who had come to live there. It is the most perfectly preserved temple in Sicily. Totally complete. Never was a church or a mosque built into it or on it and it's set in a pristine landscape. Once seen, never forgotten.'

From Alcamo to Segesta was only a half-hour drive, through groves of olives and citrus fruits, and vineyards planted with regimented rigour. However unplanned and whimsical areas of the built environment may be in certain Sicilian towns, artistic genius as well as scientific know-how is given full scope on the farms which are generally tended with love and care.

Segesta seems to have been abandoned as an outcome of long-standing, recurring war between the Greeks and the Carthaginians, and Calatafimi is the town now most closely associated with the ancient settlement, being accessible by train from the major cities and a bus ride's distance away from the monuments.

We came on the temple quite suddenly. I had some years before seen the Parthenon in Athens, but the urban clutter around that monument and the thoroughgoing restoration being undertaken on it at the time somehow diminished its impact. This Doric temple at Segesta, with its columns of unfluted, rough white stone, was a marvel of simplicity and tranquillity, almost feminine in its modesty and elegance. It stood atop a hill that arose out of a wide, plain, unadorned landscape, with nothing to spoil the view of the temple from where we were, or to obscure the great sweep of land perceived from the temple itself.

'We won't go right up to it today,' Gaby said. 'We can visit it another time, but what makes it so impressive is what we're seeing now: the perfect relationship between the temple and the setting. Can you think of anything more beautiful? In June, at the summer solstice, people come to the temple at night and sleep beside it, rising to a dawn breakfast and the music of a string quartet. It's magic, I can tell you. You should try to come in June and be there.'

I have not yet returned to the Segesta temple, but I remember it as a lyric in stone, especially because I have seen many more temples and religious buildings in Sicily since then. The building has no roof, giving rise to debate that it might not have been completed. But far from seeming unfinished, it conveyed to me an impression of total harmony and proportion, and being open above what are often cloudless skies, invited a surging spirit to arrow straight to heaven.

Agrigento

According to the simplistic cultural division that eastern Sicily is Greek and the west Arab/Carthaginian, Agrigento should be Arab, belonging with Trapani, Palermo, Alcamo, Marsala and those other towns that were oriented to Carthage rather than Greece. Indeed, unlike the other Sicilian Greek cities Agrigento had a massive trade with the Berbers of North Africa, of such volume as to make it one of the wealthiest cities in Great Greece, and the mafia, according to report, has long had a strong presence there as elsewhere in the West. (Eastern Sicilians hold that their side of Trinacria was almost mafia-free until the 1950s.)

Nonetheless Agrigento was a very Greek city, established around 582 BCE not merely by the descendants of Greeks from

Crete and Rhodes, those who founded Gela a century earlier but by direct immigration of other Greeks from these islands – a reinfusion of 'Greek' Greeks.

Population pressures and a desire to counter expansionist drives east from the 'Arab' regions had driven groups of Gelans west in search of a site for a new city, which they established rather more distant from Gela than felt secure, but desirably close to two rivers, the Hypsas and the Acragas, and a high ridge the settlers thought to incorporate in a mighty wall raised to surround and fortify the town. This ridge served for the Acropolis of Acragas. At the southern limit of Acragas, on a second, lower ridge, today inappropriately named the 'Valley of the Temples', city architects erected a line of sacred buildings during the 5th century BCE. Presumably the valley that housed the temples disappeared during an earthquake and the temples were raised up on a ridge. This might account for some of the ruins. But in the cause of encouraging Sicilians to confront modernity, I'll refer to the monuments as the Temples of Agrigento, located on the lower of two ridges that dominate the city.

Acragas developed as one of the largest, wealthiest cities in Magna Graecia with a population approaching 300,000 at its peak. Centuries later, under the Romans, the town became Agrigentum. Like Sicilian Greeks elsewhere in the region, the residents remained Greek citizens as late as the Roman occupation under Julius Caesar in 55 AD. Recurring wars between the Greeks, the Carthaginians and the Romans, and after that, clashes with marauding tribes unloosed by the fall of Rome, eventually reduced Agrigento to its current minor status, its population not now much above 55,000. When the Arabs arrived in the ninth century they changed its name to Kerkent and the Berbers later still to Girgenti, a name it bore until 1927.

In that year, the Fascists, harking back to Imperial Rome, named the city Agrigento. The original Greek name is still retained by one of the city's two ports, the other being called after Empedocles, the famous democrat who refused an offer to become a tyrant. Today the 'new town', built above the old one, has all the shambling ugliness that goes with mafia meddling, corruption at city hall, an absence of town planning with no guarantee that the buildings won't collapse on hapless residents.

But something luxuriant, relaxed and beautiful remains in Agrigento.

14

My visit to Agrigento with Gaby was the first of two. The second I undertook in early summer with my Wollongong friends, the Borghese, who spent some time with me in Syracuse, from where we drove to the south-western city along a completely different route.

The Segesta detour had us arrive in Agrigento in time for a high tea. I liked the city immediately, feeling a rush of warmth towards it when we found a spacious bar not merely with large square tables and a generous display of magazines and newspapers to read while enjoying a coffee and cake, but with clean toilets, conspicuously signed. Then we drove to the B and B Saro Portale's journalist friend had recommended and deposited our luggage, noting on the way back to the centre that Angelo Palillo had kindly lodged us very close to the Temples.

Angelo came to find us there, he being a Council press officer rather than a journalist, although a reporter at the local newspaper where we had gone first, told us he was always over at their offices. When he entered the Internet point, he took one look at us and without waiting to check whether we were his expected visitors, crossed the floor, beaming, both hands outstretched to clasp ours. He was transparently delighted to meet outsiders with more than a half-day's interest in his beloved city. Not that we were planning an extended stay.

Resettling us in a bar near the newspaper offices, he quizzed us about our schedule.

'We'll be walking round the old city,' I said, 'before we have dinner. And after that, we're hoping to find a good movie. Tomorrow we'll spend most of the day at the Temples and then go on to the Museum. We'll visit the Pirandello literary park, then head back to Alcamo – stopping for lunch at Sciacca.'

He allowed himself a slight grimace and nodded in a resigned fashion.

'Don't think I'm not grateful for such a lavish expenditure of your time on Agrigento. This town is firmly fixed in the travel agency mind as a half-day place. If only we could induce more people to stay at least overnight. It's not as if there's absolutely nothing to see but the temples. Sometimes I think they're a curse rather than a blessing. Perhaps if we lacked them, we would have had to try harder to stir up outside interest. You knew Goethe came here?'

'Yes.'

'He did at least try to describe Agrigento as it was then – in space, you know. Not just in time.'

'And he spent three days here? Six half days.'

Angelo laughed. 'He did indeed.'

I had already taken a liking to the press officer. Tall and slim, bespectacled and with a mass of silver hair at odds with a younger face, his gentle manner, warmth and obvious willingness to give us his time reminded us of how important guides of this kind had been to eighteenth- and nineteenth-century travellers in Sicily. When there were no wayside inns on overland journeys, travellers relied on letters of recommendation to the local gentry or the heads of convents and monasteries. For a long time there had not been a single facility for an overnight stay on the way to Agrigento from anywhere. And in the city itself, there had been no hotels or B and Bs that people took for granted in other towns. Only the great Greek temples would have induced travellers to confront such an inhospitable wilderness.

It did not surprise me in the least to discover our B and B host was a young German. Germans are everywhere in Sicily. You find them in the tiniest remotest villages or in the biggest cities, crowding the churches, or shepherding large groups of high school students around Agrigento with its five Doric temples and marvellous archaeological museum.

The German love affair with Sicily stems from the nineteenth century when their linguistic scientists, exponents of a new discipline declared that Egypt was not, as educated people had believed for centuries, the cradle of western civilisation. That honour belonged to Greece. Since Sicily had for centuries been part of Greater Greece – with the artefacts, the architecture and the great myths to prove it, it too has been swept up in the German-Greco romance.

Leaving Gaby to engage Angelo, I started musing whether he might ever have been a religious. He had mentioned his wife was at home looking after their three-year-old. He seemed old to have a child that age. Perhaps he had married late. Left a seminary. Children entered those places young, at twelve, generally, and a proportion sometimes found their way back to a secular life. I wondered if ex-seminarians were like ex-prisoners, always surrounded by a certain aura that other former inmates could recognise. There was something spiritual in his expression and his manner which made me think at the least he might have contemplated becoming a priest.

While we were talking, Angelo had fished out of his briefcase two unpublished manuscripts he had written, local histories of Agrigento, one dealing with personages who had visited the place, starting with famous writers from antiquity, including Pindar, who wrote an ode to the city, and another describing the growth of traveller accommodation in Agrigento. The manuscripts were printed but not bound. Angelo had been hoping the Council would have underwritten the publication and promotion of the projects, but the Christian Democrats had lost out to the left wing in the most recent elections – only, I might say, after fifty years of increasingly corrupt government. Even the Sicilians have their limits of forbearance.

'The Left simply won't countenance publishing local histories by a Christian Democrat,' Angelo said, a surprising absence of outrage or indignation in his tone. Rather an acceptance that this was the way of the world, a small cross to bear with fortitude and cheerfulness. He should have kicked up hell about it and demanded rationality from people who purported to belong to the Left, but he would have thought it futile. Sicilians are all too well drilled by the Church in the virtue of sufferance. Passion, not action, is hammered into them in every pulpit, every school book. Anything suggesting the value of action is kept hidden from them.

After scanning the pages at the B and B that night, I felt indignant on Angelo's behalf. There's little doubt that tourists would have enjoyed reading the booklets. They had been researched in great detail and were written in a very readable style, clearly intended to make Agrigento a place of interest that extended beyond its Greek ruins.

Agrigento was unique in Sicily, Angelo told us, in that the population had originally occupied the valley. 'It was the only valley big enough to house a large population. Other cities were built on the heights above valleys.'

'Wasn't that for reasons of defence?'

'No.' He shook his head. 'People always prefer to live in valleys near the rivers where they can grow their products. They may build forts on the heights and have their lookouts there, but they prefer to live in the valleys. Who wants to climb steep hills every day as part of their daily routine? Now we have the new town of Agrigento splattered over the upper ridge. You might have noticed it when you drove in. It's so ugly, totally unplanned. The mafia's work,' he added tersely.

Later, the three of us out walking together, he also sighed over the absence of any promenade along the seashore. 'Sciacca is way ahead of us in that regard. They're working hard to make their promenade attractive to tourists.'

I asked him if he had ever stood for election to the Comune. He drew back.

'*Macché!* What a horrible thought.'

I said he ought, that he had passion, he cared, he was informed and the community needed councillors like him. His family needed him more, he said. His wife worked part-time and he arranged his work so that he could take care of the child when his wife was out. It would be impossible to find the time or the resources to plan a political campaign.

'It's the will, not time, that you lack, Angelo,' I said. 'Everything can be organised. You remember what the Greeks said about people who don't take up the responsibilities of public life.'

Tilting his head a little, he gave me one of those sweet smiles so easily drawn from Italians and that I find heart-wrenching. 'You are calling me an idiot, signora!'

'Okay. So you know your Greek. Well, a private person. Isn't that what it means? Someone too wrapped up in their private affairs to perform their public role as a citizen.'

After a few more pleasantries, he offered his hand to each of us, promising to meet with us again at Pirandello's house before we left for Sciacca. We then went off to look at the town before dinner and the movie.

The next day, prowling over the temples in full sun, sweating and thirsty, I realised why Gaby had recommended we visit Segesta first. Five huge temples are a lot to take in at one visit. And it's an ordeal, puzzling how to think about them. I stood before them trembling with anxiety, conscious of my impoverished vocabulary, and the desperate need of new concepts, chewing on my lower lip while staring blankly at the fluted limestone.

But knowing how to think about the Temples wasn't just my problem. Angelo, in one of his booklets that I had read in bed, points out how competitive seventeenth- and eighteenth-century writers were when confronting the Temples. Everyone, even the great writers, looks at what others have said about them. Sadly, he offers no details of how the competition was conducted, whether the writers challenged or discounted others' opinions.

Goethe wrote about the Temples of Agrigento almost in a state of ecstasy. His joy, one suspects, was part of the general euphoria northern Europeans commonly feel when they first raise Keats's 'beaker of the warm south' to their lips. The German polymath's twenty-month trip in Italy, starting in March 1786 when he was already thirty-eight, is said to have impacted hugely on his emotional equilibrium and his artistic development. Scrutinising the pillars of the Greek temples, he was overwhelmed by the wonder of form, pursuing from then on the idea that form underlay the entire universe, a conviction allowing him to free up all his latent creative powers and place him in the top ranks of European artistic genius. Well, that reaction is on a scale few people are in a position to copy.

Our first visit was not to a major temple, but to a rocky sanctuary overhanging the valley where the river Acragas runs. This holy place is thought to be about 200 years older than Agrigento itself and was probably built for the worship of an indigenous divinity. The steps were budget-sized, few and very, very steep, practically raising my knee to my chin, meant to slow people down, I daresay and make them meditate on their sins. We arrived, panting, at a square vestibule leading to two great terraces, like the steps, hewn from rock. Merely writing that phrase suggests to me another reason why sacred sites are recycled in Sicily and no doubt elsewhere: the huge labour costs required to build the original structures.

In any case the Greeks adopted this sanctuary to build a little temple for their own immortals, mother and daughter, Demeter and Persephone, sculptures of whom are said to be the original model for the Christian Madonna/child icon. Persephone belonged to that class of *theoi* that controlled the forces of nature and bestowed civilised arts upon mankind. Her mother was one of the twelve Olympian gods who governed the universe, commanding legions of lesser gods and spirits, all these objects of worship a huge force of variously empowered divines meant to appease and regulate nature in all its capricious, whimsical, creative/destructive scary glory.

Mother and daughter shared interests in the afterlife and agriculture, especially grains, with spring growth Persephone's dedicated responsibility. Given the huge contribution of agricultural products to the wealth of Acragas and the eulogies evoked in travellers by the wonderful panorama of cultivated fields and orchards surrounding modern Agrigento, this little sanctuary and its modest temple must have found great favour with the two goddesses.

On then to the giants. At one point I tried to put my arms around a great column, pretending to take its measure – my fingers wouldn't meet – but hoping that feeling the stone might inspire me. Really, the thing was so high, I had to do what amounted to a back bend to see the capital, plain like a mortar board. They were all Doric, the Agrigento temples, nothing like the beautiful voluptuous capitals of the Egyptian ruins in Karnak. But they did have the advantage of landscape and position, and the temple at Segesta had already left me with the insight that a setting of a temple can excite the imagination as much as the architecture.

The size and location of the temples dedicated to Greek gods related to their power and status which in turn derived from their jobs, from the importance of the natural phenomena they had to grapple with or their administrative duties, organizing the lesser gods. It's amazing – or maybe not – just how much like earth and human beings are heavens and gods.

Standing at the highest point of the ridge, alongside the Temple of Hera the Queen, I looked down into the valley and then out to mountains across the sea, reportedly, the cliffs of Athens. Unfortunately there was no telescope on site to check that, apart from which, neither Gaby nor I would have recognised the cliffs of Athens had we seen them. And since Sicilians mythologise as they breathe, some corroboration of this might be advisable.

Twenty-five columns of the Queen's Temple are still standing, nine of them in various states of tortured disintegration. On the red blocks of the *cella*, the inner temple, I examined traces of the fire said to have been raised by the Carthaginians when they torched Agrigento, an event for which Carthaginian descendants later paid dearly. Placing a tentative finger on one mark, I asked myself, 'Can I believe this?'

Hera's temple might have had the best view but no other temple on the lower ridge comes anywhere near the size and mass of the Temple of Zeus, he, the King of Olympus and her husband, famed for raping Leda in the guise of a swan, and begetting on her the double-yolked egg that became the stellar constellation of Castor and Pollux.

Even the ruins of the Zeus temple are massive. The traditional rectangular platform, on five steps facing east, is the size of a soccer field. A single fallen capital, not a column, but a capital, half buried, looks as if it would require a crane to lift it. None of the columns was freestanding like those in the other temples; rather they were 'demi-columns' seven across the front and back and fourteen down each side, set in a continuous wall. Erected in the *intercolumni*, the space between the columns, were giant figures that supported the huge cornices. Imagining the size and mass of this temple, its flaunting of Agrigento's wealth, technology and power, the 'flagship' so to speak, of Magna Graecia, had I been a Carthaginian military commander my life's goal would have been to bring it to rubble. What general could resist it? And what a frustration, if an earthquake downed it first!

Tommaso Fazello, the historian considered the discoverer of the Temple of Zeus, estimated that most of the building fell to the ground on 9 December 1401. That it stood so long indicates the Carthaginians were not quite up to either the Greek or the Roman military.

If the sanctuary of Demeter was the first structure built on the ridge, the last one, fittingly reached at the end of a long, fiercely hot, tiring walk, was the Church of St Nicholas, a Roman Gothic building erected by the Cistercians – breakaway Benedictines – in the thirteenth century, by which time the originators of Gothic architecture, the French, had been invited by the Pope, himself a Frenchman, to replace the Normans as the ruling power in Sicily.

The Church is now part of the National Archaeological Museum raised behind it, a museum that will forever lodge in my mind as the glory of Agrigento. Interestingly, almost everything in it is a find from the Temples. Maybe we should have visited the Museum first and then we could have imagined the Temples as polychromatic, ornately decorated and richly furbished.

A big group of German high school students was being taken around the Museum by their teachers during our visit. What an impression it must have made on them. To judge by their silence, they were overwhelmed as we were by the beauty of the Museum building itself, of the exquisite marble and bronze statues, the vase and plate collections, all arranged chronologically and the Roman sarcophagi, their sides crowded with fully sculpted figures, old, young, babies, men and women hugging one another, or lounging, twisting round to chat, the extended family of the deceased, one thought.

Some of the teenagers were furrowing their brows, so intensely were they concentrating, particularly on plates or bowls or oil lamps, with dramatic friezes showing vigorous battle scenes or women rising from the bath, so much vitality in this society whose own members responded to beauty as much as we were responding to theirs.

It was odd, really, the feelings that these ancient artefacts can arouse in people, as if our ancestors were reaching out to us, suffusing us with their joy in being alive and human, with their sense of wonder and their delight in creating enduring records of their time and place.

But nothing prepared me, nor Gaby, nor the students and teachers, for the colossal Telamone, 7.75 metres high, that we encountered dominating an entire room, a solitary figure standing erect, back to the wall, with his foreshortened arms up, giving the illusion of bracing himself against the ceiling to support the roof. His name, in fact, means just that – support. Sometimes he is called Atlante, an allusion to Atlas who was obliged to hold the sky on his shoulders, to prevent sky and earth from resuming their primordial embrace.

Made, I assume, out of limestone tufa, since that is Agrigento's characteristic building material, his body was constructed in flat layers, like millstones, upper and lower legs in nine segments, not much worked on but giving an impression of immense strength. His facial features were barely suggested, but enough to render his expression intensely human. One felt pity for him.

Almost as impressive were the three heads and a torso of Telamoni in the same room, the heads so mysterious and mesmerising it was hard to tear oneself away from them. Everyone who came on these so human colossi was struck dumb with wonder and affection. These Telamoni were the massive supports who fitted into the *intercolumni* of the Temple of Zeus. We had seen the remains of some of them in the grounds of the Zeus temple, sunken to various depths, but barely glanced at them. Now presented with a complete figure, and imagining more than a score of them standing up between the columns, we were awed and speechless.

Like Christian churches, temples are often close to cemeteries, a practice eventually abandoned by the English Church which saw having a cemetery on the premises as inviting too great an encroachment by the laity on religious practice as well as on church property. In Acragas, however, the dead were long permitted to lodge quietly beside their temples in an area north of the buildings where a vast necropolis is dug into the rock below the road. Here there are tombs for corpses, or urns and arched cavities like the niches I saw later in the catacombs of Palermo.

On returning at night to the B and B, I looked up at the lower ridge, and saw the temples floodlit in a warm amber glow. Grand but homely. Isolated by the light, this world heritage site was eminently visible and no longer diminished by the squalid urban developments moving in on it.

Come to think of it, the 'light and sound' viewings of the Sphinx, located at Giza right on the edge of one of Cairo's most densely populated suburbs, are meant to achieve the same effect, to restore the structure to sole occupancy of its originally exclusive setting. But because the Sphinx, a man/beast is a 'living' creature with a sometimes sad tale to tell, light is actively used to create a chiaroscuro effect, generating a continuous ripple of diverse expressions over its face, readily evoking sympathy in the audiences assembled before it. At night, however, the Temples of Agrigento shine steadily like beacons in the dark, rare survivors of a very unstable environment, their endurance testimony to the diverse ways humans express their yearnings to be godlike.

Unfortunately, the exposure given to the Temples has, for tourists, devalued the city's other many interests. Yet Goethe spent three of his eleven days in Sicily, in Agrigento, tracing the configuration of the city and its buildings. Any local can say where he lodged. His observations were not confined to artefacts and archaeology but included the cultivated fields he saw stretching far and wide from the window of his lodging;

vegetable gardens, olive groves, vineyards and almond trees, noting that they had obliterated any trace of the urban development which had once characterised the Roman city of Agrigentum, with its 300,000 inhabitants.

He visited the Cathedral and was enchanted by its interior, writing: 'This has a sarcophagus, well preserved, and converted for its safety to an altar. It shows Hippolytus with his hunting companions, the horses of Phaedra's nurse alongside, and she preparing a table for him. The principal intention of the artist was to portray graceful youths, for whom old age, as expressed in the figure of the nurse, has been rendered innocuous. I do not believe I have ever seen anything more superb, in a work of bas relief. And it is enhanced by its perfect condition. For me, it is an exemplar of the loveliest period in Greek art. There is also on display a priceless vase of significant size, perfectly preserved, said to derive from a period even more remote. And there are other relics from the temples that have found places here and in the new church.'

I found the old city of Agrigento a delightful blend of Arab and medieval architecture, with narrow winding streets, their stones arranged in now familiar and pleasing geometric patterns, and iron grids in the walls. Food was as wonderful as it is everywhere else in the west of Sicily, and the B and B, so close to the Temples, was faultless, the young host serving the best German breakfast I had eaten in all Italy. Well – the only one.

When on a return trip with the Borghese I discovered the city's beautiful beaches in protected little coves where you can float happily for hours in the warm water, and the suburban houses flanking them, a mass of bougainvillea and wisteria overhanging the high walls and tall palms rising out of the gardens behind, I could really sympathise with the frustrations of Angelo Palillo, that his beloved city is accorded such scant regard by tourist agencies.

15

Ordinarily, I would have bypassed the opportunity to visit the Pirandello home-cum-museum in Agrigento. But Gaby promised we'd stay not more than five minutes. The Museum, unlike the Rembrandt Museum in Amsterdam gives practically no insight into the artist's home life. Admittedly Pirandello had not lived in the family home since he was very young, the great cholera epidemic of 1867 having driven his entire family from their farmhouse in an area named Chaos, to his uncle's residence near Girgenti, as Agrigento was then. Later, he wrote, 'I am the son of Chaos, and not only allegorically.'

The family home, only minutes from the sea had belonged to the Ricci Grammitos, Pirandello's father's family, since 1817. Declared a national monument in 1949, it merely warehouses objects relating to the writer's career as a novelist and playwright. Its rural setting has allowed the house to become the starting point of 'the Pirandello literary park', one of several parks dedicated to famous writers and a Sicilian innovation, where visitors can see what the writers saw, and walk where they walked.

But few if any of the Pirandello rooms are as they were lived in. There's no way of telling, for instance, that he was raised in a household affording numerous servants and nurses, that he was from a family of great wealth, his father having owned a mine when Sicilian mine owners were still employing nine-year-olds and producing ninety-five per cent of the world's sulphur.

Almost everything in the Pirandello museum could be displayed in the local history collection of an ordinary Australian public library: news clippings and photos, letters, theatre reviews, first edition books with autographed dedications, paintings given by the artists to Luigi Pirandello, playbills from famous overseas theatres where his plays were performed. One sees from the collection that Pirandello was a jetsetter, continually attending opening nights at major theatres across the world.

A number of photos show him over a period of years with Marta Abba, the beautiful actress who became famous as the quintessential interpreter of his characters with their swift, troubled, changing states of mind, suffering the 'chronic pain' of corruption, 'playing the game' and sadly becoming aware that that is all they are doing, playing, sustaining themselves with illusion.

Unlike Giovanni Verga, whose reputation rests on his exquisite if pessimistic observations of the Sicilian peasantry, Pirandello applies his scalpel to Italy's middle classes, lacerating them with his irony. It is impossible not to be aware, as indeed he was, that appearance is at the core of Italian existence. The look of a thing goes more than skin deep.

The mask itself as an object and symbol, a tool of the theatre is integral to Sicilian experience. In antiquity at the most basic level, men wore female masks to undertake a gender switch because women did not act on the stage. Since there were few actors in a Greek play, generally not more than three, actors often changed masks during a performance. From the audience point of view, I can say with conviction that the masks are powerfully expressive and in combination with great poetry, can make for a transfixing performance, with the audience caught up in the magnifications of the mask even if simultaneously aware that it is a device, that it is temporary, that it is consciously chosen by the actor for a limited purpose, and be asking themselves, what will I find when the mask goes?

Culturally Pirandello would certainly have been encouraged to reflect at length on the nature and function of illusion in life, while at home a long marriage to a severely disturbed woman, reportedly schizophrenic, had given him intimate experience of alienation and diverse perceptions of reality. Unlike some other writers who set out to expose hypocrisy, he did not resort to stock characters and situations.

He was curious about people as individuals and noted a few reflections on the way writers approach characters.

Some writers and they're not few, he said, portray a character of a man or woman, solely for the pleasure of portraying them or narrate a particular event or vicissitude for the sole purpose of narrating it or describe a landscape for the sole pleasure of describing it. They are properly historians. Others, like himself, seek more than this pleasure. They feel a profoundly spiritual need to evoke a character, event or landscape that absorbs a particular sense of life and that acquires a universal value. Such writers he considered properly philosophical.

Pirandello's characters are indeed universal. His plays were a sell-out when first performed in Britain and the United States even though Sicilians were his particular models.

Amazingly, though awarded the Nobel Prize for drama in 1934, Pirandello initially despised the theatre for trafficking in and enhancing stereotypes, but later he saw in it the possibility of involving the audience in his fictions, and stimulating their empathy. He was nearly fifty when he shifted his focus to the stage. It had taken time to forge his new style of drama, one that sought to turn psychoanalysis into good theatre, promoting his conviction that nothing, or nobody can be grasped completely: ten people who think they know the same person, know only their own version, while the person, under the pressure of those judgments of his or her self, is consciously trying to determine their own identity and even to change that self. Where then is the 'I'? The theatre, ironically, allowed him to give the fullest dramatic expression to that question.

To fully appreciate Pirandello's deft juggling of appearance and reality one can't go past Eric Bentley's commentary on *Liola*, a drama 'light in form, breathtakingly absurd, but which arouses the profoundest disquiet in any audience, undermining the convictions one normally has about what is real in human behaviour.'

Liola, the male protagonist of this play which Pirandello presented as a summer entertainment is its only morally positive character, one who sees himself as master of his fate. Not a hero, but determined not to let others exploit him.

His joy and self-confidence is immediately established in the song Pirandello assigns him.

Last night I slept the sleep I love
My cabin roof, the stars above
A bit of earth it was my bed,
And there were thistles near my head,
Hunger and thirst, sorrows' sting,
They touch me not:
For I can sing
My heart it jumps for joy:
Of all the earth and sea, I'm King.

It's no surprise to discover that the ebullient Liola is the gallant lover of two women: Mita, married to the wealthy and powerful Simone who has been unable to father a child on her and Tuzza who has become pregnant by Liola as part of her scheme to displace Mita in Simone's affections. She persuades Simone to pretend that the child is his. He agrees with enthusiasm because he has failed to beget an heir. Tuzza's plan is that he will dispense with Mita and Tuzza will become the mistress of Simone's household.

Liola, however, will not stand for this. He warns Tuzza and her aunt, 'I don't want to commit an outrage, nor will I let anyone else commit an outrage on me.'

When the two women ignore his warning he decides to make Mita pregnant so that she can retain her wifely dignity. Simone will disown Tuzza's child and retain Mita's.

The turning point of the action is Liola's seduction of Mita. He tells her he will not be used by the others to bring about her ruin.

In this play, Pirandello is demonstrating that reality is not more real than appearance. At the same time there are real appearances and apparent appearances and just as appearances can be more real than reality, apparent appearances may be even more real than real appearances. This proposition may seem absurd but it is perfectly logical.

To *appear* to be a father is enough for Simone: appearance establishes his paternity more than actually having begotten a child. But the appearance is itself fake because the whole town knows the truth. Simone only appears to be the father. His being a father is a legal fiction.

Simone had been part of the first pact because Tuzza had told him her child was Liola's and invited him to pretend that the child was his, but he was excluded from the second pact which included only Mita and Liola. Simone could pretend Mita's child was his.

No matter if others were telling Simone Mita's child was really Liola's. That was just unofficial gossip. The *apparent* understanding is that the father of Mita's child is Simone. It is the appearance of appearance, a shadow of a shadow that secures Mita's hold on the solid realities of Simone's wealth and power.

Prior to writing this play Pirandello asserted in an article on humour: 'The harder the struggle for life and the more one's weakness is felt, the greater becomes the need for mutual deception. The simulation of honesty, sympathy, prudence, in short, of every virtue and of that greatest virtue, veracity, is no more".

These marvellous insights originated in his own Sicilian/Italian society midway through the last century but their reality becomes more and more apparent in our own place and time.

Away from the museum and its lingering images of an old man – for there were none of the young Pirandello – drawing in deep breaths of the cool, salt air, and idling wordlessly through the park with one of Sicily's delightful gentle breezes raising a smile on our lips, I could more easily imagine Pirandello as a youth sitting or lying down under the pine tree near his father's house. The tree, they say, a gnarled, twisted, pollarded tree, craning out to sea, inspired his fantasy.

Gaby, sitting cross-legged in the lotus posture, chewing on a blade of grass, was obviously preoccupied. Finally she said: 'Funny he grew up a Fascist.'

I didn't think that funny at all. Artists are necessarily individualistic and often drawn to the triumphing will. They know what it is like to be seduced by a vision others might think mad. Some might well have felt empathetic towards Mussolini.

Many of Pirandello's admirers held that his support for Mussolini was just an illusion, a mask he wore to suit his audience. But popular opinion had supported Mussolini for his refusal to have Italy continue a victim of the western alliance, to accept the gross injustice done the Italians at the sharing of the spoils after the First World War.

Certainly Pirandello would never have been taken in by Mussolini's posturising, possibly admiring it, recognising that on the international stage illusion and the appearance of appearance is the stuff of diplomacy.

And, of course, one can't discount that he inherited certain class interests and that Mussolini on seizing power had assured the upper classes it would be business as usual – despite any appearances to the contrary.

16

Whoever heard of a seaside hamlet not on the shore but high up on a plateau so rough and rocky that Arab town planners had to divide the town into four parts, each on a separate rock which was smoothed down to the sea? Driving around for half an hour after coming off the freeway, trying to gain entry to Sciacca, we noted these little settlements high up the mountain, villages, as we thought, above the town. But that was Sciacca itself, up in the clouds.

Quarter past two already, when we arrived, not much chance of getting something to eat. The place was quiet. Siesta. In the piazza an elderly man was closing down his fruit stall, drawing the shutters with a loud rattle and securing them. Gaby asked him if he knew of some place where we could have lunch.

'Certainly,' he said. 'You can eat very well in this restaurant I will describe to you.' And he proceeded to give us an incredibly convoluted explanation of how to find our way to the place. We thought we could manage it. Soon we reached the first landmark. 'This is easy,' said Gaby. But after a long walk the second one had still not appeared when we suddenly noticed a well-dressed man in a dark suit with a collar and tie, standing on a corner about 100 metres ahead, watching us approach.

Gaby said, 'I think he's going to speak to us.'

In fact, he began signalling, hooking his arm towards himself, to say 'Come, come – on the double,' and when we reached him, feeling somewhat bemused, he smiled broadly, shaking hands with each of us in turn.

'You are the ladies looking for lunch?'

Sicily too had a bush telegraph. 'But how do you know?' I said.

The fruiterer had contacted him, knowing the difficulty of navigating the widespread rubble of urban renovation to reach the restaurant. I was a bit worried about eating in a place where custom was so lacking, the owner went trekking the streets to catch a passing tourist.

'You've been too kind,' I said, 'to come and search for us.'

His eyes twinkled: 'But, signora, who else could come? The others are all too busy.'

Arriving at the restaurant within very few minutes, he called 'Ho, Tommaso!' while pushing the door open and holding it to let us through. The waiter who responded was in mid-rush to the kitchen. He stopped abruptly and wheeled round, balancing on one leg for a few seconds.

'*Mi dica.*'

'Find our two guests a table.' Then, with a slight bow to us, 'Enjoy your lunch, ladies. You'll excuse me if I rush off. I am dining with friends.'

Even more embarrassing. He'd left his meal to come and find us. And the tables were all occupied. The room was full. Another room I saw on my left, the same. The waiter was quickly clearing a table just being vacated by two men in business suits. He slung a fresh cloth across the table, and set out the cutlery in a flurry as if he were dealing a pack of cards.

'Here you are,' he said, sliding some menus before us and hurried off. We had barely finished scanning what was on offer, when he was back, with some seafood antipasto and fresh bread, a carafe of wine and two glasses.

'This,' he said, pointing to the wine, 'goes with the antipasto. It is a local wine, very good, and there is a perfect marriage between the two'.

Everything had happened with such speed, I was half dazed, but applied myself to the platter with my usual gusto.

'A fish stock, isn't it? Made from the mussel juice and the prawn shells?'

'You'll have to ask my mum about that,' Gaby said, reaching for a piece of bread. 'She's an expert cook. I can say that for her.'

Looking around the restaurant, I wondered how a modest little town like Sciacca could come up with such a *clienti* as was sitting around us, sophisticated-looking business people, well dressed, quiet, their voices refined murmurs, more likely met in an upmarket restaurant in Rome. True, Sciacca's population, at around 45,000, was only 10,000 down on Agrigento's. But what a world of difference between the two. Though physically so close to one another, Agrigento had been a leading city of Magna Graecia for 1500 years before Sciacca came into existence, a nameless district as it was till the Romans dubbed it Thermae Selinuntinae – the place where people from Selinunte come to use the hot springs.

The local population, members of the Sicani tribe, had to wait for the ninth century arrival of the Arabs to live in a town with a wall built around it, street grids set out, the new abode in its four *quartieri* to accommodate the difficult terrain, and a name, Sciacca, said to mean 'Rocky Heights' or 'Cliffs by the Sea'. During its Arab period, a mere 200 years long, Sciacca flourished like the rest of Arab Sicily, developing a thriving fishing industry and becoming Sicily's major outlet for the grain exports to North Africa. Couscous was on the menu, I noted. I felt as if I should like to run backwards and forwards between the two places to compare the two, one for so long the product of Greco-Roman civilisation and the other, twenty-five kilometres distant, rooted in Arab culture.

Quietly happy, I sat without talking, astounded that we had been led here by the hand of the owner. The restaurant was winding down. We had arrived late after all. Tables were being cleared and reset, for dinner, I presumed. We waived dessert and the waiter brought us our coffees on a tray, a bowl filled with Swiss chocolates, and two small glasses of *nocino*, locally made, he told us, to accompany them.

'On the house,' he said, surprisingly warmly, given that he must have been waiting for his own meal. Then, knowing I was a foreigner, asked: 'Do you like *nocino*?'

Did I! Australian Italians I knew were always bringing *nocino* back with them and would hand it around after a specially substantial meal. They call it a 'digestive' and amazingly a small glass very quickly eases that uncomfortable post-gluttony feeling of really wishing you hadn't... It is much more palatable than Fernet, a popular digestive tasting like medicine, and more treasured, because of the rituals and hocus pocus incorporated into the process of infusing green walnuts, shells as well as kernels, in a syrup with alcohol and spices. The dedication required to make *nocino* creates yet another Italian occasion for lip smacking and delivering an entire rhetoric of gratitude to man and God.

When the bill finally arrived, I was surprised to find it much less than I had anticipated. Eventually we were ready to depart, having left a generous tip, and as we reached the door, the owner was suddenly on hand to open it for us.

'Everything all right, ladies?' he enquired, solicitously.

I looked at him for a moment, my head heavy with food and wine, 'Well, the experience has been quite overwhelming.'

Gaby joined in, enthusiastically, praising the food and the service. 'We will remember Sciacca,' she said.

The owner offered us a little bow. 'It has been our pleasure, ladies. Come and visit us again.'

Oddly enough, we had no trouble finding our way back to the piazza. We debated going to look for the new promenade then decided against it. I had every intention of coming back to Agrigento for a longer stay, and that visit would include a day or two in Sciacca. The promenade would probably be finished by then.

On the road to Alcamo, Gaby fell silent. On impulse, I told her I would like to cut my visit a little short and return to Favignana that afternoon.

'I can go back to your place, get my gear, and then if you drive me to the coach station I'll take a coach for Trapani.'

Voicing this aloud made me feel like cheering. Now I would avoid being involved in the money squabbles that were very likely to ensue within the family. And not have to listen to people screaming at one another. Gaby groaned.

'Oh don't let me have to do everything on my own. I don't have the strength. I need you to give me confidence when I'm dealing with them. You'll stop them screaming.'

'Look, Gaby' I said, firmly, 'I do not intend to become embroiled in family squabbles. You have to adopt a strategy of being agreeable when your parents return. Your conflict with your dad is about power, as you said. Bend a little, but consciously. Give him an opportunity to be magnanimous. You absolutely must not shout and argue because power will always win in that circumstance.'

Gaby smiled, despite herself. 'What a schemer you are. Is that the kind of thing you do, yourself?'

'No need, 'I said. 'I don't have a wealthy dad who's trying to keep my moiety from me. I don't come from a patriarchal family. But I did live for decades with a patriarchal husband and thought it worth while learning a few tactics to keep us close, not drive us apart.'

After a few minutes when we sat in a 'what now' silence, she suddenly turned to me and her voice ringing with triumph, declared, 'You have to stay another day or two. We've got something important to do before you leave.'

'Important? For whom?'

'Both of us. Danilo Dolci,' she said, smiling happily. 'You don't want to miss visiting the Centre, do you?'

I did not.

17

Oddly enough, every foreigner that visits Italy knows it as a sumptuously rich country. An astonishing number of Italian writers, however, mainly middle and upper class themselves, 'know' Italy instead as poor, poor, poor. Poverty in Italy, especially in the south, allures writers, I've decided, because observing that poverty leads unerringly to the awareness of an endless and pervasive continuum of social and political evils unimaginable by ordinary people in Western liberal democracies.

Danilo Dolci, a sociologist by profession, but poet and reformer by inclination, made his name outside Italy in the 1960s with *Poverty in Sicily*, a book that combined passion and compassion with intellect and enormous energy. Gaby had experienced the same admiration for Dolci as I, though encountering his work decades later and had promptly suggested my time in Alcamo offered an ideal opportunity to visit the Centre for Creative Development, Danilo Dolci, still located in Partinico, an appallingly neglected little municipality of Palermo in 1952 when Dolci, after moving to Sicily, selected the district as a kind of social laboratory.

His decision had been influenced by a paper prepared for him by a local writer, Germana Fizzotti, who wrote: 'In Spine Sante (where madness reigns) of 330 families, 300 live in the depths of misery, 319 without water in the house and with a public fountain operating only four hours a day, with women forming a queue for all of that time, waiting their turn to get some water.

'Two thirds of the streets, half of whose cobblestones have gone, are without sewerage. They are also dusty and dirty, but among the filth, there is not a single skerrick of food, not a piece of orange peel, nor a tea leaf, not a cabbage stalk, no cans, no bones: emaciated dogs sniff the ground as if half demented.

'Seventeen people officially declared insane live in two or three houses and who knows how many others there are, less evident and less clamorous?

'We saw standing in front of one door, a young girl, her arms dangling at her sides, and her face and eyes seeming to have dried out, calm now, but according to neighbours, when seized by hunger, flies into a rage.

'We entered another house where one man was shut up in a cage. The little room which housed all the family had been divided by iron bars similar to those used to cage wild beasts, and in his prison, pacing to and fro was a young man with a bestial face and dark, mad eyes. Next door the head of the family had been lying in bed without moving for months, shut off from the world. It hardly need be said that among the various diseases, mental illness occurs with an unusually high frequency.'

A profound dispiritedness was ingrained in the local villagers by chronic unemployment, poverty and the lack of resources personal or communal to feed themselves or look after their bodies. Their self-esteem was so low they thought themselves unworthy even to have a want. But, encouraged by Dolci, they gradually talked themselves into realising that more than anything else they must have water. They needed a dam on the Jato.

The effort required to have them arrive at this level of assertiveness was a clear indictment of the pastors and the nobility, those in daily authority over the people of Partinico. Indeed, when Dolci later reproached a priest for not throwing his weight behind infant community projects, the priest yelled at him:

'I'm here to save souls! To save souls.'

In October 1952, after learning of a little child found dead in the street from starvation, Dolci announced that no food would pass his lips until the government acknowledged its responsibilities to the people in the area. Fasting alarmed both the Church and the government. It too closely resembled

Christ-like behaviour. So the government passed a law making it an offence to fast for political reasons. Arrests and publicity were assured every time Dolci and his followers began starving themselves.

Four years later national interest again focused on Dolci when he organised a 'strike in reverse', that is, working without pay: leading 150 unemployed locals to a public road in very bad repair and beginning work on it, with Dolci right in the middle, setting an example.

This 'strike for work' was based on article IV of the Italian Constitution which stipulates that (1) *The republic recognizes the right of all citizens to work and promotes conditions to fulfil this right.* (2) *According to capability and choice, every citizen has the duty to undertake an activity or a function that will contribute to the material and moral progress of society.* Dolci, with three union leaders, was hauled off to gaol.

Viewing a documentary film on Dolci's work in Partinico Gaby and I were stunned by images of a settlement such as might have been found in Europe when the Black Death had swept the continent, and villages became ruins with no one to maintain streets or municipal services. One main street was broken up in a ravine formed years earlier by an earthquake.

When Dolci arrived, the ravine was unchanged and still a barrier to communication between those living on opposite sides of the street. To compound the misery of the municipality the Palermo mafia were committing a murder a day there, gang warfare going through one of its periodic surges.

Only Dolci's international renown kept him safe in Partinico. His survival there and his achievements with the local people speak volumes for his tenacity and an astonishing array of skills.

With money accruing from his 1958 Lenin Peace Prize award – though Dolci was explicitly not a communist – he bought land at Mirto, a little hamlet between Partinico and Borgetto. There he built a house that drew others to erect similar dwellings alongside him, giving rise to a colony of like-minded people.

Later, in 1971 he set up the Educative Centre of Mirto, holding that contemporary Sicilian schools (read, Church-inspired educators) dealt violently with children, not merely physically but emotionally and spiritually, bent on reducing them to obedient automatons, independent thought and the spirit of creativity being destroyed in the egg, so to speak.

Amazingly, the Dolci Centre is today hidden away in a corner of a local junior high school. Whatever its earlier glory, it is now a sheepish remnant of nearly five decades' struggle with the State, the mafia and the Church. Isolated and embarrassingly tiny, its premises are little bigger than an average living room, unimaginable as having housed the vibrant presence of a Danilo Dolci.

Today, three Dolci devotees keep it functioning: Dolci's son, Amico, Luca Dai, the young volunteer publisher of the newsletter that revealed the plight of the disabled Neapolitans whose radio signal had been unlawfully usurped by Vatican Radio, and Dolci's former secretary Giusi Martinetti. Together they run the Centre as an information clearing house, organising innumerable conferences, seminars and workshops for scholars, largely sociologists and educators from the five continents, still meeting today to discuss and disseminate Dolci's philosophy and pedagogy.

Martinetti, Dolci's loyal assistant of many years, told us that famous educationists, philosophers, psychologists, architects, economists and writers visited, commented on and contributed ideas to the Mirto Centre. Some became close friends of Dolci's, like Paolo Freire, the renowned Brazilian educationist whose adult mass literacy project added tens of thousands of peasants to electoral rolls and had him expelled from Brazil for a decade before a new government granted him an amnesty.

A German foundation had supplied 30,000 marks to buy the land for building the school. Other funds from *The Swiss Committee for Danilo Dolci* had paid for the construction. 'But foreign support gradually ebbed away,' the secretary recalled sadly. 'Nowadays we've become accustomed to living off euros we find on the floor.'

She said that the reform drive had come totally from Dolci himself, for the teachers took the view that while the Socratic method was excellent it required too much effort and time.

Luca Dai, a quietly spoken, helpful and unpretentious person who seemed to get through an enormous amount of work and whose diffidence occasionally gave way to the odd sardonic interpolation, described conditions today for the children in the junior high school hosting the Centre as 'appalling'.

'They've turned the children's playground into a car park. All that remains is a basketball ring rusted right through.'

Given that Partinico is a mafia fiefdom and the mafia and the Church joint oppressors, it takes little imagination to figure out why Dolci got no support from the local council or from the State.

Gaby had arranged for me to meet the school principal. On the way to her office, we were suddenly caught up in a bunch of older students, thirteen- or fourteen-year-olds, running out of the buildings, their backpacks bouncing, in a hurry to catch the school bus or meet a friend to walk home with. On impulse I stopped one, a girl, her black hair drawn back tightly into a thick, heavy plait that hung over one shoulder.

'Hello,' I said. 'I wonder if you can help me. Have you time for a little chat? It won't take a minute.' She paused, blinking with surprise. I hurried on. 'I just want to know if you might have heard of Danilo Dolci?'

She looked uncertainly down at her feet. Embarrassed. 'I'm sorry. I cannot help you. I am not from here. I am Moroccan.'

'Moroccan? How long have you been in Partinico?'

'Three years,' she said, raising her head shyly.

'And you have never heard of Danilo Dolci?'

'Who is he?' she asked.

I ignored that for a moment. 'You don't know there is a place in this school not many metres away, called the Creative Development Centre, Danilo Dolci?'

The girl took hold of her plait and absentmindedly began to chew on it. 'No. Ought one to know about it?'

'Yes,' I assured her. 'Dolci was a great man who made Partinico famous.'

'Who said?' Gaby asked me, disgustedly, when we had sent the girl on her way, 'Partinico's famous with you and me. That's about it.'

The visit to the principal proved disappointing but not surprising. While she enthused over Dolci's pedagogy and supported it to the point that she had sent her young children to his infant school she could give no good reason why her own school had reverted to traditional Catholic instruction. Nor did she see anything odd in the fact that children in her school were totally unaware of the Dolci Centre inside their own playground.

We saw nothing of Partinico except for the high school, the Dolci Centre and one or two side streets where we went searching for a bakery at lunchtime. Two young mothers with children were buying bread when we arrived at one shop and while we waited our turn, examining the pastries in the meantime, an old man, slim and trim, in his eighties perhaps, and wearing a hat, entered the shop, carrying a little basket on his arm. On impulse I told him I was a foreigner from Australia, researching a book about Sicily and asked him:

'Signore, were you here when Danilo Dolci came to Partinico? Do you know of him?'

Startled, he froze for a moment, trying to gather his thoughts. Then a wonderfully beatific expression lit up his face.

'Do I know of him? Do I know of Dolci? Of course I do, Signora, I took part in the reverse strike for work, when the police came and arrested Dolci and beat us.' Then, twisting his hat in his hands and with a note of regret creeping into his tone, he added, 'But I never took part in a fast. No, I never did that.'

'Fasts can't be done safely by everyone,' I said, soothingly. 'Were you here before the dam was built?'

'Yes,' he said.

'You remember how it was then?'

His shoulders rode right up to his ears and he spread his hands slightly, shaking his head. 'Bad. Really bad. Not knowing if you would have water or not. This is very worrying. For those with babies and children especially. It frightened people. And it took a long time to get the dam. Seventeen years. There was a lot of trouble. But we found it exciting. It gave us hope. And something to strive for. Things weren't so boring any more. Especially for the young.' Nodding his head slowly. 'We got jobs. We made cooperatives and planned little projects. We worried a lot about Dolci, but he was not afraid. He became a very important person. Many, many people, very big people in their own countries, came here to visit him. The mafia thought it too risky to kill him. Besides, he used to walk up the middle of the street with a group around him.' After a pause, he added. 'We miss him.'

Partinico is still a mafia stronghold. When Bernardo Provenzano, a long-sought aging mafia chieftain reportedly responsible for 600 murders, was finally seized by the police on his own home ground, Corleone, a village in the interior, now rendered a tourist attraction by Mario Puzo's 'Godfather' novels, they found no funds or financial records there, but discovered them later, stashed away in Partinico.

One or two local visionary groups dedicated to Dolci's memory operate in the district, The Stone Theatre and a small television station, but none has the stature, energy or Christ-like combination of compassion and political understanding that awed those who encountered Dolci. They are weak and fragile, allowed to continue because they are not seen as a serious threat, more as a safety valve.

In the EU report included later in this book it can be seen that very little of substance has changed for Sicily's poor since Dolci's struggle to invigorate Partinico.

18

After the visit to the Dolci Centre, I agreed to remain home with Gaby for several more days (when she would be pressing her parents for the allowance) and bear with whatever conflicts arose.

Initially I thought her mother a poor creature, a vacuous little doll. She appeared to have nothing whatever to say of any consequence and spent a great deal of her time spoiling her tiny little dog, a chihuahua even smaller and yappier than the norm, turning it out for a dinner she'd offered us, in a kind of regimental dress, emerald green with blonde tassels, and a stiff collar that held the little creature's head on high. Seated erect on its chair, which had been turned away from the table in the pizzeria where we were eating, the dog, sensing it was on parade, looked straight ahead, bearing itself with a hauteur that had the other diners chortling.

Ariadne had joined us for the pizza. In a certain way she was a silent supporter of Gaby, envying her intelligence, wit and her higher level of education, I felt, and at the same time, admiring her spunk, willing to see her thwarted in minor ways, but not crushed. I wondered how she managed, working for her father. During the squabble which erupted on the second night after the parents arrived back, neither she nor her mother intervened between Gaby and her father. But I did not see any need for me as a guest to have to endure the boredom of their mindless reproaches.

Listening to the father, a short, stocky man with a good head of light brown hair, ruddy complexion and slightly prominent blue eyes, I decided he was looking for recognition from Gaby, from his family, really, seeking acknowledgment of his achievements and if that were forthcoming, they all might be a lot happier.

In English, I said to Gaby, 'For goodness sake be quiet and let your father speak.' But she was so fired up by her own grievances she had no patience to listen to Dad's. In Italian then, I said to him, 'Look, Mr de Santis, I'd love to have a chat with you about the big career change you made, from tailoring to what you're doing today. It strikes me as having been quite extraordinary. Since I'm leaving in the morning, would it be possible to talk now?' And I reached into my bag for my notepad and pen.

The effect was magic. He flushed a little, with embarrassment. 'Oh, I've never -er -er...' I made the usual soothing noises required by the occasion and raised my pen, preparing to go through the motions of interviewing him. In the meantime, Mamma went off to the kitchen and peace reigned except for periodic snorts of disapproval from Gaby. Ariadne was leaning forward, chin in hands, watching with a little smile, no doubt recollecting the Englishman's presence at the last public squabble.

Their father began by saying that his mother's main ambition for her son was to see him in a trade. She didn't care what he earned so long as he learned. 'I became an apprentice tailor at twelve.' He looked too bulky and nuggetty to be a tailor, but seemed tailor-made to run a tough transport business, being hard and tanned, lacking a tailor's pallor, and with the kind of baleful expression blue eyes can often assume when their owner wants to exude menace. Nowhere evident was the usual meekness of most tailors who live with their heads bowed over the cloth. His expansive manner with its hint of steel and the overflowing confidence were much more suited to a macho environment than to the pleasantries associated with measuring up bodies and running one's hands over them, making light of physical irregularities and reassuring the client not merely regarding their appearance, but also satisfying them that the tailor would deserve every lira put on the coming bill.

'I really enjoyed the work.' The conviction in his voice and the light in the blue eyes surprised me. 'I thought of myself as an artisan. Someone creative. I did everything around the workshop, lit the fire, cleaned the floor, took deliveries on foot to the rich. And I was always sewing. It was clear that I had an aptitude for the art, and I started having fantasies of being a designer. Yes, like Armani. I kept pushing myself to do more, and to find ways of doing things better. I was like a hot iron at the forge waiting to be shaped by the blacksmith.'

From the age of fifteen he worked twelve hours a day, six days a week and sometimes on Sundays for one hundred and fifty lire a day. It was a game to him, rather than work. 'At night, I dreamed of sewing, faster and faster.'

At seventeen he took the first step to riches. 'I went to another post where my expertise earned me better money on piece rates. And I also employed on my own behalf two men working from their homes. I cut and they sewed. I loved it. I felt I was well on the way to becoming a designer. A year later I was employing five outworkers. With that number I could make ten suits in a week. My clients were mainly professionals, doctors and lawyers, dentists, bankers, persons like that. I never put a price on my work. I sent the garment to them for a final fitting and they returned it for finishing touches, with the payment they thought appropriate. At the age of twenty-five I owned a house but not a car. Some years later I went on holidays in August and found a wife. Eventually I was invited to sit on the board of a local bank. They thought I was honest but stupid.' He assumed a vacant expression to make the point, and followed it up with a gleeful smile, flashing a perfectly groomed set of teeth: 'They soon got a surprise.'

In his late thirties he felt obliged to quit tailoring. He had his own label, of course, but every tailor has a label. His had not made the salons of Milan. Not only that, he was experiencing a shortage of manpower. No one wanted to become a tailor.

'So I went into buying and selling. I borrowed money from the bank, went north and bought trucks, selling them on hire purchase. The banks charged four per cent interest and I charged eight per cent. It's important to know prices. The commodity is not important. And you have to take risks but without becoming addicted to risk taking.

'I built this house: It's what I call brutta/bella, but its defects are all mine. I like to create. Public life? What? No I've never contributed anything to public life. Why should I?'

It was easy enough to bring the conversation round to the fact that neither had he seen any need to contribute time at home. Being at home bored him as it bores many Italian men. The Church's cult of the madonna may take much of the credit for this: spending endless hours on one's own with children does not equip women to offer stimulating chat by the home fire. Since Gaby's dad valued creativity and had married someone who was barely out of her childhood, had he done anything to help her develop her own creativity? To guide her or encourage her? He had given her money, of course. Time?

He frowned. He was no fool. He saw where I was leading him. If one took away the money and left his wife in the street in a ragged dress, what inner resources would she be able to draw on? What had he contributed other than money, to her development, to the marriage? To fatherhood? Ariadne was hugging herself, smiling more broadly. Gaby raging. I raised a warning finger to her. Her father was silent. Then he heaved a sigh. 'I've been talking too long. Got to make some phone calls.'

I thanked him, said he had a lot to be proud of, and turned to Ariadne: 'What about a little chat with you, Ariadne?' To my surprise, she accepted with alacrity.

Ariadne had never intended to work with her father. She wanted to be a dentist but hadn't gained the points necessary to undertake the study. When she was still trying to settle on what she might do, one of her father's staff left and he invited her to fill the vacant position. She had to go on the road a lot, rising at four a.m. to drive to Syracuse and other cities on the east coast. She hated it. The roads were so bumpy and the trips so long she began to suffer from headaches. Her mission was to purchase licences from companies that were closing down. (Licences exist for everything in Italy. They offer golden opportunities for corruption.) One man who was angered by the price she had offered for the family's licences, tore up all the documentation prepared for the bureaucracy. The man's father came to apologise and she told him that his son's anger had frightened her. The father said: 'Afraid of my son? The hell you were,' and his own tones were so fierce that she was afraid of him, too.

However, she had learned over time that every workplace has issues, abuses and mistreatment of staff. 'So I'll get by here.'

She had a delegated authority to sign documents on her father's behalf. As her administration of the business became more expert and her knowledge and range of contacts widened, her father and she became more competitive. He checked everything she did, not concerned to discover what had been done well, but what was done badly. Once he found that she had achieved something on her own initiative without telling him and he couldn't find any fault with it. So he admonished her: 'Don't forget. This business is mine.' But other people praised her. 'I learned to work for myself, to do well for myself. I set my own goals and standards.'

She had frequent contact with the truck drivers. 'Their lives are shit. They're always on the road, driving endlessly. And I can tell you, the roads south of Naples are really terrible. Dangerous. I do feel sorry for them.'

She had been working for the firm for fifteen years. Generally men did not like to have her present at meetings, with lawyers and managers and the like. They raised their eyebrows when she raised her voice. They were always patronising. 'Here's a woman, and here am I, stronger, more intelligent.'

When she made a good suggestion, their reflex action was to say 'Bullshit' but eventually they would get around to saying 'Oh well, maybe.'

'I make it clear to men that I won't put up with any of their crap. It's nothing like working in a shoe shop. Here men try to cheat and exploit what they think might be my weakness.

'Sometimes I feel I could kill my dad. At other times I turn to him when my partner is being difficult.'

Her father will eventually sell the business. She doesn't want to carry it on. Shaking her head. 'No, no. I'm thinking of doing a three-year course in nutrition.'

****

When we sat down to dinner, a simple but very tasty meal with a lavish array of vegetables and crispy spatchcocks, beautifully presented, I decided that all four members of the family had already been experiencing the benefits of good nutrition, for the glow in their skin and the smooth pink complexions of the mother and her daughters, combined with their apparently unlimited energy, pointed to excellent health. Conversation was polite and friendly. Gaby had cooled down. I was feeling warm towards the father and the sister.

In this relaxed state, congratulating myself on having deflected the family quarrel, I was completely unprepared when Mamma suddenly confessed that she too would like to have a little chat. My God, I thought, at my patronising worst, what on earth can this little woman have to say? Gaby caught my eye, and grimaced, shaking her head. But it was impossible that I could refuse. Besides, it wouldn't take long. That was certain. Mamma wanted to talk while she was doing the ironing. Fine, I said.

Unfortunately, I could hardly understand a word she was saying, whether because of her accent, or her speaking dialect, I was unsure. So I had to ask Gaby to interpret for us. At least to convert her mother's speech to Italian. Gaby sat opposite me at the table where I was taking my notes, her back to her mother, drumming her fingers and huffing and puffing while her mother was speaking, then hurrying through the translation.

'Listen, Gaby,' I muttered to her in English, 'if you don't stop acting like a spoiled brat I'll find a B and B and go back to Favignana in the morning.'

Gaby banged her head on the table and groaned loudly. Then she sat up, exaggeratedly straight, and said briskly:

'Right then, let's get it over and done with. And don't blame me if you fall asleep.'

Mamma was the youngest of a family of twelve, six boys and six girls, born to a woman almost old enough to be her great-grandmother. Fifty-six years of age.

'She was seventy-six when I was twenty'.

One of her brothers had a disability. The other brothers had to move to find work, one settling in Agrigento where he found a job in a factory making horsehair mattresses, the others taking up long term residence in Piemonte, Palermo and Calabria. Their father had been a forestry guard but was no longer working when Mamma was growing up. In that period, two of her big sisters were still at home and looking after the house. Their only future was in marriage. Mamma herself was selected for special schooling in the country. Her mother worked every day as a house cleaner, coming home in the afternoons.

Mamma would say of herself that she was always someone who knew how to make her way in life. Initially she had thoughts of becoming a hairdresser but found instead a position as a legal secretary. She prepared drafts of documents as well as typing. She was very happy in the work and was the only one of the six girls in her family *ever* in employment. Ever. Gaby's father was quite a bit older than she when they married, and his mother was *very* old. But Mamma was content to marry him.

'He had four houses,' she said. 'He was a person of substance.' A man of property, a person of means, how reassuring the phrase is in the making of a marriage.

The house they lived in when she married was only a little smaller than the one they presently occupied. Her life vastly improved after she married.

'My husband maintained me. I never had to bring money home. We had a lovely family. The three children were always here with their friends. The house was full of fun. When the youngest left, I was very sad. I thought they might return. It is a joy to have become a *nonna*. I am always speaking of my grandchild. If I could live my life again I would be much firmer with my children. I'm a person who could never say 'no'. My children exploited that. They treat me as if I'm the child and they the parent.'

Gaby gave a little snort of incredulity.

'I think men and women are significantly different. They are meant to have different roles. When you're modern you must realise that you place yourself outside the family. I'm modern, myself, in certain aspects. I visit Palermo, for instance. Before, women never used to go out much. However, I had my car licence when I was only eighteen. I think modernity is one thing and education another. They're not necessarily linked'.

Gaby was making so many noises, grimaces and rolling her eyes heavenward that, despite my disapproval, I nearly burst out laughing. Mamma, seemingly oblivious of the pantomime, was pushing the iron backwards and forwards over some pillow slips, looking into space, and pausing every so often to collect her thoughts. Eventually she said, 'That's all I can think of for now.'

****

Back in my room, Ariadne's room, Gaby settled down to text Simon. 'Did you catch what she said about being modern? She was referring to me, of course. Warning me that it puts me outside the family.'

'It's true, though,' I said, impressed by the distinction her mother had made between education and modernity. The whole point about 'education' in Sicily is that the Church maintains a stranglehold on intellectual development, reducing the whole of human existence to 'a mystery' and relentlessly waging its counter-reformation against modernity.

Mamma, empty-headed though she had seemed to me on first appearance, understood the significance of modernity. She had been unable to say no to her marvellously talented and intelligent daughter, indulging her demands for a superb education beyond Sicily and was now desperately regretting it. Gaby was lost to theocracy. She rejected the Church's doctrines, all belief in the supernatural, patriarchy, clientelism with its disgusting outcomes, lawlessness and domestic terror, lifelong unemployment, no hope for the many of ever finding paid work.

She was fiercely unforgiving of those benefiting from the status quo. She understood the value of a public life and wanted to be involved in the reform of Sicily, but from a safe base in Australia. And she was totally unapologetic in demanding her share of the family substance to give her a sound foundation in the new life she was intent on having.

If she were a man living fifty years ago, she would have become a *gabellotto*, more than likely achieving the status of a mafia *capo*, for she was made of that stuff, it seemed to me. But now she was a modern, for the time being, impatient of and deaf to her family's plaints of loss.

The following morning, I made my farewells to her family, who were very cordial, and she drove me to the bus station in Palermo, where buses left every twenty minutes or so for Catania.

While we waited for the next bus, I asked her what progress she had made with the research into the ferries. I knew she had hardly done a scrap of work on the subject, in effect ignoring my attempt to make the money she had hounded me into giving her the basis of a trade.

In an offhand manner, as if she hardly knew what I was talking about, she said she had made a few phone calls but one needed to go to Naples to talk to people at the head offices. 'You'll have to do that, yourself,' she said. 'I'm returning to Australia very soon, so I don't have time.'

'Fine,' I said. 'Good luck.'

'Oh, but we'll meet up in Sydney when you get back,' she assured me.

She had been a good companion and when she contacted me later for a reference she needed to gain permanent residency in Australia, I acknowledged the many virtues and talents she would bring to the Australian community. She was thrilled.

'I hardly recognised myself. Thank you so much.'

But I had no intention of pursuing the friendship.

Part IV Palermo

Nobody ever asked me why I visited Palermo when in Sicily, though I always had to explain my stay in Catania, that it's on the East Coast, that it has the oldest university in Sicily and is conspicuously a university town where students and their teachers throng the streets in the small hours of the morning. Palermo instead has somehow seeped into the consciousness of most people – even my own before I went to Sicily. I knew its name, and yet felt uneasy about going there. Before leaving Australia, I booked myself into a monastery on the outskirts of the city, timing my arrival for late September, at the far end of my trip.

The Alcamo mayor had told Gaby and me that he loved it, that it was his most favourite city in the world.

And a delightful image of the city appears in an article earlier referred to, The pleasures of Palermo *by Baron di Denone who portrayed Palermo as a thoroughly pleasing and liberal society, citing his approval of The Società Generale, 'a kind of club, magnificently maintained, and charging only a modest fee from the nobility, both men and women, who contributed to it.' The Frenchman wrote a tactful account of the 'conversations' that is, the social gatherings, parties and discussions these club members enjoyed nightly, either before or after a* passeggiata *along the promenade, where the lighting of torches was 'prohibited' to ensure that no one could detect who was married and who single. The atmosphere was so relaxed and easy, so agreeable to Di Denone, that 'I began to consider the famous Sicilian jealousy of which people still speak today, was a thing of the past, of two hundred years ago'.*

Three decades later it was a radically different story: a post-Revolution French diplomat posted to Palermo was so terrified by its lawlessness and violence, he refused to step beyond the city for a year, fearful that the rest of Sicily was even worse. When eventually he decided to risk a trip to Messina, Syracuse and Catania and was rendered euphoric by the beauty and tranquillity of these East Coast cities, their prosperity, the courtesy and generosity of their citizens he then had to inquire into why Palermo was so different, so poor, so lawless and scary. His research showed that the city had been ruined by an irresponsible and self-centred regime whose economic mismanagement had reduced the bulk of the population to starvation and desperation.

Why did I elect to stay in Casa Diocesana, Baida, for several weeks? Seeking some kind of security? The monastery was certainly a safe place, neither easy to exit or enter, especially for guests. I became rather fond of the nuns I met there. Suor Myriam was the classic 'sergeant-major' seizing on breaches of discipline and calling one to account, inclined to naysaying but with a smile and offer of a coffee. It was a pleasant environment, save that the nuns' belief in what seemed to be an overcrowded supernatural parallel universe, took my breath away. How could they believe the nonsense they spouted? At the same time, their understanding of control and power over others demonstrated a very firm footing in the real world.

On the whole I found Palermo generally oppressive compared to other Sicilian cities. Perhaps the fact that it is the headquarters of the Church, the mafia and the Regional Parliament, the three together a closed fist of duplicity, ruthlessness and oppression, is just too much. It's an edgy place. Yet it is also the home of the sunniest natured dentist I've ever met, whom I simply could not persuade to accept payment for the five visits I made to him, after arriving in the city with an abscessed tooth. 'Via, via, signora, I've done nothing,' he said, when I asked for the bill. And he knew I was leaving the city. Where else in the world would one find such another dentist? I beam on Palermo every time I clean my teeth.

I decided to keep a journal when I was there. To recognise its special character.

19

Sunday, 10 September 2006

Woke this morning at three thirty to the clinking and clanking of the train carriages trundling onto the ferry at Villa San Giovanni, with the shunters hurling commands to and fro and their feet pounding along the tracks. They seemed to have dismantled the entire train in ten minutes and loaded each set of carriages in a pattern so as to allow rapid reassembly of the segments at the other end when we reached Messina, just across the Strait.

Lying in my bunk with the blinds drawn, listening to the bustle, I was surprised to find the whole expedition so stable that only the slow drift of fumes into my compartment and the drone of the ferry engines signalled we were moving at all. The crossing took half an hour with just a momentary hint of a rocking motion, making me wonder whether the carriages were bolted to the decks or could slide about if a sudden swell should arise. Probably no swell of any magnitude would be unforeseen, unless a sudden earthquake under the sea.

We got into Palermo about ten a.m., a thirteen-hour trip from Rome. I was relieved to find a surfeit of taxis queued at the station. I knew the Casa Diocesana where I was heading to be on the outskirts of Palermo, and that the fare would probably be higher than normal. Happily, the driver drove very fast, no turns or wriggles on the way, the streets being mostly empty early on a Sunday morning. The monastery was some distance, in fact, and at a high altitude.

When we drew up at its great open gates I reached for my wallet and asked the driver brightly, 'How much?' Obviously anticipating a wail, he pointed wordlessly to the meter before hurriedly exiting the car and making for the boot to get my two heavy suitcases.

'My God,' I said, catching up with him. 'That's more than I paid from Fiumicino to Rome.' But with everything I had to carry, the cost was immaterial. I rounded up the figure and gave him a tip.

The monastery, originally built as the summer palace of the first Archbishop of Palermo, a Spaniard, predictably enjoys a peak position, atop a hill set well back from the bay in the crescent shaped mountain range that throws a protective arm around Palermo, offering refuge of a temporary sort from raiders and invading forces wading ashore.

An immense terrace large enough to hold a great ball gives a 270-degree view of city and sea. The Palace is on a ridge with a wood below and around it where shady little paths lead from the terrace into the trees, the kind suited for quiet complicit conversations on ecclesiastic politics – as fierce and furious as any in the secular world. Statues in the classical style, only one or two, disported to their best advantage, seem somehow frivolous, lightening the atmosphere.

Everybody outside on this terrace was totally involved with whatever they were doing. Nobody even cast a glance in my direction. I pushed open the front doors, the ease of access a rare event as it transpired, their being a component of a very modern security system and saw facing me a U-shaped reception area similar to that of a standard hotel.

The building seemed to have been substantially restructured within, changes originating probably with the Benedictines who occupied it for a time, but more radically in the era of Cardinal Pappalardo, the retired Archbishop of Palermo who has apparently spent twenty-six years overseeing the renovation and – as seems evident – its conversion into an income-generating conference centre and resource for clerics, laity and some tourists.

Its formerly palatial character is now evident only in the huge gates, wide enough to allow entry to horse-drawn carriages, in the baroque facades of the main building, in the marble terrace and possibly a meeting room that might once have been a grand reception room whose floor is totally covered with glorious majolica tiles in the traditional style.

Not a soul was in sight when I entered and dumped my things in front of the counter. I waited a few minutes, crossing back to the front doors to look through the glass panes at a little lock-up of some description on the terrace and then turning back to the desk, humphing to myself, caught sight of a bell resting on top. Within a few minutes of my pressing it, a nun appeared. I told her I was booked in. She checked the register and with barely a word, let alone a smile, handed me a key carrying a tag stamped 162 and went off. We would settle payment later.

Blinking a little at the speed of events, I took note that I was standing at the foot of a wide staircase leading up to a small landing before it turned left and continued to rise, vanishing into the upper reaches. Could there be a lift? As quick as thought it appeared in my peripheral vision, a small lift on the other side of the office, its doors invitingly open. Feeling like Alice in Wonderland looking for signs, I entered it. Three people of normal stature could have squeezed inside. Or two with a monster suitcase. The buttons indicated there might be only three floors in this part of the building. I'd try the top one.

When I got out and walked along the corridor peering at the room numbers, there was no number anywhere near a hundred let alone 162. In a three-storey building the tag could hardly refer to room number two on the sixteenth floor. I must be looking for room sixteen on the second floor. But on the second floor the highest number was fifteen. Oh dear. How can a simple thing be so difficult? Then I noticed a door immediately beside the lift and immediately preceding entry to the corridor. Perhaps kept for a supervisor or such. Thankfully it bore the elusive number sixteen.

The keys opened the door. Wiping my brow with relief, I dropped my things inside, shed my coat and went down by the stairs onto the terrace, to breathe in the air. What a view. The ridge sloped down in a great sweep to the foreshores, Palermo covering the entire expanse and reminding me that it was once a great capital of Europe. The bay was too far away to see any details on the waterfront, just a shimmering crescent in the sun.

Back inside, after some deep breathing to settle myself, I wandered down some corridors on the lookout for cooking and eventually came upon the kitchen where several staff were obviously very busy. One of the women looked up and saw me in the doorway.

'Just go into the dining room,' she instructed me. 'You will be shown your table.'

By mistake I poked my head into a small utilitarian room, plainly furnished with a table and chairs, the walls bare except for a single crucifix. This is the Archbishop's private dining room.

The public dining room can easily seat 200 people. It's a vast, well-lit space one of the two longest walls being entirely of glass, with French doors set into it in several places, all soundly locked, and the roof supported by wide columns.

Tuesday, September 12 2006

Well, the first two days have gone off quietly. Numerous Sunday visitors had been fed and despatched. By bedtime I realised that the taxi driver was the last person with whom I had exchanged more than four words since the forenoon. But the next morning I spent five minutes with Suor Myriam who was pretty relaxed about the financial side of things. No rush to pay. Maybe before you leave. *Per noi, uguale.* It's all the same to us.

I'm being shifted around the dining room when a religious visits so that I don't pollute their gaze, I think. The monk's ideal. To be solitary. To retreat from the world and its distractions. To be alone to meditate and pray for all the souls that need saving whether they want it or not. It goes on the great Domesday report card.

Having grown up in a family of seven children and being of a gregarious nature that allowed me to fit well into the Italian community at home, it's a shock to be alone in the monastery with Italians who speak very little and are fairly resistant to communicating. To be fair, this is in the monkish tradition of providing hospitality to travellers, but not associating with them.

Yesterday I had to go into Palermo to perform a few essential commissions. With the exception of my trip to Etna, I didn't travel on a single bus in Catania or Syracuse but I can see that in Palermo I'll be spending half my life in buses. To get into town I have to take two, one from Piazza Baida to Campo Reale, and another into Palermo Station, each trip half an hour. The connection was immediate going in, but coming back I missed the one from Campo Reale and had to wait an hour for the next.

Tomorrow I'm going up to Monreale, to see the famous mosaics in the cathedral and the wonderful cloisters of the Benedictine abbey, the two structures being part of a complex that includes two palaces, the Archbishop's Palace and the Royal Palace – the Church as usual careful to ensure that its glory overshadows the secular presence.

My travel brochure says that Monreale Cathedral was the dream vision of the third Norman king, William II, who was only twenty when he initiated the project as an ardent expression of his new faith. It's commonly seen as an architectural mishmash because artisans from every faith and many different parts of the world were welcomed by the Normans, and contributed their diverse genius to William's great project. But the bulk of the population at the time in Palermo were Muslims and Byzantine Greeks and their styles predominate.

Monreale is only a fifteen-minute drive from Baida in a car but it's a two-hour trip by bus. To understand the socio-political character of any country or region, I've decided, it's enough to travel on the public transport system. Where it serves users badly, requiring the poor to take an entire day off work to deal with bureaucracies private or public, it goes without saying that the regime is corrupt and the general population not educationally equipped to reflect on deficits in governance.

Rita rang me last night to tell me she was off to Favignana for a week and when she returns, Saro and her other friends will be arranging a dinner for me in Catania. She wanted to know when I was coming for a visit.

'I miss you. I miss our intellectual battles.'

'Me too,' I had assured her. 'Maybe at the end of next week.'

In response to her queries I said the food at the Casa was excellent, very simple but good, and varied. Fruit on the table at every meal including breakfast. Excellent coffee at breakfast. Pasta twice a day plus meat cooked in different ways and various vegetables or salads. Last night, parboiled roasted chips, hand cut from big potatoes, were served with steak and chargrilled eggplant. In fact, I'm going to tell the kitchen that I'll have only two meals a day.

My room is small, as you might expect in a house essentially for priests and nuns, with a narrow bed, a very old plain desk, scratched all over as if it might have come from an education department, a man's wardrobe, two kitchen chairs, a bedside table with reading lamp, central heating for winter (roll on, November) and a standard fan to help me through the hot, humid nights. Leading off the bedroom and very little smaller is a good sized bathroom.

However, in Palermo yesterday I had to buy a multiple electric plug device with a universal plug. Otherwise I won't able to use the fan and my computer together. I trailed up and down the usual long streets till I found a kind of emporium where the owner, a man probably close to seventy, told me he knew what I wanted, but he didn't have it in stock and to come back at four thirty p.m. He would have it then. I returned at the appointed time and he handed it to me, with a slight nod. It cost only a few euros. We were perfect strangers and had had no option but to trust one another. We had both kept our word. A flush of warmth between us brought out smiles. One of those moments when you think being a human isn't such a nightmare.

This morning I spent an hour trying to find a new mini mouse for my laptop. The one Jack gave me seems to be kaput. I was also checking out the Internet points that had telephone booths, visiting the tourist information kiosks and collecting maps, brochures and digests. It took ages trying to find the Sicilian Regional Art Gallery where lives Antonio da Messina's exquisite *Annunziata*, the divine lady in blue, surely the loveliest Madonna ever painted.

I can't overlook an opportunity to see her for a second time. Such an intelligent, thoughtful, composed expression on her face and even in the posture of her hands, as if she has instantly grasped the nature of the responsibility devolving on her and is quietly figuring out the new arrangements she will have to make. It's a mystery to me how I've managed to remain completely ignorant of da Messina until this year when by chance I saw his blue Madonna on a website advertising the first ever exhibition of his work in Rome. Perhaps that's the reason. The first ever exhibition.

He is called da Messina because he worked in that city, (also in Holland) but he was born in Cefalu, seven minutes on the express train from Palermo. I made the effort to go to the Rome exhibition from Catania, basically only to see the *Annunziata*, but then, fickle me, was mesmerized by another superb portrait da Messina had named *A Sicilian Sailor*, powerfully interactive like the Madonna, and I couldn't help thinking, just maybe a little more impressive. But in the Madonna stakes, the blue lady for me has no peers.

The Sicilian Regional Art Gallery is in a long sleazy street. It was shut by the time I found it. On starting to wend my way back to Via Vittorio Emanuele I suddenly became aware that the only other persons in the street were a boy wheeling aimlessly up and down and round about on his bicycle and a little cluster of young men squatting on the threshold of what a hurried glance over their heads showed me was an empty room. The cyclist was hovering very close. Suspiciously close. Casually, I hoped, I shifted my handbag away from kerb side to wall side, clutching it tightly under my oxter. I stepped up my pace almost but not quite running, not daring to look behind me but listening acutely. Then I made myself furious and thought if this youth lays a finger on me I'll punch him in the face and push his bike over. By the time I'd reached the cross street, I was sweating and could hardly breathe.

My imagination is ruinous. When I cautioned Petra about travelling late at night in New York subways, she said, 'Don't be absurd. Nobody touches you unless you look a victim – and they can tell.' How did she become so bold?

At a more mundane level, I've had to deal with the laundry problem. Despite the fact that the monastery does its own massive laundering on the premises, the only facility for me, I've been crisply assured, requires a few stops on the bus. No ironing either, the housekeeper says.

But I found a blanket folded in the bottom of the wardrobe. The desk is over a metre long. So at Camporeale this afternoon I bought an iron, two big cakes of washing soap and two of hand soap and then searched for a household linen shop to buy a tablecloth.

For six or twelve at table? the assistant asked me.

Six would be fine, I told her.

The blanket is protecting the desk. The tablecloth is acting as an ironing cover over the blanket and my computer is resting on top. That settled, I washed two tops and two cotton blouses in the bidet and three hours later they are all dry. Even without a breath of wind. What's this drying out doing to me?

On Sunday, so I learned today, there were actually seventy visitors from Caltanisetta, in the centre of Sicily. The Bishop of Caltanisetta had brought his party to the monastery for a long weekend. Not simply to pray and receive religious instruction but also to be tourists. Seventy more were lodged with the brothers in the John the Baptist monastery down the street a bit.

Today I was alone except for a little priest also eating in solitary state on the other side of the room from me.

Never before having exchanged words with priests or nuns, or, come to think of it, even Protestant ministers, I felt a little uncertain of the proprieties. But with nobody else in sight I risked calling to him in a low voice, 'Will a cold wind come some time soon?'

Above the table, with his fine, bony face and narrow shoulders, he looks small and slight, but standing he carries a huge belly in front, like one of those big drums they beat on the sides in pipe bands, and when he walks, he leans right back the way some drummers do, to retain their balance.

He was silent for a bit, laying his cutlery down carefully, to deliberate and said, 'It's too early yet. A cold wind won't come till late October or November.' Then he gave me a happy smile. 'Sicily has a very good climate. It's generally warm. We *are* close to Africa, you know.'

But I remember Favignana in February and the tiny heater in Rita's summer house. I froze then and I long to freeze again.

Wednesday, September 13 2006

No little resident priest, as I thought of him, anywhere to be seen this morning. I felt mildly disappointed. Then I heard his greeting come from behind me, '*Buon giorno, signora*,' and I turned round to see him in the company of a very tall priest with a thatch of wiry white hair so ruffled and awry it looked as if he might have been chopping at it himself. He gave the impression of being tired still and crumpled all over, his face and his clothing slept in. But his friendly '*Buon giorno*' seemed more natural and assured than that of the other priest who is obviously less at ease with people, or maybe just with me.

'I heard a terrific alarm go off early this morning,' I said to both of them. 'Was someone trying to break in?'

'My car,' said the tall priest. 'Sorry.'

He must have been in a deep sleep, I thought, to have taken so long to respond to it. Or perhaps he had just let the alarm run out.

I now know the name of the body that runs this monastery. Not an order but something more and something less, the Istituto Religioso, Le Suore del Bell'Amore. The Sisters of Beautiful Love. Suora Nunziella, the founder of Beautiful Love, was born in Messina and educated at the university there. Her doctoral thesis seems to have been on the idea of love and was the basis of her drive to found the Institute.

'And why on earth do they need to add another order?' my brother Jack asked crankily when I made my telephone report to him. 'Don't they have enough?'

'C'mon,' I said, 'Every age needs its own idiom. You might as well say, we've got wonderful Renaissance art, why does anyone else need to have painted since.'

Jack grunted. 'Well, don't tell me beautiful love is something the Catholic Church has still to learn about after all these centuries.'

Ha! Little does he know. Love has yet to find a place in the Church's lexicon and it won't be any time soon. These sisters are bent on reformation, if not revolution.

Thursday, 14 September 2006

This morning I finally made it to Monreale, famously associated with the renowned bandit, Salvatore Giuliano who helped his father and other prisoners on remand escape from the prison there. Giuliano was one among many 'primitive rebels' as the British historian Eric Hobsbawm has christened bandits in Sicily and elsewhere. His youthful fantasy somewhat distinguished him: like Ho Chi Minh, he wrote to President Truman professing his admiration for the American dedication to liberty, the Sicilian, however, proposing that his land should be annexed to the United States. Ho Chi Minh was seeking only support for Vietnam's liberation from France, but neither he nor Salvatore struck a chord with Truman. On the contrary, they both became wanted men.

****

I was right about the other priest's being assured. At dinner last night, when the house assistant was carrying in his pasta, he got up and walked straight over to my table.

'I'll have it here, signorina,' he said to her and sat down, and, 'I hear you're a writer,' with hardly a pause, not looking directly at me but appraisingly over his plate. 'What are you writing about?'

'Sicily,' I said.

'Hmph. Will it be a picture book?'

I controlled my indignation. 'No, not at all.' He remained silent until I said, 'You're not Sicilian,' then unfolded himself and sat upright, without expending too much energy.

'No, I'm from Toscana. Firenze. San Miniato.'

He was a writer of sorts, himself, he eventually volunteered, after eating steadily and with concentration for a few minutes, during which time I kept quiet too. 'I write poetry.' He let me know his work had been published by well regarded publishing houses and within a few minutes an animated discussion had flared up between us on poets and poetry. He told me American troops had put Ezra Pound in gaol in Pisa in 1945 after the Allied invasion and then forgotten about him, letting him languish there until a twelve-year-old Florentine boy who had admired him and monitored his plight had contacted a newspaper. The editor had run an article protesting Pound's continued imprisonment and, 'Two days later, he was released.'

'They said Pound was a Fascist,' I recollected. 'And a traitorous broadcaster. The Italian Lord Haw Haw.' I explained the term to him.

The priest contented himself with saying that Pound believed women had no talent for poetry. Obviously I couldn't let that pass and declared that some of Australia's most powerful poetry had come from women. Likewise in the USA.

The only Australian writer the priest had ever heard of was a woman who had written a wonderful story about the friendship of a country priest and a *fanciulla*, a maiden. That stopped me dead. Who could the writer be? Had I read it, he asked. I shook my head, puzzled.

He was surprised I knew nothing of this book. It was famous. In America too. They made a film out of it.

'Can't you think of the title? What was it in Italian?''

He mentioned *uccelli*. Birds.

'What kind of birds?' I asked.

'Ones that scratched,' he said, drawing his nails across his arms and pinching the skin. 'Spine.' (Thorns). And I remembered.

'Oh, you're talking about *The Thorn Birds*. So – a story about a priest and a *fanciulla*, eh? That's what allured the world, was it?'

Months later a friend told me the priest and the young girl in the story had ended up having a child. The Tuscan had talked of the relationship as a 'lovely friendship'. A very liberal attitude. Perhaps the very liberal part of the friendship had been suppressed in a special edition for clerics.

Wanting to needle him, I said, 'But surely there have been hundreds of books on that theme over the ages, given the Church's mandate on sacerdotal celibacy. I thought priests were always supposed to be having problems with women fantasizing over them – though I believe some don't always consider it a problem.'

He raised his eyes and looked at me for a second, then returned his attention to his plate, and we both lapsed into silence.

When he had finished eating, he rose abruptly and said: 'I had to bring some of my things with me to show someone. Would you like to see one or two?' I assured him I would. 'Then I'll go and get them. But I want to have a cigarette outside first. Wait a little while, then come to the terrace. And be sure to wash your hands.'

On the way to the washroom I suddenly recollected that at some point the priest had said, apropos of what escaped me at the time, 'I had to go and find my father whom I hadn't seen for twenty-seven years, and I found him in Addis Ababa.' That was a topic I would have to pursue when an opportunity arose.

As soon as I saw the bundle of antique papers that were his poetry publications I wished I had had pockets to imprison my hands. But he held out a slim volume toward me, invitingly, and said, 'You see how beautiful this paper is. Feel it.' The paper was thicker than any other paper I had ever known, full of substance but not coarse, quite silken. Holding both his arms wide, he showed me how the verses fitted neatly into each page, saying, 'This is a long poem,' and with a grin, 'But you can see that.'

There were various imprints on the books. One publication he showed me had a brief biographical note inside the back cover, revealing his date of birth. He was born in 1929.

'You are learning my age,' he said, with a note of resignation and regret. He was in his seventy-seventh year. That surprised me. But I didn't think it appropriate to tell him that despite his crumpled appearance he looked much younger and was somehow compelling. Attractive even. Gracious. Then I realized from the publication dates that he was forty-three when most of these poems came out.

'You arrived at poetry quite late in life,' I said.

'To publication, yes,' he said. 'I had a long apprenticeship, but I was determined to be a writer from the time I was in high school.'

A pity he'd had to become a priest to get the opportunity, I thought.

Finally he handed me a very tiny book, measuring maybe five by seven centimetres. It had been published in San Miniato in 1988 and was entitled, *A dictionary of the first two years*.

'Take this,' he said. 'It's for you.' A quick glance at the cover and contents revealed that the book was a perfect miniature, containing all the elements of a standard paperback: imprint, a preface and introduction by the author himself, twenty-eight pages of text and a substantial appendix. Feeling somewhat embarrassed, I thanked him and rose, anxious to go.

'I have work to do.'

He nodded. 'Good night, then.'

And I made off, leaving him to continue puffing on his reed-like cigarette. I'm not at all comfortable with that Tuscan priest, but it's a pleasantly disturbing kind of discomfort.

Friday, 15 September 2006

Last night I sat on the edge of my bed and went carefully through the miniature dictionary page by page. According to a note, the cover illustration comes from a bookshop in Florence. It's a delightful etching by someone with a German name, of a toddler, a little girl, seated on the floor with an open book across her legs, holding one page down with her right hand and pointing at the opposite page with the index finger of her left hand. Since the vocabulary of children in their first two years is smaller than the sounds they can make, it amounts to only forty-two words, carefully laid out with their meanings, like a normal dictionary. The introduction says that the vocabulary is Tuscan, from both city and country, in an area forming the triangle of Florence, Pisa and Siena.

This morning when I arrived in the dining room the little priest was already bent over his caffè latte across the way and the Tuscan priest came in a bit later. We exchanged greetings and I complimented him on the miniature dictionary. He told me (after I asked) that the Church had been pretty supportive of his writing, even if the topics were not specifically religious, but when they were, nothing was too much trouble. He did not belong to any order, nor was he a parish priest.

'You don't have to belong to an order if you're a priest. You don't have to have a congregation. I used to teach philosophy in a well-known seminary.'

Then a sudden jab of pain in my mouth made me gasp. Fortunately the priest had his gaze on his plate and I had made very little sound, but the strain of keeping my chewing to one side of my mouth distracted me, and, worried that the toothache would return, I quickly excused myself to go off in search of Suor Myriam whom I asked this morning if she knew of a dentist I could see straight away.

'That's not going to be easy, I can tell you,' was her encouraging response. 'I will interest myself in it, but I can't promise anything.'

At the books section near the bar where a notice says the books are not to be taken away but to be paid for – they are for sale – I found a new nun obviously busy changing the stock, removing some books and replacing them with others. I'd browsed the racks a few times and knew the titles might change but the content would remain constant, being strongly oriented towards religious philosophy and testimonial narratives.

I asked if she had seen Suor Myriam.

She gave a little smile and answered in English. 'She should be coming down soon. Are you English?'

'Scottish,' I said. 'But I've lived in Australia all my adult life.'

The smile suddenly engulfed her face and her eyes shone with the delight that overwhelms you in a strange place where you unexpectedly meet someone who knows where you're from and where you've been.

Depositing her books on a nearby table, she said: 'I lived in Australia for twenty years.'

She had managed the Catholic Bookshop in Sydney's Castlereagh Street on the opposite side to David Jones, but further west. I told her that until a few months ago I had been Senior Writer for the NSW Law Society Journal and that walking to work in Phillip Street from Central Station I'd often looked in the window to see what new religious bestsellers were out but that Pascal's thoughts were usually in the foreground.

When I remarked that she must have been happy to return to Italy and be united with her family, she started sorting the books again, arranging them with jerky movements, pushing them too close together on the racks. Then she stopped, drew in her breath and said evenly, 'No. No, I wasn't happy to come back at all. I didn't want to come. I'd even lost my fluency in my own tongue and found it difficult to think in Italian.'

It didn't take much to read between the lines. I felt sorry for her. She had succumbed to Australian culture that combines poor cookery and tepid conversation with the seductions of quiet and stable democracy.

'What,' Jack hooted later when I was recounting my meeting with the nun. 'You're talking about this NSW government?'

Then I asked the nun if she might know where I could find a good dentist. She disappeared for a few minutes, returning with a phone book and ran a finger down the Os, seeking her dentist's address and phone number.

'His name's Orsino. In Via Rocciello. He's very good. And clean. Clean. But you should ring first. Tell him I recommended you go to him. The nun, say.'

She was sorry he was in a spot awkward to get to. (Isn't everybody, here?) She suggested I make my way to the station (take the two buses) and go by taxi from there. When I was about to move off, she suddenly touched my arm briefly and said, 'I'm at the Paulines right opposite the Cathedral. Why don't you call in and see me some time? Sister Rita's my name.'

I've promised her I will. I like her. But I can't imagine being friends with a nun.

Saturday, 16 September 2006

Scores of people were milling about at the bus terminal this morning when I arrived at Camporeale and immediately I alighted, I heard the dreaded word *sciopero*, strike, on everyone's lips. What a nuisance. And I had to get to that dentist. Heavens, can that be me hoping for a miracle? I don't want to go home with any bad habits.

I crossed the street and at the AMAT compound where the bus drivers were drinking deep and enviably from their iced water tank, I asked the room, 'Is there any chance a bus will be going to the Station?' One driver glanced around at the others to see if anyone else might respond and since they were all apparently busy doing other things, he looked directly at me and shrugged. As he made to turn away, I called to him.

'Can you be more specific? I can't always interpret a gesture.'

'Somebody may be rostered, signora,' he said. 'But we'd have no idea who or when.'

'You mean someone who has decided not to go on strike?'

He wasn't entirely sure about that. Perhaps they had been allocated to work a few hours.

When Italians are most exasperating the religious spirit is generally in evidence. A strike's a strike. Rationally meant to cause inconvenience. No use having prayers in the piazza, as the billboards were advertising. Imagine it. Prayers in Martin Place to resolve the capital-labour conflict. Eroding a strike's force by sentimental, ill-thought-out Christian charity just makes the whole thing a waste of time. That's the point, though. Solidarity is a no no in a vertically constructed society like Sicily's. Different in Poland, though. But it was a different kind of theocracy there. Not run by the Church. If one theocratic power wants to replace another, solidarity has to be forged among the commons who are being wooed.

It was blazing hot in the sun. I became uncomfortably aware that even at this early hour sweat was already trickling down the back of my neck and between my shoulder blades. My eye fell gratefully on an empty space on a marble bench under a shady tree in the little park beside the AMAT office. An elderly man was sprawled along the middle of the bench, but I could perch on the end. Then I would think what to do. I walked towards the bench and sat down, relieved to be out of the sun. Funny that I hadn't noticed this park before, or the shady trees. I'd make more use of it in future. The man beside me was dozing. I took a look at him and startled, looked again.

The tall priest.

'*Buon giorno*, but what are you doing here?' I cried, jumping to my feet.

He opened his eyes and said calmly, 'If you're going to the Station you will have to walk.'

I made a little moue of rebuttal. 'Not in this heat, I won't.'

A few metres away, a strapping young woman caught my attention. Taller than I, robust, in jeans and a T-shirt, with long dark curls cascading down her back, she was announcing to the piazza that she intended to walk to the Station, where she had to catch a pullman at eleven a.m.

'See you later,' I said to the priest, abandoning him to hurry after the girl who was already stepping out. 'May I come along with you?' I asked her, lengthening my stride. 'I need to reach the Station but I don't know how to get there.'

'Okay,' she said. 'I don't know either, but we'll find the way.'

There was nothing indecisive about the streets she chose to follow, no stopping to take her bearings by the sun or to consult her compass, just intuition I decided, noting that we had arrived at the Station ten minutes earlier than it took to go by bus.

'Many stops,' she commented laconically after I remarked on this marvel. I couldn't imagine her unemployed, and she wasn't, she explained on the walk.

'I arrange myself. I am a masseuse. I do house calls.'

Her husband worked in Palermo and dropped her off in town in the morning. She had built up a regular house *clienti* who lived near one another so that she didn't have to walk too far. But today she had to be home early. The plumber was coming and she couldn't miss the pullman. She smiled when I invited her to join me in a coffee at the Station kiosk.

'No. I can see the pullman over there,' pointing, 'and I don't want to risk missing it, now that I'm here. Goodbye, lovely to have met you.'

The visit to the dentist consumed only three hours, counting the time taken to get a non-strikebound bus back from his place to the Station. Dottore Orsino had scratched his head when I mentioned the nun, trying to recollect her.

'Sister Rita,' I said. 'She's a Pauline.'

He nodded but without comprehension, I could see.

'She said you're clean.'

That brought a hearty laugh. He gave me a prescription for antibiotics I should take for a week and come back to see him next Friday. He couldn't touch my tooth till I got rid of the huge abscess he had discovered, shocked, in the first ten seconds. Hadn't I realized I had a giant abscess? Was there no pain?

Only this morning, I had explained. And I had attributed it to having lost a part of my tooth. It wasn't my tooth I'd lost but on old repair, he informed me. There could be no more repairs. When I returned on Friday he would start root canal therapy.

'Take this,' he said, handing me a carton as he ushered me out the door. It's a mouthwash that will help reduce the inflammation.'

****

At dinner that night, the little priest was at his table. The poet priest was sitting with me. We were a happy trio.

'Did you go to Monreale the other day?' the little priest called across.

When I called back, 'Yes', he spread his arms wide.

'You saw the *Pantocratore*?' He meant the colossal Christ figure, head and shoulders only, that takes up an entire vault above and behind the altar in Monreale Cathedral. It's actually a larger copy of one in Cefalu done by the original Byzantine artist. I stood up to make myself more easily heard by the little priest, and said that I thought the figure the manliest Jesus I had ever seen, the only one I could imagine capable of leading a revolution or trouncing the Pharisees. I said I didn't favour the *mammone* (mother's boy) type of Jesus who is so common in Italian iconography. How could he whip the moneylenders in the temple?

Both priests looked taken aback. Jesus a mummy's boy? It's the sort of thing you wouldn't think twice about saying among your friends. Maybe it seemed irreverent to clerics.

However, the priests quickly recovered their composure and we went on to talk about the sumptuous Monreale Cathedral, founded by young King William II. Externally, Monreale's not to be compared with Palermo Cathedral, built much earlier by William II's brother, William I, but inside, it is unforgettable. I don't remember looking at the floors but the ceiling and walls are entirely covered with mosaics, reportedly the greatest mosaic expanse in any church outside Hagia Sofia in Istanbul.

'It's amazing to think of the entire Bible being illustrated in mosaic,' I remarked to my friendly cleric when we were eating.

'They couldn't read print in those days,' he said, 'but they could understand pictures and in the sixth century Pope Gregory the Great made a plea that scriptural scenes be depicted on the walls of churches for the benefit of those who were unlettered.'

I had read somewhere that the Synod of Arras in 1025, the Norman period, had also recommended pictures for the illiterate, 'to learn what books cannot teach them.'

Illiterate people would nonetheless have had to be taught orally about the symbols and the stories before the pictures made sense. As a Scot I know the Bible quite well, but I recognised very few of the events dramatized in the one hundred and thirty two pictures at Monreale until I checked out postcards at a newsagent's and found the captions. Then I remembered the stories. The pictures are only aides-memoire.

Thus ends my first week at the Casa.

Monday, 18 September 2006

Both priests have departed. This morning at breakfast, I asked the Tuscan how I should address Cardinal Pappalardo when I'm interviewing him.

'*Eccellenza*,' he said.

'Not Cardinal?'

'No.'

I couldn't hide a grimace.

'There's a problem?'

'Calling him *Eccellenza*. I've grown up in two egalitarian cultures, you know – Scotland and Australia. Not places to encourage deference to rank'.

He knew some English, so I recited slowly Burns's memorable contribution to egalitarianism, 'the rank is but the guinea's stamp, the man's the gowd for a' that.'

The principle was easy enough to communicate but translating Burns's Ayrshire dialect took more effort and time.

While the priest was cogitating, something he required little encouragement to do, my thoughts started roaming over Burns's poem *The Liberty Tree* and suddenly I heard myself saying, 'Security is an obsession with Italians, don't you think? Horrible, really. To feel unfree.'

Oh, that brought the genie right out of the bottle. If there's anything the Church deplores more than equality, it's liberty. Well, one's a prerequisite for the other. He thumped his fist on the table, rattling the cutlery. 'You're not a *Catholic*, are you!' Before I could answer, he hissed fiercely, sounding out each word between closed teeth. 'You're not even a Protestant. You're one of those' – sweeping his arm right across the table, 'one of those' – I shrank away from him, tilting my chair onto its back legs, and held my breath – 'Yes?' – *atei*, atheists, he finished heavily, regretful, I think, for having momentarily lost control. Flattening himself out on the table, his chin practically resting on the cloth, he looked up at me and asked sadly, 'You're not reverent?'

I shook my head.

He stood up, easefully, all put together again and announced he was moving closer to the Centre, Baida was too far out of town. Suor Myriam had found him a monastery that was central. Dropping his contact card on the table, he said, 'You can find me there. We have a guest post at San Miniato.'

After he'd gone I sat nursing my abscessed tooth, poking it all about with my tongue to see if the swelling was going down. No luck. A nervous cough disturbed my reverie. The little priest was standing a few feet away, poised as usual to flee, but smiling warmly.

'I thought I'd tell you this is my last day here. I'm leaving now.'

He lived in another house quite close by and had come to the Casa Diocesana for spiritual refreshment.

'Thank you for letting me know,' I said, restraining an urge to pat him on the shoulder. 'It was lovely to meet you.'

Tonight I was the only person in the dining room. Eating alone and thinking. The Tuscan priest had eventually told me about the search for his father, who had climbed into his truck when his son was three, and gone off, never to return. I wondered if the priest had become friends with the *mulatta* sister, he encountered after tracking his father down in Ethiopia. It's a disgusting word, *mulatta*, but an expression of the time. The priest's tale was almost comic. Craving to know his father and assisted by the Church, he had travelled to Ethiopia in civvies, and been flatteringly well regarded by everyone on the ship, including a group of nuns returning to the Italian colony, but when he let slip that he was a priest, the entire shipboard company, nuns and all, had scorned him.

Suor Myriam looked in to say that His Excellency the Cardinal had returned from his several days' sojourn in Pisa and would be able to talk to me tomorrow night at six o'clock.

Tuesday, 19 September 2006

I'd made a few enquiries about Pappalardo since my arrival at the monastery. He was from Catania, not Palermo. While archbishop from 1970 to 1996, he was dubbed the 'anti-mafia' bishop, for having persuaded Sicilian bishops to state publicly in 1994 that 'The mafia is part of the reign of sin, and those who belong to it are agents of the Evil One. Whoever is part of the mafia is outside ecclesial communion.'

Nonetheless the Sicilian bishops spoke out only when a Palermo priest, Giuseppe (Pino) Puglisi was murdered by the mafia, a year after the judges, Falcone and Borsellino were car-bombed.

The opening scenes of *Into the Light,* the movie based on Puglisi's struggle to collapse the mafia's nursery recruitment program, show a group of little boys about seven or eight years old, hurling kittens with all their strength against a wall and laughing at the animals' terror and pain. Behind them stand several bulky, older males watching po-faced and pitiless, deliberately setting out to crush every feeling of human compassion in these very young children.

Lady Macbeth's attempts to purge her own self of conscience came to mind:

> *... make thick my blood;*
> *Stop up the access and passage to remorse,*
> *That no compunctious visitings of nature*
> *Shake my fell purpose ...*

Tonight, trotting behind an assistant down the long corridor leading to the Cardinal's apartment, I was surprised to see him poking his head well out the door, waiting and smiling a welcome.

'Come, come and sit down with me,' he invited warmly, leading the way, but slowly, steps tentative, the assistant hovering, and the Cardinal taking his seat on a sofa before directing me to the armchair beside it. The assistant slipped away. We were in a bright and cheerful room, homely, not over furnished. Pleasant and relaxing. Not the place to think of Cardinals Richelieu or Spellman.

'You know I'm rather deaf,' he said to me, in a cultivated English accent that took me by surprise.

'Yes, Excellency.' I was shouting as loud as I dared, nervous that I might be overdoing it or not be speaking loudly enough.

Dissenters don't generally advance to the top of hierarchies and the eighty-eight-year-old, thoroughly Vaticanised Pappalardo was no exception. I asked him if he'd like to talk to me about the Church's problems in Sicily in the post-War period.

Then I sank deep into my armchair, and waited, resigned to the inevitable, for the reigning orthodoxy. Perhaps it's impossible to be a cleric and avoid using nothing but stock phrases when commenting on the Church, but having read the Church's mission statement, I would imagine that discussing how it actually achieves salvation for its subjects, the methods it uses, how it assesses their efficacy, whether or not the methods have altered, and what kind of state best creates conditions that allow the Church to perform its mission more effectively, could be quite interesting. Would it be possible to recognise 'saved' persons by their behaviour? How would the Church know that its methods of 'saving souls' work?

Instead I listened while phrases like 'justice and order', 'peace not war,' 'collaboration not competition', 'faith not virtues', 'reciprocity is the basis of Christian civilisation,' floated in the air like soap bubbles. It was startling to hear him say that the Church had been in Sicily for 2000 years. This is not true. Sicily was part of the Byzantine Empire and the Greek Orthodox Church until the Normans conquered the region in the 1060s and invited the Church of Rome to move in, making it overnight a huge landowner with immense riches in prospect.

Likewise I blinked to hear that 'two thousand years of Christianity have created a mentality that thinks you should be honest, free, just, kind and loving.' The very opposite of what Pirandello has written. Here, in the land of Provenzano, Borsellino and Falcone, where reciprocity and clientelism are synonyms, where Church and State have stood idly by and seen their Sicilian subjects suffer privations of a brutal and hateful kind, matched only by the degree of force used to suppress revolt among them, such an assertion reeks of self-delusion.

Moving into the real world, I asked him what he thought of Giorgio La Pira and Luigi Sturzo, the two Sicilian religious/politicos now awaiting canonisation. Of La Pira, he said, smiling, 'Some people thought he was mad, you know. In the early days. Ingenuous, perhaps, thinking he could bring peace to the world.'

I said he hadn't struck me as in the slightest mad, or especially ingenuous in his goals. I admired the way La Pira set about housing thousands of homeless people in Florence within months, first asking owners of real estate to rent to the Council empty apartments for those who had been evicted until permanent solutions could be found and when that brought no response, ordering the requisition of these apartments, drawing on a law of 1865 that allows mayors to do this in an emergency situation or one that threatens public order.

La Pira was assailed by denunciations and legal suits and responded to them by declaring that 'a mayor who from fear of the rich and powerful abandons the poor, the homeless, retrenched, unemployed and so on, is like a shepherd who for fear of the wolf abandons his flock.'

I was pretty sure the Cardinal would not yet have read a new book released only days ago in Florence revealing that La Pira had refused to let Pignone, a local company proceed with closing down and retrenching over 500 staff, and that he helped it to switch to a radical new technology which has made it today a global giant in its field, employing over 4000 people and with offices worldwide. Many Florentines, even Communists, remember La Pira with gratitude.

'Really?' he said. 'Well I didn't ever know the details of what he was doing in Florence, whether he actually paid much attention to routine administration.'

In that same book the author had in fact reported La Pira's lament to an assembly of jurists that he was being overwhelmed by administrative matters: *'In Florence, the magistrate Bernardino every day writes me letters from morning till night: There are 500 evicted people, that is people who till now must go away and there is no room available in Florence even for an hour. We are trying to construct 3000 apartments but we need time and money. The employment office records that there are 9000 unemployed. These people come to me. I have had to put a 'don't disturb' notice on my door, otherwise I can't get any work done. I must go to bed at night, but how?'*

Though Communists knew him as 'the priest' everyone else thought La Pira a communist, not surprisingly, when he said that the only political issue is poverty. Mind you, he did grow up in a very poor anti-clerical family, and was drawn to the Church by a Dominican while a student at the University of Messina.

I found myself pushing on, doing my little bit for La Pira's canonisation. 'I think his idea that cities are privileged entities, with historic rights that should be recognised, and that they ought to become individually and collectively activist in international affairs, is brilliant. Organising conferences of Mediterranean mayors was a sound practical beginning. I don't know why his successor hasn't pursued the process.'

The Cardinal reflected on this for a few moments, suddenly recalling: 'He even went to Moscow, you know. There was a war on at the time. Yet he went to talk to the Russians about peace.'

Surely a sensible thing to do. 'Could there be a better time, Excellency? Isn't war, however it turns out, supposed to be intended as a short term diplomatic stratagem?'

I debated asking him what he thought about La Pira's writing the Pope, advising him, pressing him urgently, in fact, to open more closed orders in Morocco, some male and some female, but mainly female, so that there could be a bigger concentration of prayer to convert the Moroccans to Christianity. It was the silliest thing La Pira had come up with so far as I was concerned, and did tend to confirm his ingenuousness. So I kept quiet.

The Cardinal was recommending that I read some books on Don Luigi Sturzo, and remembering that he had two books on his shelves, fetched them and lent them to me.

Now I'm really loaded down with Catholic vision. Sturzo and La Pira. La Pira was a jolly sort of fellow and died at seventy-three. Sturzo, a priest, activist and philosopher lived well into his eighties. The son of a baron, brother of a bishop, with a sister a nun, on the cover of one book he looks lugubrious. But I suppose you'd look like that if both the Pope and Mussolini had told you to get out of Italy, with Mussolini indicating that you would be murdered if you delayed and the Pope making plain you were a thorn in the flesh.

Sunday 23 September 2006

Behind the old city's superabundance of ancient churches, fortresses, palaces and the thirteen monumental gates, those grand triumphal arches raised by invaders to celebrate their forced entry into Palermo, hundreds and hundreds of tall, modern and often very colourful apartment blocks stretch right back to the mountains, housing close to a million people – plus their cars.

The streets, though broad and straight, a mile long in the city centre, struggle to cope with the traffic load on a normal day. When it rains – what can I say? A nightmare ensues. I took four hours to reach the monastery tonight, just in time to meet the curfew.

'It's because of the rain, signora,' the bus driver responded calmly when I observed that we hadn't moved a metre in the last half-hour.

Initially I was quite happy to see torrential rain in Sicily, till I observed that Palermo's drains can't handle the volume of water and the rain just flows straight across the streets, making them difficult to negotiate on foot. The bus driver said that sometimes the force of the water running under the street is such that it sends manhole covers suddenly shooting up into the air. The Palermitani, to avoid being saturated, take their cars out of storage and drive them into the torrents. Gridlock keeps them there.

But leaving Central Station at six ten p.m., warm and dry inside the bus, I was unfazed by the rain. On reaching Camporeale terminus an hour later, that is half an hour behind schedule, and waiting another hour in the bus shelter, I was starting to feel exasperated. Even being seated inside the connecting bus brought no relief. After ten metres we crept to a stop. Hours later, it seemed, we crawled forward again, a metre at a time.

Most of the passengers were destined for an area normally five minutes from the bus station. Only a few were heading right out to Baida. A large group eventually alighted at the major stop, leaving a young girl, an old man and me in the bus.

The rain was now falling in heavy torrents, bouncing off the pavements. We remained stock still for the next half an hour while buses on our left scooted along the freeway on their way to the airport. The girl grew tired of making calls on her cellphone, and sat chewing her fingernails. The old man, slim, well dressed in suit and tie and carrying a large umbrella stood patiently the whole time clasping a rail with his free hand. The bus driver lay across his steering wheel, head resting on his arms, serene, relaxed and listening to pop music on the radio. When it comes to patience, Sicilians sweat it out.

At last, the old man decided the situation was hopeless and he would have to brave the swirling waters. After he vanished up a street on our right, we eased forward several more metres and then the bus driver called the girl. She moved up to his cabin and during their brief exchange I heard her say she was going to her yoga class. Whatever he advised her, she decided to walk. Unlike the old man, she was targeting some place to the left, across the freeway and the traffic beyond. I watched her, holding my breath, and wanting to clutch my head, while she splashed through the speeding traffic on the freeway, reaching the stalled cars on the local streets and beginning to wind her way tentatively between cars nudging forward in no order whatsoever, with every car prodding the one next to it on the left, on the right, or ahead, and itself being butted from behind, people on motorbikes appearing suddenly at both elbows, the rain teeming, lights blinding, streets shining, and this young girl of about fourteen teetering over water on her high heeled sandals, both arms outstretched for balance

'But this is normal for wet weather,' the bus driver, still a model of patience, informed me when I paced the empty bus, watching the solid choke-up ahead of us and despairing of reaching the monastery before curfew.

'Basically it's the drains. If the streets didn't flood, everybody wouldn't want to take their cars.'

In fact, while there are no gratings in the gutters to receive water, and no obvious camber to direct it there, most of the pavements have close to their buildings a continuous succession of large gratings, less than a metre apart in some pavements, and water can escape so quickly down into the drains it's no surprise there's an overflow.

The driver went on to tell me he had another 100 kilometres to go, after he dropped me off at Baida. He lived in a tiny village of 2,800 people, 'The place where Cinema Paradiso was filmed,' he revealed proudly, adding with a sidelong glance, 'not so far from Corleone.'

'Aaagh,' I said, shrinking back in feigned terror, and he laughed, smiling in his cabin in the dark, his eyes still purposefully on the road ahead.

We were silent for a few minutes while I was searching hopefully for any signs that the traffic was unknotting itself. But how could it? 'Why are cars allowed to squeeze in from streets on the right?' I complained. 'It's ridiculous. Haven't you got traffic policemen? If these people on the right were held back for fifteen minutes the main stream could move quite fast, actually, and then these others would have a chance to move too. I mean, do you bus drivers never sit down and try to work this out?'

'It works out by itself, signora,' he said. 'You wait and see.'

He pretended to be concentrating on the road, but was continually letting cars on the right through in front of us. They can be infuriatingly courteous at times, the Sicilians.

Then he said, his mind still on Corleone, perhaps, 'The mafia today are different from what they used to be. They used to take from the rich to give to the poor.'

I told him that was nonsense. 'It's one of your million myths. The mafia have always been thugs, bent on living like the nobles, on acquiring power and wealth. They have never been interested in helping the poor, only in subduing and exploiting the weak. Their so-called protection – against the disorder they themselves create – is offered to the nobles, not to the poor.'

'What about Salvatore Giuliano?' he asked triumphantly.

'What about him?' I said. 'He was just a poor silly man. Wanting to annex Sicily to the US. A fantasy, a dream. How can you have faith in such a ridiculous person?

For the rest of the trip the bus driver remained silent, not responding to any more questions. Had I offended him? I started musing: there's always plenty to muse about in Sicily. How did someone from a tiny village on the periphery manage to find a prized, not overtaxed, regular government job, with a pension at the end? How could he afford to send his two teenage children as weekly school boarders to Agrigento, another mafia domain, to ensure they attended senior high school and would get the education he had missed out on? He probably reasoned he was doing all right, as a *raccomandato* and wasn't going to say or even think anything that would put him or his family's goals at risk.

At Baida, on exiting, I bade him good night and he called something back, in an amiable tone. Pressing the buzzer at the gate of the Casa Diocesana, I turned to look after the bus vanishing into the gloom. It would be midnight before he reached home, and would maybe have to skip supper, but that was all right with him. He had a secure job and all the patience he needed in the world.

Monday, 25 September 2006

Young Palermitani often use the phrase, '*Ci si sente soffocare*' (one feels choked), to describe the dark pall that the mafia presence throws over their city. Perhaps, however, the feeling of suffocation stems not merely from the frustrations of living with the want of employment, income and even personal safety attributable to mafia malefactions, but also from a sense of being physically penned in.

One stands in the middle of Via Roma, an arterial street, looking south to the station and the eye is immediately drawn to the slope of a bare mountain rising starkly behind the railway station and appearing to wall off the street. Turn to the north and even if far in the distance, high-rise modern apartment buildings straddle the other end. There are many streets in the city with vistas that reveal a mountain slope seeming to hem one in. More remarkably, some of the very narrow streets, from a certain perspective form the apex of a triangle, a very constricting configuration.

Palermo, like Pandemonium, has its seductions nonetheless. The city's wealth and long-standing status as a major European capital is reflected in its baroque treasures, the tall, elegant palazzi whose curlicues, almost feminine in their lightness and delicacy, and prow-like wrought iron terraces swelling over the streets below, ever varied and sometimes playful in design, are backgrounded in sage greens, rosy terracottas, rich chocolate, all with their quiet and harmonious contrasts and pleasing symmetry.

Tourists, on encountering the facades at the famous Quattro Canti, where Via Vittorio Emanuele intersects with Via Maqueda, almost break out in applause, so enchanted are they by the unexpected sight. A simple concept but totally novel to me: to slice, as it were, across the corners of the four buildings that meet at an intersection, creating four large concave panels, in this instance about four storeys high, each surface divided horizontally into five panels for a sculptor to revel in: top and bottom panels short like borders, the three middle ones each a storey high. At ground level, a fountain anchors each facade: On the panel above the fountain is a woman sculptured to personify spring, summer, autumn or winter, above her a king, two of the four monarchs in jovial mood, and above them, four saints staking hierarchical precedence for heaven. Right at the very top, poised on the edge of the roof, are ceramic coats of arms, three on each surface, and a bunch of eagles, several, crowding each other, not the usual solitary one.

Strange how many want the eagle for an emblem. Yet another human folly, as Erasmus saw it: 'Of all birds, the eagle alone has seemed to wise men the type of royalty – not beautiful, not musical, not fit for food, but carnivorous, greedy, hateful to all, the curse of all, and with its great powers of doing harm, surpassing them in their desire of doing it.' Wouldn't that take a man to the tower!

Palermo, despite its grandeur and vastly greater population than Catania, is a city that seems to observe a curfew. After eight at night, it's graveyard quiet. Even in Baida, there's no one about. Makes me think of the children's nursery rhyme:

Wee Willie Winkie rins through the toon,
Upstairs and doonstairs in his nicht goon,
Rapping at the window and crying through the lock,
Are all the bairns in their beds, it's past eight o'clock?

Except of course, that Wee Willie Winkie is the mafia, and the word 'bairns' describes not children but dependency.

In flight from boredom, crowds of young Palermitani jam into cars, and speed to Catania for a night or a weekend, attracted by the eastern city's freer atmosphere, its rich all-night life, and the morning after, by its beaches, where the revellers can bathe in the sea and stretch out on lava platforms on rugs, sleeping till late in the afternoon, when they rise and prowl about, making contacts and planning the coming night's festivities.

Setting out for Catania on the packed intercity coach departing from the bus interchange adjoining the station, I knew how these young people felt. Not that I was fleeing from boredom, but rather, seeking lightness of being.

At Rita's place on Saturday I found the apartment radically reconfigured. The transformation that has awaited their daughter Rossana's formal departure, after her wonderful July wedding to Marco at Ravello, is complete. Giordano, ever closer to finishing his doctorate, has moved to an apartment which he shares with friends, conducting his transfer in instalments, and still using storage facilities at his parents' house. His room, the noisiest from street traffic, has been converted into a study for Grzegorz. Some of the scores of Polish icons painted on glass or wood have been relocated from the entry hall to the living room, where they have greater exposure and are already a talking point for visitors. A new phase of life is in evidence. This is no longer the family home, but that of Rita and Grzegorz, one day to become the grandparents' home.

Wednesday, 27 September 2006

Today I had a facial. No easy matter in Baida with its scant half dozen or so shops. I got the contact details from the hairdresser who cut and coloured my hair last week. On the point of paying my bill and readying to leave, I had a sudden inspiration and enquired, 'Would there be a place in Baida where I could have a facial?' Without immediately answering, the hairdresser opened a drawer and withdrew a card that she handed me.

'This woman is just a few paces along.'

My eyebrows arched. Not as cleanly as they might have. That's why I needed a facial. I had walked past this little cluster of shops any number of times and never seen a beauty salon.

'Where? I haven't seen it.'

'Oh it's very near us,' she repeated. 'But you must ring her first.'

Back in my room I examined the business card. A little cryptic. 'Health and beauty treatments for women' plus a phone number. A recorded message told me to leave my own phone number. The next day a call came through on my cellphone. 'How can I help you?' The tone was cautious.

'I'm told you do facials,' I said.

'Yes.'

'When may I come?'

She suggested two days hence and we fixed on a time. 'But where? I must have overlooked your salon. You're near the hairdresser?'

She referred me to a small palazzo that I had noticed in passing but which seemed to be only apartments, instructing me to press the buzzer on a particular floor and she would let me in. This afternoon I arrived at the palazzo at four p.m. and discovered to my annoyance that I had forgotten the floor number and left the card on my bedside table. I'd have to press any buzzer and hope the occupant would overlook the intrusion. A woman responded to my first attempt. I asked if she knew the floor where I could find the beauty salon.

'There is no beauty salon here,' she said and hung up.

Fortunately the beautician, concerned that I might have a problem, called me on my cellphone and gave me the code for the lift. Within a few minutes she was leading me through a small foyer, past a bathroom and into a massive room, only half its space exhausted by large and very solid furniture all in a deep pink oak, a modern version of nineteenth-century stolidity. The head and footboard of the king-size bed were serpentine shaped, like the end of a chaise longue, an elaborate rose carved in the centre of each board.

Through the large French windows that opened on to a terrace I could see a clothes-horse covered by an assortment of linen and other garments airing. The beautician stepped out onto the terrace returning with a gown that she proffered me with a quick smile. Then she vanished, to assemble her lotions and unguents, no doubt, leaving me to wonder where I might be lying down.

Her salon cubicle turned out to be hidden behind some heavy drapes I thought had been covering a window. It had all the standard appurtenances. I was a bit surprised when she had me sit on a chair and drew one of my feet towards her. Starting at the wrong end. What on earth...

'I begin with a little foot massage,' she said. 'It helps relax one.'

The second foot received the same pampering. Finally, she patted my feet dry with another towel and slipped them into a pair of disposable slippers, bidding me get up on the table.

'Have you had a facial before?' she asked, after several minutes spent tucking a blanket round me and drawing my hair inside a turban.

'Many, many,' I answered, pleasantly aware that the bed had started vibrating beneath me, intermittently producing a wavelike motion. And since I liked to induce competition in beauticians, I added. 'Actually, I've had facials in quite a few cities: London, Paris, Rome, Sydney, Auckland, Lerwick, Milan, Cairo, Catania – and now Palermo.

'You are very fortunate,' she said, politely. 'To see so much of the world. I have never been out of Sicily.'

'Mm, that's a misfortune, more than most.'

She paused, resting slender, pointy fingers with pointy knuckles on my shoulders. You could categorise her as a digger and kneader among beauticians.

'Why do you say that? Tourists always tell us Sicily is a paradise. One of the most beautiful places in the world.'

'It is,' I said. 'It's even quite rich. Not a poor place at all, as we outsiders tend to think. But too many people are unnecessarily poor. And many seem to work in hiding. I had quite a problem finding you. Whom are you hiding from? The mafia and the pizzo or the financial police and state taxes? Or both?'

Above my head I heard her thin, reedy little laugh. 'Ah, so you know something of Sicily.'

I told her I knew only the things that were readily knowable.

'I'm cleansing your skin,' she said, laying hot damp towels over my face. 'Then I will exfoliate it.'

'Fine.'

For a few minutes she worked on in silence and I was on the point of dozing off when she spoke again. 'Our problems are like a roundabout. We see them. They go round and round in front of us, but we don't know how to stop the process.'

I kept quiet and she continued going round and round my face with her exfoliant disc. But she knew when to stop.

'You have very sensitive skin, signora. So I will focus on calming it. We can stimulate it another day.'

'Sure.'

A minute or so later.

'I never go to church.'

'What?'

'No. I don't feel I need priests to mediate between me and God. I hate the idea of confessing my sins to a man. Why should I? Are you a Protestant?'

'I'm an agnostic,' I said. 'And an economics graduate. I really detest monopolies because they're so inefficient, but religious monopolies such as you have here in Sicily, are also pretty scary. Yes, I was raised a Protestant in Scotland.'

'Protestants don't have priests, right?'

Never before had I encountered an Italian remotely interested in Protestantism or even aware of it. In fact, the beautician's knowledge didn't amount to much, but she was keen to know more.

However, I wanted to avoid being embroiled in a complex discussion. Otherwise at the end I shouldn't even know I'd had a facial. And it's the process rather than the outcome that's the source of pleasure. Wrinkled faces remain wrinkled.

'Maybe we should talk about this over a coffee or tea,' I murmured, forcing myself to pay attention.

'Are you sure you can spare the time, signora?' I could hear the thrill in her voice. 'I have a machine. I can make you a beautiful cappuccino.'

'That would be lovely,' I said. Then I closed my eyes and let myself sink with a sigh down into the bed. She took the hint and I floated off.

When the procedure was completed, a moment signalled by a series of controlled slaps around my face and neck, I pronounced her handiwork the equal of any in Paris or Rome.

'You're making me compliments, signora.'

'No, no,' I said. 'You have a deft touch.'

I asked her what she thought was Sicily's biggest problem, but only if it were her problem too.

'Work,' she answered promptly. 'Not enough work. That is the worst problem. For me too, because if women don't have jobs, they cannot afford beauty treatment.'

I asked her if she had any idea why unemployment was so high in Sicily.

'Because we're poor. Because foreigners who're poorer than we are take our jobs. Because we have too many people. Because the mafia bleeds those of us who have small businesses, not enough to kill us, but to tire us out.'

We sat and talked for over an hour. In the end I had to acknowledge that however maleficent the regime is, and its pernicious character is simply appalling, it has succeeded in fending off change for a thousand years and can easily continue to do so because it has a well-armed brutal force, able and willing to kill off any reformer attracting a following.

The beautician sat with her chin in her hands. She heaved a sigh. 'So there's nothing we can do.'

'*Macché*, there's a lot you can do as an individual,' I assured her, 'if you are prepared to make the effort. Start a little book club with your friends and try to read as much as you can about Sicilian history and the history of the Church here. You need to understand how you've arrived at where you are. Try and find history enthusiasts who might come and speak to you at your club. Once you have made some advance in that area, you can study economics and political theory in the club. And learn how to organise and chair meetings according to international rules. How to make presentations. You can also contact the Italian Women for Democracy Association. Email Luca Dai at the Dolci Centre in Partinico. He and Amico Dolci will help you. Enormously I'm sure. They may be able to arrange seminars for your book club and get people from Pisa University to come and talk to you. You will be so busy you will hardly find time for your business. You will have great fun. And you will change Sicily as well as yourself.'

Waiting together for the lift outside her flat, she asked: 'Signora, will you be coming for another treatment before you move on?'

It was most likely, I told her. Probably the day before leaving for a break in Florence.

'I have a friend who would like to meet you, I think. And to talk. About this club. You can't imagine what it is like to hear the same words every day, over and over, and over and then to hear something very different.'

I laughed at that. 'Oh – be assured we have similar problems in the democracies. But it's not so difficult to find different thoughts and modes of speech there.'

Monday, 2 October 2006

Tried to keep my appointment with the dentist at noon. I was worried about it, because yesterday I finished off the second course of antibiotics and my abscess is as resistant as ever.

As it happened, I didn't make it. I'd forgotten the 234 bus that goes to Via Rocciella stops five minutes after it leaves the Station, to give the driver a fifteen-to-twenty minute break, during which time one person after another puts their head in the bus to ask, '*Quando passa?*' When does it leave?

But siesta was coming up. Rain was forecast for the afternoon. I had to get back quickly. I didn't want to be caught up again in a four-hour two-bus odyssey back to the Casa. So I rang the dentist on my cellphone and explained about the bus delay. Said that the abscess had not improved. I could hear the tsk at the other end, but he gave me a new appointment.

Wednesday, 4 October 2006

Today is my father's birthday. I don't remember his death day, but it was in June some time, in 1986. He was only seventy. When he died I thought bones had been ripped right out of my chest: I could feel the sound of them tearing like sheets of sticking plaster. I would never recover. He had always been there ever since I was born. He was a fixture in my world. Nobody else had known me as long except my mother. But she was alive, watering her plants, taking her little dog to the vet.

A good day then, to visit the mummies in the Palermo catacombs.

I arrived on the heels of a group of French visitors who hurtled past the monk seated at a table inside the porch, waiting, uselessly as it turned out, to accept their entry fee, an agreeably modest sum. Accustomed as they are to the beneficence of their strong central State, it probably did not occur to the French that they were required to pay.

Inside, I had to squeeze myself past the group who had hurriedly gathered round their tour leader, and were busily taking notes while he gave them a short history of the catacombs and an interpretation of what they were seeing.

The corpses ranged in date from the late 1500s to 1920 and most were embalmed before their display. The last person to be lodged in the catacombs and a drawcard for everyone who comes upon her was a four-year-old girl, now a tenant for close to a hundred years and looking very, very much alive and childlike.

Some people wrote into their wills the clothes they wanted to wear when they went on show and asked that they be changed from time to time – wanting to remain fashionable, perhaps.

Interestingly, the only writer who has reported on the mummification process used by the monks is John Dryden junior, son of the great poet, whose *Ode to Saint Cecilia* I loved at school. Young Dryden visited Sicily and Malta between October 1700 and January 1701. Alas, though he lived till 1757, he never saw his manuscript published. According to Saro Portale, the manuscript went astray until 1776, when it was discovered and published, once only, in London. Saro found the book, edited it, translated it and wrote all the notes. I cannot do better than present the mummification extract here, apologising for any mistakes I have made in the back translation:

The most unusual and surprising assemblage of the dead I have ever seen, was that on view at the monastery of the Capuchin monks, about half a mile outside the gate that leads to Monreale.

Once arrived, you are led by one of the monks into a long subterranean cross vault which extends under the Church and the convent (monastery).

There I saw many Capuchins lined up, one beside the other against the wall, apparently attending to their devotions. It was only as I drew nearer that I became aware they were all dead and mummified but with their flesh and skin still intact on their hands and face. Not even the nerves had decomposed. The Capuchins practised this marvellous technique of preserving the corpse in a form easier than one could possibly imagine: They limited themselves to laying the cadaver on four or five crossed poles erected over a hollow in the earth or a little receptacle made of some bricks and in the form of a coffin. In such wise, the corpse, always stretched over this cavity and supported on the poles, eliminates all its corruptible parts and in the span of a year the skin and the flesh dry on the bones.

I saw many corpses that after barely a year were on their feet and erect against the wall, wearing on their bodies an inscription with their basic details. Even if these were all dressed in the vestments of the Capuchins there were, however, many laity and other persons that had had positions of social importance. The most incredible thing was that their faces looked remarkably as they were when alive.

Some, not only our host, Mr Gifford, addressed them by name, saying of each one, 'This was so and so and this was another,' but also the monk who was our guide pointed to the corpse of one particular Capuchin and said, 'He was a very handsome man.'

To tell the truth, in comparison with other dead, he did appear handsome, not only there, underground, but also on the floor above, where our Capuchin guide showed us the portrait of this Capuchin to convince us that the dead had not lost all resemblance to the person they had been when alive.

Among these mummies were some about a hundred years old and, like the more recent ones, they had been so well preserved that it would have been possible to touch their faces or hands without damaging them.

This method of mummifying the dead can easily be achieved by any nation. In my opinion, however, to see them in this condition is a very melancholy way of renewing a friendship.

But in Catholic countries, the practice serves to remember them to those who come to visit them and to pray for their souls. Mr Gifford said he had already booked a place for himself in the catacombs among them.

A surprising note was struck in the postures of two mummies: one was on his knees with his arms extended and his hands joined as if he were praying, the other with arms opened wide in the crucified position. The priests told us that in life these persons had been very devout and that the crucifixion posture had not been arranged like that by the fathers.

When the corpse was still fresh they had fastened the arms to the body more than once, but a little while later they found that the body had resumed the other posture. From the moment they knew that this man had been an illustrious and devoted worshipper of the Passion of Our Lord, they thought that the body had assumed its position by divine will.

The same kind of story applied to the person on his knees; they said that they had found him in that position when they had gone to visit the bodies laid out to dry in the underground area which had always remained closed except for this purpose, and to place there someone recently deceased.

Although nearly three centuries have passed since the Dryden visit, mummification having ceased, the corpses still look oddly human despite the fact that their lower parts seem to be packed about with straw and covered up with a long tunic, a bit like a scarecrow built around a broom. The garments are now quite uniform, the originals perhaps not having lasted as long as the bodies.

What attracted most comment from the French was the arrangement of the corpses by profession – doctors, lawyers, magistrates, clerics and such, and the corpse of the little girl in the glass case. The bodies certainly retain some vestigial humanity and individuality. Nonetheless I prefer my animal remains to return to the oceans sooner than later.

I am now reminded of the Bishop of Monreale who recently died. Only in his fifties. Suor Myriam invited me to go to the requiem mass, a prospect I initially found intriguing, but changed my mind after one of the nuns caught up with me at the lift on the way to breakfast to tell me that Suor Myriam and the others might not make it to Monreale and that I should go on my own. She used the word 'autonomous' at some stage. It sounded like: You're a solid grown-up person with a sense of responsibility who doesn't give in to every abscessed tooth plus cold, but struggles up the mountain to the Cathedral to represent us at Baida.

'Well, my cold's really become worse,' I said to the nun. 'I should be very embarrassed if I had a coughing fit during a prayer at the service. Please tell Suor Myriam I'll be staying in bed most of the day.'

I had rung the dentist who advised me to come back on 18 October. That means nearly every subsequent visit will require me to travel from Messina, a three hour trip both ways. If he can take the nerve out, I'll have to find a Messina dentist to continue from there. Although I'm planning six weeks in Messina I'm told root canal therapy takes a very long time. I'll have to ask Rita. She had all her teeth done. In the meantime, will this abscess lie mute, improve or worsen? I feel like the Messinese after a big earthquake. Sock it to me, Goddess.

Sunday, 8 October 2006

During siesta I often find the owner of my Palermo Internet point, a Bangladeshi, catnapping, stretched out on top of two chairs in front of the work stations. He and his wife are easy going, humorous and amiable, seeming to enjoy the chaos around them when Africans or Indians who frequent the place kid one another at the tops of their voices and convulse themselves laughing as if they hadn't a problem in the world. The occasional Anglo-Saxon sitting at a computer might blink once or twice, but makes no effort to hurry away.

Today, when I pointed to a phone cabin, the Bangladeshi nodded and offered a slight ripple of fingers from his makeshift bed.

He looked exhausted. Thank goodness I was the only person in the shop. It was much cooler than usual inside. And quieter. Everyone I ring in Australia often has to listen to African women shouting in a variety of languages. If they're in an advanced state of pregnancy as they sometimes are, they keep the cabin door open for a bit of air and I can sometimes hardly hear what I'm saying, myself, let alone the person I'm ringing.

But this afternoon, everything was lovely. My brother Jack was home. Poor Jack. He must have groaned to himself on hearing my voice and wished he were already tucked in. I never ring for only five minutes and I blush to confess that I'm the one who does most of the talking. When I apologised to him and asked him to tell me first his news, he said, 'But we're doing the same old things, you're the one that chats up cardinals in their apartments.'

With that encouragement, I burbled on happily, and Jack was careful to ask me the right questions so that I didn't suspect he might be dozing off. Then I asked him for a family update.

While he was talking, and I listening, looking idly out the glass door of the cabin, I suddenly registered that the Bangladeshi was no longer napping, but on his feet, fully alert, and having a an exchange with two youths who had come into the shop.

There was a curious intensity in the postures of the little group, in the tightly hunched shoulders of the bigger youth and the way he kept jabbing the air with his index finger.

The younger boy, about sixteen or seventeen, initially had his back to me but had walked around the owner and was now facing me offside.

Totally unconscious of my presence, head thrown back, he had begun laughing inanely like a horse, his mouth wide open, all teeth, and eyes rapturous with some secret joy. He was pressing his palms together across his chest, ready, I thought, to start clapping or dancing. '*Of Mice and Men*' flitted across my brain like one of those distracting electronic ads that glide past on the television screen just when Inspector Montalbano is wrapping up the plot for his awed superior.

Then I hissed into the phone: 'Oh, my God, Jack, you should see what's going on here. Two hoods have come in. I think they're mafia lowlife demanding the *pizzo*. You should see the big one and the Bangladeshi, they're confronting each other like fighting cocks. The hood is contorting his face like a gargoyle, but you can see it's an act: he's raising himself on his toes and kind of swelling out, snarling. Really ugly. The Bangladeshi is responding in a more controlled fashion. He's putting all his aggression into his eyes, glaring, making his eyes seem to smoke. Swelling out his chest. What a charade. Men are incredible. They're starting to shout now and the hood is pointing his forefinger as if it were a gun.

'Oh, God. The Bangladeshi has told him to "Fuck off!" Can you imagine! But they're Bengalis of old, aren't they? Famous warriors?'

'Did you tell me to get fucked?' the hood was saying. 'I'm not interested in a fuck at the moment'.

'Bloody hell, Jack, he's reaching into his back pocket. I hope it's not for a knife. There's only me and the Bangladeshi here. You won't believe it. He's taken out a packet of cigarettes and he's clutching it in his hands. An expert in anticlimax if nothing else. He's leaving. He can't wait to have a smoke because he's all wound up. Imagine it as a cigarette commercial. Oh, I don't know if I heard him right. I think he said, 'I'm going to burn you down'. I have to go, Jack and find out what's happened. I'll let you know next time.'

'Hah, and you wanted to know my news,' Jack said, 'You're in a place where the news happens even while you're on the phone. Don't get involved.'

I rushed over to the Bangladeshi.

'Were they mafia?'

He nodded briefly.

'Did they want money?'

'Yes.' He was trembling a little and making an effort to control himself.

'You're not going to give it to them.'

'I haven't got it,' he said. He looked drained.

'Did I hear them right? Did one say, "I'll burn you down?" *Faccio bruciare?*'

'Yes.'

He clung to a chair for a moment before sinking into it. Two tourists were crouched low, peering in the shop window.

They had been examining the opening hours pasted on the glass and were puzzled as to why the door was still closed. Now they would be more puzzled. The door was suddenly flung open and four Bangladeshi men walked straight through in Indian file and out the door at the back. They were what once might have been called 'stalwarts'. Not very tall, but solid. Not scared looking. It was the first time those particular youths had come to the shop, the owner told me, barely glancing at the men who swiftly disappeared from view, and ignoring the tourists making faces through the glass. 'But many, many have come in the years that I've been here.'

'How many?'

'Eleven and a half.' He meant the years.

'Do you think they're the mafia or just individuals working the system the mafia has opened up?'

'*Bassi*, I think.' (Low down the pecking order).

'Why don't you leave?'

He looked around at his computers and phone booths: 'This is everything I have in the world. I have nowhere else to go.'

The tourists had decided to open the door and let themselves in. They were bowing and smiling and waiting. I would have to talk to him at another siesta time.

'You're very brave,' I said. '*Buon coraggio.*'

Maybe he should move to Catania. The pollution in Via Vittoria Emanuele is fierce. And that little place is really just too small. The mafia are mean-minded to pick on someone as poor as he is. But they want to train their recruits in savagery.

Tuesday, 17 October 2006

Today I finally kept my twice-delayed appointment with the dentist. The abscess is definitely shrinking, he said approvingly, but I must wait till it has 'dried out' before he can complete his task. No matter if I'm leaving for Messina tomorrow, or if I'll be finishing up on the island on 30 November. He would make me an appointment for 5

November and we might be able to fit in one or two dates before the 30th. He laughed when I suggested paying for my visits up to now. 'Later,' he said.

I caught the bus back to the centre and went straight to the little Internet point to send some last emails before I left Palermo.

The owner was very busy, but later, when that particular rush was over, he came and sat beside me: 'Only last night, signora, two more men came, this time with a pistol. One of them held it to my head. My wife and child were here. They took all the money in the till and about 900 international phone cards I had.'

To my consternation I thought I saw a white pallor under his brown skin.

'But surely you have reported *that* to the police? It's a very serious offence.'

'No, no. It's useless. They won't do a thing. How can I carry on? What can I do?' He was dispirited. I felt murderous.

I dug into my bag for my contacts book and gave him the address of an anti-rackets website to look up; also contact details for Bruno Piazzese, whose Syracuse discotheque had been burned down twice by the mafia when he refused to pay the *pizzo*, and who had agreed to a government proposal to rebuild the disco yet again if he would become a symbol of resistance. On the two occasions I had interviewed him we had met late in the evening on a seafront, he arriving in a black car and accompanied by two bodyguards.

'Maybe there's a different way to get justice,' I said to the Bangladeshi, urging him: 'Go to lawyers, young lawyers, women lawyers. Find an anti-rackets group and tell them it may be possible to demonstrate that because almost the entire city of Palermo pays extortion to criminals, the Italian government can be sued at the European Court of Justice for failing in its duty of care to its citizens. They can take out a class action. This would be very humiliating to the government.'

He stared at me. 'You think people can do this?'

'There's one way to find out,' I said. 'And you'll be much the stronger and wiser for making the effort.'

Part III The East

Aside from widely touting their Greek and Roman origins, East Coast Sicilians used to think their side of Sicily was a mafia-free zone. They took pride in that. Saw it as a reason for self-respect. It might once have been true, but World War II brought an end to any such quarantining of the mafia when the Church of Rome and the US government decided that an illegal terrorist force was just the thing to combat Italian communists at the polls and wherever else they might surface in solidarity.

For me, what really differentiates east and west Sicily are natural phenomena. Immense earthquakes that can completely empty a large city of its population and raise mountains of rubble on top of main streets so that for years survivors have no access to whatever property or people dear to them are buried there; volcanic eruptions that cause alarmed seas to rear up, hiss, sizzle, steam and retract before onslaughts of red hot lava plunging into them at eighty kilometres an hour; and one of the world's most desirable ports, beloved by ships' captains for the protection and services it offers – so long as you can survive the dangers of getting into it.

I give these things a lot more thought than I do the mafia. I draw up tables showing when the last big eruption or earthquake occurred and try to estimate when the next one might be due. Messina was uprooted and thrown about like a tree trunk in 1783 and 1908. There's a gap of a hundred and twenty-five years between the two events. It is now a hundred and two years since the last earthquake in Messina. The next could be any time. That Berlusconi could imagine any private or public body investing over a billion dollars in a bridge across the Strait is so perversely opposed to reality, even Pirandello would cringe before it.

And there are always mementoes around to maintain my apprehensions. Whenever I visit any of the beautiful late baroque cities on the south-east coast, like Palazzolo Acreide, Modica, Sicli and Noto or admire Syracuse's baroque buildings – Syracuse that was Archimedes' birthplace and the largest city in Magna Graecia – I remember that these baroque buildings and monuments arose out of the 1693 earthquake, second only in horror to the massive 1669 volcanic eruption that preceded it. The earthquake reportedly destroyed at least forty-five towns and cities in Sicily and Malta and killed two thirds of Catania's entire population.

Fine. Destruction generates creation. New babies. New people. New buildings go up. New styles of architecture. Architects and town planners love working on greenfield sites. For the entire eighteenth century Sicily splurged on baroque, in its late form a style so extreme it was labelled 'Sicilian' baroque. It makes the heart sing, even if the Jesuits conceived it as a counter-Reformation stratagem in re-asserting the Church's wealth and power.

Lavic art, lavic paving, lavic jewellery, lavic sea sculpture, even lavically fertile hectares of land are other beautiful but scary reminders of the east coast's particular attributes. I love the lava when it is cool and quiet, grey and detached. But – what if one becomes caught up in the cataclysm that precedes the rebirth of all this beauty? I hold my breath when I go back east and never forget to keep an eye on Etna.

Catania

Catania is often labelled 'a bit of a dump' by tourists and in truth it has a grotty feel about it. The old sulphur chimneys are highly visible beside the railway tracks that were once a conduit of sulphur from the interior to the port, and which, with the freeway running parallel to the railway, now block off the foreshores from the town. Etna throws up varying amounts of volcanic dust almost every day, the colour of the smoke always meticulously assessed to gauge the intensity of the interior activity. A ghastly burnt-out skeleton of a Standa store remains in full view to menace citizens and intensify their anxiety. The pocket-sized botanical gardens are sere, weedy and boring, a disgrace to a city of half a million people. It took me days to find them because no one had heard of them. And that's the way some people prefer it.

But... Catania is my kind of dump. Especially when I'm sitting in a restaurant deep in a cave in the heart of the city, where my friend Rita and I can revel in cool, damp air, the walls sweaty to the touch and an ice-cold stream that rises somewhere on Etna, bubbling over our naked feet while we sip our wine and share a plate of antipasto. Or when I'm equally captivated admiring a great yellow sun rimmed by peaks in an artisan's shop window and wondering if I will ever get the money to buy one of a size that will drench me in golden smiles all day.

Grotty or not, it's a warm-hearted city that exerts a strong pull on the affections and coming back to it makes me feel that I'm coming home.

20

On my return to Catania after my tour with Gaby, at my insistence, Rita found me a room at Just Like Home, a relaxed and comfortable B and B located in a palazzo right in the heart of Catania and only a five minutes' walk from the pungent odours of the sprawling city markets where a small Chinese restaurant was the only place I could order soup.

I loved the personality of the palazzo from the moment I stood before its massive wooden entry door, solid as a wall, failing repeatedly to push it open after sounding the buzzer. A mechanic watching me from his workshop across the street and grinning broadly, finally pointed out the smaller door within the giant frame. 'Enter by the little door, signora.'

The *pensione*, owned by Silvana Cirrone, a professor of theoretical philosophy at Catania University occupied the fourth and fifth floors of what was once an eight-storey palatial mansion, now a condominium. The upper floor had been her parents' home. Silvana was born there and raised her son within its comfort till he was thirteen and went off to Milan to school and to live with his father.

About eight bedrooms were tucked away in a corner of the upper floor of the B and B, my room among them. Bypassing the lift, it was exactly 120 steps up from the ground, a perfect number for a bit of exercise, especially since I went in and out of the building several times a day.

The entry to the B and B, here on this upper floor, opened directly into a very large sitting room, whose southern wall, largely comprising floor-to-ceiling windows, overlooked an extensive roofscape and a busy main street. Simply furnished, a great round family-size table was its central focus. Every bedroom, high ceilinged and spacious, had its own sunny terrace and a bathroom, except for one very small bedroom where Silvana's friends would stay. They had their own bathroom opposite, not en suite. The bedroom furniture was often old style Sicilian, dark, heavy and creaky but warm and mellow.

A flight of wooden steps just inside the entry door and on the right, oddly inconspicuous, led up from the sitting room to Silvana's large attic apartment/solarium, where a vast open space served as an office-cum-living room. Her bedroom – doorless and with an en suite, was a steep step down on the left of the socialising area. A small scullery on the far side led out to the solarium where her women friends, most of them academics at various universities throughout Italy, seized every opportunity to deepen their all-over polished tans.

When I first arrived at the B and B Silvana was on sick leave from the University and for some weeks had been undergoing radio and chemical therapy for cancer of the pancreas. In her early sixties but looking younger despite her illness, she insisted on driving herself to her morning appointments at Taormina hospital, returning in the afternoon drained, falling asleep across her bed, sometimes without undressing, often in pain until a friend or one of her two assistants at the B and B could give her an injection.

She had good days, nonetheless, sometimes extending to a week, with less pain and more energy, and would engage me in conversation when I reached the top of the steeply raked wooden steps, heading for her computer to check my emails.

'Habermas was so impressed by my analysis of his work and my assessment of the direction it was taking, that he arranged to come and see me in Catania,' she confided once, finding me examining a very considerable private library that wound through halls, foyers and other public rooms of the B and B on two floors, as well as along every wall of her own apartment.

'But unfortunately, as you may know, he got a stroke and had to cancel his visit.'

She waved a casual hand across several walls of books.

'Those books are from a much earlier part of my career. These others here' – pointing to about six or seven shelves – 'are the very most recent ones.'

They were all on the subject of computers and the mind. Some in German and others in English translation.

'In computer terms the mind is seen as software and the brain as hardware,' she explained. 'Children's language is what we are looking at now. That's where the software development commences.'

Rita had been very curious to meet Silvana. Though she had contacted her to negotiate the room for me, they did not know one another. As she put it to me, 'Silvana's a friend of a friend and very clever, I'm told.'

I rather suspected that Silvana's interest in Habermas suggested she might have been a Communist or Socialist or left-wing in some form, whereas I was pretty certain Rita and Grzegorz were firmly conservative.

I had overheard Rita on the phone, speaking to Silvana on my behalf. Impressing her: 'She is a journalist from Australia. *Intelligentissima*. She has been staying with us since she returned from the West but now she needs to be independent. She requires a place for six weeks, with an Internet connection and a bedroom with a bathroom. One is rather hoping –' a pause '– for a *bon prezzo*, [a good price]'.

Silvana could not have been more co-operative. A bedroom with a bathroom. Of course. I could even make my choice of room. And she herself had a computer with an ADSL connection. Since she was for the most part at the university, I could use it any time I liked. A good price was always arranged for a friend of a friend. That was her policy. But with taxes so high as they were, especially because she had another job, and with domestic wages hitting the roof, and with a mortgage to pay, thirty-five euros a night was absolutely as low as she could go. Rita had thought the price very good indeed and it was agreed I should move to Silvana's place at the end of that week.

Arranging a time for them to meet was the problem. Silvana was brightest and most energetic in the morning and usually debilitated or asleep in the afternoon. Rita could only rarely contemplate going out before the siesta ended, about four p.m. or even later, but then she might not go to bed until the early hours of the morning. I had forgotten forenoons were not for her when I arranged a time to suit Silvana. Rita kept her eleven a.m. appointment at one p.m. But Silvana proved understanding.

They were both expert in the opening courtesies, with Rita offering judicious flattery to warm the atmosphere. It embraced me as well as Silvana. I was *simpaticissima*. She was first to ask permission to give the tu, briskly crossing Silvana's attic floor to fetch an ashtray while Silvana took out her tobacco and began to roll her own cigarette. She talked about her cancer. Rita commiserated, relating the story of her thyroid, lamenting that her eyes were protruding too much. Silvana pointed to the parting on the top of her head. It was more than two centimetres wide. She was losing her hair.

Rita explained at surprising length how I had arrived for a few days but had been talked into staying another week, as a 'paying guest'. This was something completely unknown to her, she told Silvana, but I had insisted. Apparently it was an Anglo-Saxon custom.

One new myth coming up. 'Only with people you don't know,' I said.

Silvana nodded, tweaking the ends of her cigarette clean of tobacco threads. As a student in Germany she had learned to roll her own. Satisfied the cigarette was ready for use, she rang Melan, her Sri Lankan assistant, asking him to bring tea, and then began quizzing Rita about the cottage for rent on Favignana. Did it have a high occupancy rate in the winter? Rita was regretfully negative about that. Even June dates were proving difficult to fill. But then, it was a very new purchase. One had to wait. She and Silvana then turned to the problems of running a bed and breakfast.

The way the two put their heads together, excited to share their experiences, reminded me of a dinner party I'd attended during my first week in Catania where I saw a woman lean across the table and quietly invite another, 'Tell me, *gioia*, how are your investments going at X?' This was not a casual inquiry. Middle-class Sicilian women like Rita and her friends are increasingly alert to the rental capacity of a second, or even third house in the international holiday market and to the returns available on bed and breakfast accommodation.

The woman's friend had responded with a description of the house she had purchased, the locale, its beauty, comfort, utility and especially intriguing details like receipts and outgoings, gradually attracting the attention of other guests and deciding them to abruptly terminate their own conversations, the better to learn the risks and rewards of property development in the hospitality industry.

Once the details were grasped, anecdotes started emerging, often hearsay, some producing gasps of horror – a tenant thought to have been paying rent for three months had cleared out without having paid a penny. But did you not have an agent? An agent? (Agents cost money). Well, one had faith. One trusted. Yes. That's what one prefers to do. But then...? Someone leaned forward and inconspicuously adjusted their hearing aid. Property values had quadrupled since they bought the place. How long ago? Eight months. Silently the worth of the couple was reflected on and reassessed by others around the table.

The host, a man with a sardonic cast of mind, recalled Giovanni Verga's memorable short story, *La Roba*, 'Things' where over a long period of time, a poor peasant turns himself into a rich landowner, so mindlessly attached to his 'things' that in a momentary consciousness of his pending death, he rushes about his farmyards in a rage, whacking his animals with a stick, and shouting, 'You're coming with me.'

That raised a few rueful smiles.

Silvana, enjoying high status as a university professor had particular concerns. 'My preferred *clienti* are colleagues from the University or their friends, at the least, friends of friends,' she was confessing, 'but over the past two years I've had to take quite a number of vulgar people – I don't want to sound snobbish, but some have no appreciation of books or antique furniture. All they want is laminex and plastic.'

Rita sucked in her breath up to her chin. That was precisely her own problem. She and Grzegorz had debated what kind of furniture to put in Favignana. They had an eighteenth-century pasta-making trough in the living room. The Palermitana architect who had renovated the house after purchasing it had also installed some antique majolica tiles on the kitchen floor. Silvana was impressed. They went on to talk about the taxes. Particularly onerous if you had a job, but how could Silvana survive without a job? She had a son that had to be maintained at Milan University. He was working at Prada now but not financially independent yet. Imagine how much it had cost to keep him schooled for years: the fees, the books, the accommodation, living expenses. Year after year. Milan was shockingly expensive. Rita reached out her hand in sympathy and the two of them sat, hands clasped, nodding and empathizing.

Some Sicilian women have a habit of enclosing your hand in theirs and just pressing it gently while they talk to you. The first one who did that to me (a magistrate friend of Rita's) made me feel quite wriggly, but now that I have become more accustomed to the practice, I find it pleasant and reassuring.

When I first arrived at Silvana's she took my hand to lead me up the narrow stairs to her attic, to show me where her Mac computer was lodged. And she kept on holding it and pressing my fingers while we were talking. It's an extraordinarily friendly and sympathetic practice. I've never known other Italian women do it, but I've seen several Sicilian women, usually in a party situation, sitting on a sofa or in chairs next to each other, with their fingers entwined, chatting amiably.

****

Everything was clean and bright at Just Like Home, kept that way by Silvana's two assistants, Melan, a disco habitué with a wonderfully sculpted body that he displayed to maximum advantage, and Minta, a young Mauritian, mother of two small children.

Melan rented a flat near Rita's place but a room was kept free for him next to the B and B kitchen because he often had to welcome guests arriving either very late at night, or early in the morning. He and Minta were perfect choices for the job, always good humoured and cheerful, nothing too much trouble for them, and Melan, an excellent cook, would often rise earlier than need be, to make large raspberry jam tarts as a breakfast surprise.

Minta was intelligent and full of common sense, quick to resolve any little difficulties that arose, while Melan was a bit of a drama queen, but kind, generous and reliable. Both were very loyal to Silvana who trusted them and encouraged them to act on their initiative. Though she rarely saw her guests, her two devoted staff kept Silvana fully informed of everything that went on. Their wit and sense of comedy certainly made my stay at the B and B dramatic and entertaining.

Their domain was largely on the lower floor of the *pensione* where the dining room, several bedrooms, and the kitchen and laundry had been constructed out of the original apartment that, becoming unexpectedly vacant, offered Silvana an opportunity to enter the hospitality business.

Melan and Minta had a formidable talent for making instant friendships with people and Melan seemed to know everyone in Catania, especially members of the military whom he frequently met at the gym. He was like a character in Armistead Maupin's *Tales of the City* and frequently found himself in parlous situations that could throw him into such a funk he would retreat under the bedclothes in his little room beside the kitchen and swear he could not possibly face the world again. Then Minta, full of sympathy, would take over his duties until he had recovered his equilibrium.

While I was at the B and B, an attractive young couple arrived, with a delightful four-year-old son in tow, a child with a deep bass voice that made me smile every time I heard him talk.

The husband looked like a romantic villain from the silent movies epoch. Even Dracula. Slim and limber and close to two metres tall, he moved everywhere like a cat, an impression intensified by thickly lashed, magnificent green eyes which were an unfailing magnet for anyone, male or female, meeting him, something he was well aware of, and responded to with a dreamy, languorous expression, half-closing his eyes sometimes when appraising what was being said to him.

He spoke little, happy to leave the chitchat to his wife, but could be very funny when regaling listeners with tales of his work as a police officer in one of those interior towns where everyone lives within a hundred steps of a mafia capo.

On one occasion he imitated the terror of a colleague charged with responsibility for arresting a man known to be associated with the mafia. This colleague had absolutely refused to perform the task.

'He's mafia,' the officer had protested. 'He'll wipe me out. You come with me.'

'And did you?' I asked.

'He did it on his own,' the wife burst in, indignantly. 'He didn't care about us, if he got shot.'

'Ah, you were confident of the outcome, then,' I said to him, 'Perhaps you knew something you're not telling us about?'

He gave me one of his appraising green-eyed looks, and smiled, radiantly.

'I know how to do my job.'

His wife was seething with some deep-seated resentment, but I forbore to enquire into it. She seemed to have modelled herself on the Sicilian vamp, perhaps what she thought an appropriate image for someone married to an old-fashioned movie villain, but the thick greasy make-up, big hoops on the ears, frilly red blouse with a plunging neckline, short tight skirt and embroidered black fishnet stockings, sat oddly with the unexpectedly maternal devotion she showed to her little boy, whom she adored, and whose every wish, she thought, should be gratified on the instant.

Within hours of the couple's arrival, they had Melan waiting on them hand and foot, enchanted by their beauty which he lavishly discoursed upon. Minta and I, constrained by our 'handsome is as handsome does' reservations, kept quiet.

Although Just Like Home was a breakfast-only establishment, the wife swiftly installed herself in Melan's kitchen and the little family could be found cooking and eating there at all hours of the day and night, sometimes alongside Melan, or me, I being a friend of a friend of Silvana, having the run of the kitchen too and regularly sharing lunch with Melan.

One day he notified me somewhat anxiously that the wife had used up my bottle of olive oil that was parked on a shelf.

'I told her it was yours,' he said. 'But she paid no attention.'

'Don't worry about it, they'll be gone soon,' I said.

He sighed deeply. On his mind was also the fact that the couple were living off the land, so to speak: hoeing into Silvana's resources for the guests, coffee, mineral water, milk, butter, croissants. Raspberry tart. Fruit. All but the tart had to be accounted for by Melan.

Still, no one stayed more than a few days, generally. Likewise the couple. But within a very short time they were back on the doorstep.

'We love Catania. We love Just Like Home.' They loved it better than home.

They started getting into my new bottle of olive oil, my fruit and Melan's prawns that he packed in the freezer. Robbers-in-residence.

But they were fond of Melan. And I quite enjoyed their company. One night I found the wife in the kitchen with the little boy who was on the floor surrounded by enough toys to open a shop, a new amusement being thrust on him every single day.

'Where's your husband?' I asked her, stepping around the clutter.

'Gone out to a disco.'

My eyebrows went up. 'That's not a wise development. There are a lot of predatory females out there waiting to devour good looking husbands like yours.'

'What can I do? He likes to dance. We always went dancing before our son was born. But I have to stay home with him.'

Never having lost sight of my mother's dictum that 'the shadow of the other woman darkens every marriage' I recommended she find a baby-sitter but the idea was repugnant to her.

She tossed her thick curls and pouted fiercely. 'My son is number one in my life. Nobody comes between me and him. I love him. He is the joy of my life.'

'And what about your husband?'

She gave a hopeless little shrug of her shoulders, naked in her peasant blouse.

Sicilian husbands are notorious philanderers and no wonder. Of course it's the Church that goes on with all the hullabaloo about mothers and mothering, trying to turn ordinary women into living icons. Augustine's mean-spirited campaign to convince people that sex between humans exists only to transmit original sin through the generations is said to be a source of mass neurosis among Catholics.

Fortunately my mother had never heard of Augustine and in one of her heart to hearts with my sister and me, both still prepubescent and sticking our fingers in our ears to block off the latest disgusting information about body parts, she assured us, 'If God had anything better than sex he must have kept it for himself.'

Not too long after the latest encounter with Sicilian motherhood I came downstairs to have an early breakfast in preparation for going out with Rita, and found Melan and Minta in the kitchen, earnestly conversing, Melan talking at high speed, Minta obviously in the role of comforter. When she saw me, she grasped Melan's arm and turned him towards me.

'Tell Mary Rose. She'll advise you what to do.'

It was a tragic tale he had to tell.

He had been asleep in his little bed the previous night. In the early hours of the morning he heard a tap-tapping on his door. 'Like this,' he said, knocking on the fridge door in a repetitive pattern. The sound immediately triggered a Walter de la Mare poem from my childhood and set it running through my head, though I continued to favour Melan with an appearance of close attention.

*Someone came knocking
At my wee, small door;
Someone came knocking
I'm sure-sure-sure.*

*I listened, I opened,
I looked to left and right,
But naught there was a-stirring
In the still dark night.*

*Only the busy beetle
Tap-tapping in the wall,
Only from the forest
The screech-owl's call.*

*Only the cricket whistling
While the dewdrops fall,
So I know not who came knocking,
At all, at all, at all.*

But Melan knew.

'I got up and put on my dressing gown, the short one, you know, and went to the door and whispered, 'Who is it?' It was her. You know, the wife of the policeman. She said she had a headache and asked me if I could give her a tablet. I opened the door and saw she was in her nightwear. Not that there was much of it. One of those flimsy see-through things. She followed me into the kitchen and was right behind me when I opened the drawer where we keep the headache pills. When I turned round, she kind of threw herself up against me, pressing me, and before I could gather my wits, grabbed the hem of my dressing gown with one hand and said, breathing all over me, I love your shortie dressing gown. Have you anything on underneath? And before I could reply, had shoved her hand right up and grabbed my, you know' – and he swayed on his feet, wiping the sweat from his brow.

He was genuinely revulsed, I could see. Not the normal male reaction to such an opportunity. But then... she hadn't shown much judgment. I couldn't help it. I started laughing.

"Don't laugh," he reproached me. 'I'm not finished. She threw her arms round my neck and started kissing me – and then her husband walked into the kitchen.'

Oh, that snapped me to attention. One of those situations set up by a couple to blackmail a hapless third party? But no. No such nefarious intention. Another kind of peculiarly Sicilian sin? The husband had ambled past the couple into the kitchen, seating himself at the table. His wife was in no hurry to stop kissing Melan, but she eventually detached herself and sat down beside her husband who asked her conversationally, 'What were you doing with Melan?'

'Oh, just giving him a thank-you kiss for fetching me a headache tablet.'

That was all right, then. A kiss between friends. No jealousy. No worries. The policeman invited the Sri Lankan to join them, offering to pour them all a juice. Silvana's, of course.

'And was that it, then?' I asked.

Melan nodded. 'But they told me they had just bought a flat in Taormina and invited me to come and stay with them for a few days.'

He was certainly agitated. Not his usual confident self.

'I don't know what to do,' he moaned. 'I don't like it. I'm very worried. I think I'll have to go away somewhere for awhile. They're leaving tomorrow but they told me they'll be back on Monday.'

'When does the husband do his police work?' I wondered aloud. 'They're hardly ever home these days. Always coming to Catania.'

'What do you think I should do?' Melan asked me. Despite the iron man physique he laboured at in the gym he was a gentle soul and surprisingly innocent.

'Absolutely do not go to Taormina,' I said. 'They may be the kind of couple that want a threesome, or foursome or whatever. You don't want to become involved in that kind of activity especially since the husband is a police officer and very likely has ties with the mafia who reportedly frown on marital infidelities.

'I'll write the wife a letter. She gave me her email address because she wants to maintain contact with me, she said. After she gets the letter, I'm pretty sure they won't come back again. If they should try, you can ask Silvana to refuse them a room. Just say they're not appropriate guests. But we don't want to bother Silvana unnecessarily when she's so sick. Cheer up,' I said to Melan. 'This is just a little incident. And they won't be back here again. I'll write the wife an email this afternoon.'

I did. And they never contacted the *pensione* again. Not that I wrote anything nasty or even uncivil. I felt sad for the isolated young wife, and regretted that the circumstances were not such that I could give her the support she obviously needed. I simply pointed out that she and her husband had not being doing the right thing and that if they wanted to keep returning to Like at Home Silvana would want them to do so on a different basis.

****

Though I knew Silvana for only six weeks she impressed me mightily. Incredibly brave, forcing herself to go regularly to her office at the university up to a few weeks before her death, trying to act normally, she lived by a philosophy which, non-religious or otherwise, proved a source of strength to her.

Not very long before she died, when I was climbing the 120 stairs to my room and had arrived at the landing of the lower floor I was astonished to hear screams and yells coming from inside. I recognised Silvana's voice above the clamour.

What could be happening? Melan answered the door when I pressed the buzzer. I pretended I wanted to go to the fridge for some fruit. Another round of screams rent the air. They were coming from the salon where we had breakfast in the morning.

'What's all that racket?' I asked Melan. 'Why is everyone screaming?'

'That's mainly Silvana,' he answered, a grin spreading across his face. 'It's the condominium quarterly meeting – for the whole building. It's always a bunfight. Silvana really gives it to them because they talk such rubbish.'

He paused a moment. 'I think she enjoys it.'

Then he stared at the floor. 'They'll miss her at the next meeting.'

She knew she was dying but her first thought was always for other people's welfare. When she asked you how you were, it was a fervent enquiry. She lavished hugs on everybody. Even me. Twice on the day that I was preparing to leave for Syracuse she had come and searched for me, to hug me tightly and thank me for coming to stay at Just Like Home, telling me that it had been such a pleasure to meet me, that my presence had lit up the place.

I was dumbfounded. Our brief encounters would hardly have amounted to more than two hours. On the other hand, she never made small talk, plunging straight into literature or philosophy, searching for books to show me, beaming and waving as she departed, thinning fast and tightly wrapped in her slim grey overcoat, with a beret drawn down over her ears.

It was easy to imagine the warmth between Silvana and the old friends of her youth, though 'old' didn't immediately leap to mind with these Catanese women. Silvana, herself, looked much younger than her age if you subtracted the effects of the illness.

Her friends, some of whom were working on campuses in other Italian cities, were totally at her service. As her deterioration became increasingly evident a group of six rostered themselves so that at least two came every day, one or another staying overnight, cooking and washing for her. But often they all came. The solidarity between them was as important to them as to Silvana. They were grieving in concert.

One night I returned to the B and B and crept up the stairs to her attic, thinking her out and that I would check my emails. I was flabbergasted to find her there, not out, seated at her round table with her six friends: I had arrived in a moment of sudden silence when each was peering at the hand of cards they had been dealt. The sky had darkened, but they hadn't noticed. They were all smokers and the fug around them was like the Glasgow pea soupers of my childhood. 'Come up, *tesoro*,' Silvana said, hearing me reach the top step, and turning to stretch out her hand to me.

'Come up and say hello to everyone,' and she drew me into her side, clasping me round the waist.

'You know Mary Rose.'

They looked at me, briefly, running knowing eyes over my new gear from Upim, the cheap chain store. Thoughtful, their minds on their cards and their luck. All blonde and deeply tanned, slim, with generous décolletage boldly displayed. Each one was with a cigarette, dangling between the fingers, hanging from their lips while they frowned over their cards, or flattened between them in a grimace, when they were breathing deeply to get at the nicotine.

On a one to one basis, her friends were warm and chatty towards me if I met them in the lift or sometimes in the spare bathroom doing Silvana's washing. Then they would talk to me like old friends, holding my hand or throwing an arm around my waist, encircling me in their mourning.

In late May, when I was settled in Syracuse, Minta rang me to let me know Silvana had died from her pancreatic cancer on the twenty-second. She had known she was close to dying and had chosen to spend her last hours at home. Minta and Melan both thought I should send her son a telegram.

'They're read out at the funeral service,' Minta said. 'It's essential that you do it.'

As a Mauritian immigrant she had had to familiarise herself with Sicilian customs and she was always attentive to ritual propriety. So I wrote a fairly formal note of the sort I thought might be appropriate from someone who had known Silvana for only six weeks. To ensure that the Italian was comprehensible I showed the note to Maria, the owner of B and B Oikos where I was staying in Syracuse's old city, Ortygia, she being a former high school teacher of Italian language and literature. She gave it a cursory glance and without a word, wrote off something completely different.

I goggled on reading it. It was full of baroque clichés and effusions. I hardly recognised myself as this warm, expansive person overflowing with affection for Silvana, and even her son whom I'd met only fleetingly, affection of an intensity I might have reserved for a very close friend or member of my family.

At the end Maria had written, 'Remember that I'm here for you.'

No, no. Never. I felt sick. My hand rose to cover my mouth. A nightmare of embarrassment. What would Sergio think? He'd know it was fake. Surely he would. He was thirty years old and had lived in Milan since he was thirteen. He now worked for Prada. So he had spent a large part of his life in a post-Enlightenment environment in a very tough town. He would probably be stunned to receive such rococo condolences from an Anglo whom he hardly knew.

21

Silvana's body was sent to the university and afterwards removed to Palermo for cremation. She was thought to have been an atheist, but more likely, I think, had adhered to Giordano Bruno's heresy, the one that took him to the stake, 'God is either within you, or he is nowhere.'

After the funeral Sergio emailed me a warm thank-you note, writing in a surprisingly personal tone for someone normally reserved. Maria's telegram had apparently been accepted at face value.

His quandary now, he said, when we met up in Catania was what to do with the B and B. His girlfriend had recently broken off their engagement. He was bereft. He couldn't stop thinking about her and his loss. The loss of his mother. The loss of his fiancée.

'I don't know where I am', he said.

The melancholy in his eyes gave him the look of a religious icon.

'Why did your fiancée break off the engagement?'

I wouldn't normally have been so inquisitive, but with the new-found intimacy forced on me by Maria's telegram, I could see no impropriety. Is the situation irremediable? Has she met another man? Or is it a problem you know how to resolve?'

She did not want to live in Catania and his flat in Milan was very tiny. He was thinking of selling that flat and the B and B and buying a place in Milan where they could live together. At this moment he had not quite made up his mind. But I knew he had. His mind was solidly made up.

Minta and Melan were quite capable of managing the B and B. They were both honest and hardworking and with a little extra salary, would have been overjoyed to do it. Clients loved them. They were efficient and great fun. Unfortunately, the law said that the owner of a B and B had to live on the premises. Sergio could not live in Milan and have the B and B managed on his behalf. The law allegedly was intended to prevent crime but more likely represented vigorous lobbying from the hotel movement who were finding B and Bs increasingly tough competition.

As mere real estate in the heart of Catania, two floors and an attic should have fetched an impressive price: demand was assured, and there were scores of people in Catania well able to pay. I knew Sergio was aching to shed the property, to leave Catania quickly, forever, and complete his metamorphosis to a Milanese. So he sold it for a song, the quicker to go. His mother's friends were shocked. Horrified. Even Rita and Grzegorz.

'We'd get more than that for our apartment,' Grzegorz said, 'and it's much smaller than the B and B.'

'Then you should have sold your flat and bought it,' I said, 'Rita would be fabulous in a B and B. You too.'

They considered it for a moment and Rita said thoughtfully: 'Perhaps when I'm retired.'

'You'd have such fun, Rita,' I assured her. 'Handpicking your guests like Silvana to keep you amused. You would reign over a court.'

Once the deal was completed, and despite Sergio's urgency it couldn't be done overnight, given the convolutions of Italian law, the B and B was scheduled to close down for six months, the time it would take for the purchaser to get their licence without which they couldn't move in.

Minta and Melan would have to look for other jobs. They could not assume that the new owner mightn't be bringing their own staff with them from elsewhere.

Minta, when I saw her last had black rings under her eyes. Melan looked moody. He had booked a plane to Sri Lanka to see his family and when he returned had plans to go to Pisa.

What a shame. The whole sequence of events.

When I returned to Catania the next year, I went straightaway to see what had happened to Just Like Home. Plasterers were working in the empty rooms. They had no idea that the place had been a B and B, and knew nothing about its future.

I'd lived in the *pensione* for only two months and felt a deep sense of loss that a vibrant little world had passed away forever.

22

One day Rita suggested I go buy us tickets for something at Teatro Massimo Bellini. The theatre, in a seedy part of Catania was looking more roughed up than usual, sprayed in thick dust by workers jackhammering the entire piazza.

'What's on?' I asked a male in the box office, eyeing his white overalls and the specks of plaster caught in his eyebrows.

'Omelette,' he said promptly.

Covering both ears, I fixed my eyes on his lip movements. 'Again, please.'

With an airy flip of the fingers. 'Omelette. By Shakespeare. You are not English?'

It took a few seconds to register.

'You mean *Hamlet*?'

'Yes,' he said, beaming. '*Omelette*'.

Never having seen that play staged by Italians, I bought two tickets for the gallery but was frustrated to learn that programs would be available at the box office only on the night of the performance. Night regardless, when we arrived the following week we both blinked to see half of Catania's schoolgirls, mothers and teachers filling the seats.

More surprises were in store. First, a bunch of women in tutus appeared on stage. This was not a play by Shakespeare but a ballet by Diaghilev. Even on a good day I wouldn't cross the street to see a ballet. I can't stand the thought of the anorexia, the drugs and the mutilated feet, or that there will never be a black swan in *Swan Lake*.

Omelette himself was very short, and surprisingly well padded for a male. With a wide pelvis. Unusual in a younger man, though he didn't exactly generate youthful vitality, seeming to do a lot of plain old walking rather than scheduled ballet movements.

Where had the story gone? The dancing was sluggish and heavy. Not one dancer went up on points. They seemed to have trouble hiking themselves aloft, manifesting lumbering strength rather than grace. Then my eyes lit on the powerful throats and the big Adam's apples. Blokes, every one.

By the interval, I had it worked out. All the dancers were men, in drag or out of it. Ophelia was so hefty she could have panned Omelette with an egg slice. He, I was willing to bet, was a woman. Pregnant at that. Slow and cumbersome, but fragile with it, because whenever she landed in the arms of a male dancer, two others rushed up to help move her.

At the interval I asked the ushers – are they all men in this performance? Yes. Except Hamlet. She was Carla Fracci.

'Is she pregnant?' I asked. They fell back in horror.

'No, no, she is seventy-four. She is Italy's Fonteyn.'

'Fonteyn's dead,' I said, absently.

Rita didn't share my indignation in the slightest. What did she care about Hamlet? Instead, she adored la Fracci and was thrilled to wait in a freezing alley to get her autograph. When I finally managed to borrow a program from a schoolgirl I learned that the whole menagerie had been assembled and directed by Carla Fracci's husband. The males were a small group from Rome, their energies, I suspected, normally going into fancy dress.

My scenario was this: la Fracci and her husband were an aging couple, probably a bit short of money since artists often end up in poor circumstances, Fonteyn herself a prime example. Going on tour was a way of recouping some income. The male dancers would have come cheap. Maybe the cost of an outing to Sicily. Young ballerinas would be excluded not to dim further a crippled diva's faded lustre, or simply because they were beyond the budget.

But what a transformation when la Fracci finally appeared in the alley! Every inch the famous ballerina, petite, her dainty head turbaned, wrapped in a long faux leopard mantella, she greeted her Catanese fans with serene composure.

Rita was right up front, thrusting a notepad and pen into the dancer's black-gloved hand while one of the ballet teachers had deftly handed Fracci a bundle of programs on a clipboard to flip through, signing quickly.

Among the stage door johnnies I spied two of the three military men from Palermo that had booked into my B and B the night before. They were obviously gay, and waiting to pick up a chorus boy. In fact, I saw one marching off with a member of the cast, a tall macho-looking fellow still in his long blond curls, sad eyes peering out from under furred eyelashes and big male feet jammed into high heeled pointy shoes.

In the car, on the way home, Rita, euphoric after a night out, said, wittily, 'Well it's been all Fracci and *froci* [queers] tonight.'

And there was always the theatre itself to rejoice in, she comforted, patting me. Late baroque. The opulence of the foyer had almost made me swoon; an extravaganza of scenes from Bellini's operas splashed across the ceilings, intensifying the sensuality of the ornate stuccoed walls, rose pink marble columns, vast expanses of gold-framed mirrors, marble floors and enormous glass chandeliers, potentially lethal, I decided, if they should come down on heads in an earthquake.

The acoustics were unsurpassable, Rita assured me. Callas sang *Norma* in Catania and Gigli preferred to sing at the Bellini more than in any other theatre of the world.

'Hah!' I snorted my derision. 'Is this another dodgy Sicilian myth you're giving me? Can you prove he said that? Or that he meant it when he said it?'

After nearly a year in a region where counterfeit notes turn up in the wallet and truth is traditionally 'revealed' or masked, for me, evidence is a must.

23

Mildly curious to find out what was at the top of Catania's dauntingly steep Via Antonino Giuliano, I one day climbed its far too many steps, saw to my right a rough-hewn archway and strode through it, totally unaware that I had just entered a great Benedictine monastery, once the second biggest in Europe.

Until I visited Sicily I had never been in cooee of a monastery. I had no idea that it was often a great manorial estate with a vast assortment of buildings, and I entered the former Benedictine property thinking I was simply in another part of town.

The Scottish scientist and traveller, Patrick Brydone was similarly puzzled when in 1770 he encountered the stupendous staircase that rose out of the monastery's entry court and thought he must be in a king's palace. Such a huge piece of real estate in the heart of Catania was exactly the kind of status symbol roundly denounced by Peter Abelard and other eleventh-century critics when the 'reformed' Benedictines first arrived in Catania from Calabria.

These Benedictines were seeking to return to the solitariness of the monk and to isolation from worldly distractions. They shortly quit the relative comfort of lodging next to the city Cathedral and relocated on a high, bleak and isolated part of Mount Etna. The rigours of the site and its isolation were meant to repel unwelcome visitors with their idle chatter and to keep the monks on the strait and narrow. Said quickly it's easy to undervalue the hundreds of years during which the monks endured severe winters on the volcano so that their aged began to complain and ask to be lodged in a milder region of the mountain. Entire generations of them would have been functioning in the reformist mode.

Although Benedictines met the requirements of their Rule in the way of each independent monastery, all had two obligations they could be publicly measured by: extending hospitality to strangers or guests, and reproducing a page of print a day – by hand, with illuminated rubrics. The Catania 'state' library of 24,000 volumes includes 132 incunabula produced by the monks, a truly monumental labour. Reportedly, one long manuscript could require an entire life. I saw one with extremely large print, designed to serve choristers who had to be able to read together from a single copy on the lectern. Benedictine choirs, incidentally, are famous and today they have the reputation of organising the world's best concerts of sacred music.

But factors beyond their control were at work making it almost impossible for them to keep the world from camping on their doorstep. The evangelical Normans having given a third of Sicilian landholdings to the Church of Rome, also decreed that every village must be in the jurisdiction of a monastery. This necessarily involved monasteries in local activities, and since the Emperor Constantine in 321 had made it legal for the Church to be a beneficiary of a will, including property left to a saint (!!!) there could be no stopping the rise and rise of the Church to temporal power and eminence as the largest landholder in Italy.

Moreover, in a society where any kind of labour other than war was thought despicable, and the Church had funnelled all administrative offices into itself, there was no other option for the aristocracy but to focus on assisting the churches so as to provide opportunities for their sons and daughters to engage in some kind of professional activity. Keep in mind that many monks and nuns were lay persons, not ordained priests.

Thus a local Catania count donated to the new Benedictines the Church of Saint Leone high up on Etna. In 1150, the count's son, more liberal even than his father, gave them the Church of Saint Nicholas l'Arena, some distance below the other church, in a more agreeable climatic zone and embracing a large expanse of vineyards and other agricultural land. Two more lots of land very soon afterwards came from the same family, one from the wife, and another from the son.

Named the Benedictine Monastery of St Nicholas l'Arena, the second monastery in Catania gave rise to a small town to its south-west, called Nicolosi, (still extant) a town shaken by earthquakes and covered by ash time and again but invariably rebuilt around a large common cistern that once dominated an open area.

These gifts from the landowners were expected to gain benefices for their children. Even Heloise, Abelard's famous wife, sought a prebend for her son Astrolabe, from the Abbot of Cluny who wrote her he would try to 'find something.'

The Benedictines were particularly attractive to the aristocracy because their competence and skill added huge value to their lands, which in turn generated new villages and towns within their jurisdiction. Benedictine abbots became prominent among members of the black aristocracy, those princes whose rank originates in the Papacy and not the Crown. Many abbots became Princes of the Church, much to the delight of the nobles who shared in their burgeoning wealth and rejoiced to have their sons and daughters under their tutelage. As for the nobles, reduced like Lampedusa's prince in *The Leopard*, to hunting, visiting brothels and travelling between their far flung estates, if they were at all bright and active what could they do but join the Catania monastery? Abelard's own parents in later life entered separate monasteries.

The large scale of the monks' agriculture and animal husbandry, their storage of snow for the flourishing ice-cream market and their other, more professional, 'scientific' and artistic achievements are often written about in lyrical terms. Missing from the story of their conspicuous wealth, however, is the means whereby they bound to themselves a large, cheap labour force.

A desire for security in the feudal age and dependence on big landowners like the Benedictines persuaded small landowners and labourers to become serfs as an expression of humility before God, the monks enthusing them by citing their own humility and the spartan lifestyle congregations were pursuing in the reform period. But as Marx pointed out, nothing generates wealth so effectively as gaining the surplus value of other people's labour.

Serfs had certain rights like the use of common lands and the retention of gleanings after the harvest. But flight, especially after plagues when the price of labour might otherwise soar, attracted severe penalties like torture or even death. So too did disobeying the lord of the manor, (the offence of contumacy) equivalent to disobeying the Lord in heaven. This is the origin of the strange Sicilian custom where labourers have until very recently greeted the local baron with 'bless me, Lord.'

If the locals, serf and non-serf, working for the monastery were notoriously poorly rewarded for their labour, the monks reproached complainants by pointing out how they had been trained in modern agricultural methods, how to make the grain more fertile, develop apiaries and artificially inseminate fish. Besides, earning their salvation in the other world, not their bread in this world, was to be every Christian's primary objective.

But the serfs, paid in kind not money, a practice that discourages price rises, and being unable to move away and exchange their new skills for higher wages, the monks retained the entire added value from increased productivity. And in reminding the peasants of the primacy of earning salvation, they were ignoring their own palatial lifestyle.

In 1578, earthquakes having turned various of their habitats to rubble, the Catanese Benedictines took possession of further new buildings. By the start of the next century they were ready to raise yet another church, initially deciding its columns should be of limestone, but ultimately seduced by richly ornamented marble. So much for asceticism.

On account of its size and immense holdings, this version of Catania's Benedictine monastery eventually became the second biggest in Europe after the Portuguese Palace, Abbey of Mafra. It has to be conceded, however, that social values had changed considerably since the high middle ages. Then cities were in a state of confusion and the Benedictines wanted to reform themselves. But in the sixteenth century, post-

Renaissance, competition for wealth, power and status among nations and institutions was intense and mounting with every decade. And the Benedictines sought to be admired by all.

In 1669 a tsunami of hot lava surged right over the top of the city walls and into the city, burying the monastery walls in the north and southern parts of the complex. Only a Job's comforter would attribute such catastrophes of the seventeenth century to the monks' failure to please God. Within a mere two decades, the monastery was resurrected. Damaged walls were restored and strengthened. Since the old church had been shattered, an architect was brought from Rome to design a new church attached to the monastery. Everything was well advanced by 1693. Think of the funds that had had to be raised! But in that year a great earthquake struck all Sicily, worst in Catania where thirty-two monks in the act of performing a requiem mass in the old church were buried under its ruins. Surely God must be punishing the wicked? The Greeks aver that justice and suffering simply have no connection. That's the nature of tragedy, according to them. I think so, too.

Eventually a new establishment was raised far from the bleak and isolated spot where the few Calabrian Benedictines had first settled on Mount Etna. The monks were well and truly back *in* the world, dominating the city, right on the highest part of Catania, overseeing cloisters, dormitories, refectories, a museum, a library in what was called "Arab-modern" style and with the first stone laid of an even grander church than the previous one. Abelard would have fulminated against such grandiloquence.

For the next two centuries, these members of the 'black aristocracy' enjoyed their glorious palace, its prestige and power, before the new national government gave them their marching orders, handing the monastery over to the Comune during a period of intense anti-clericalism. Undoubtedly most of the labour and the resources that had gone into the complex had in any case come almost freely from the community.

While still in its massive entirety, the expropriated monastery was initially occupied by the military and scholastics. Then for a long period it was subdivided, with cell walls knocked down and classrooms, offices and workshops set up everywhere, even in the corridors and in the cloisters. During the Second World War thousands of people sheltered from the bombing in the cellars. In the post-War period the complex was starting to disintegrate.

Now it has been resurrected by the University of Catania, Sicily's first and largest university, founded in 1445, its current student population around 60,000. The Faculty of Literature and Philosophy took possession of it in 1977 after persuading the Comune that the growing number of campuses scattered about the city and elsewhere was stretching the University's resources, students and staff having to move about from one place to another, and that gaining possession of the monastery would allow more departments to be brought together right in the centre of town. This seems to have had an impact on night life in Catania because every night, between ten p.m. and three a.m., the streets are crowded with students and staff, dining out, walking and talking, and scooting about on their *motorini*.

A staff member invited Rita and me to enter his office, a former cell, in order to show us two very narrow staircases, no wider than a ladder and steeply raked, one on the left and the other on the right of a wall, that led up to a mezzanine nook, the sleeping quarters of the monk's servant, probably the very smallest occupied space in the entire monastery. But the cells themselves were actually very spacious, while the public rooms, like the refectory, the library and the museum were on a grand scale, oval in shape with domed frescoed ceilings, and filled with light – except for the library – from the many windows.

The University's new library has been installed in an enclosed area marked out from the old cellars of the convent. How wonderful are these underground caverns that have been wrested from the lava. Since the space available is no less than that above ground, they're enormous, with ample rugged pillars left standing to support barrelled arches. Some of the supporting columns are thought to have survived from the Greek period and to have come from other parts of the monastery. The library seems to be soundproofed, a naturally occurring condition, I imagine, and one observes a high level of security consciousness against illicit entry and theft.

To my surprise, sections of the long and wide convent corridors had been cordoned off as computer areas, where we saw students quietly engaged in writing or research. "Cordoned off" shouldn't indicate anything temporary or makeshift in the design, whose understated beauty brought whispers of delight from Rita and me. The students were on a level below us when we first saw them and scrutinising their environment we could see how the lighting in these study sections had primacy in the design, almost as on the stage, together with a spartan economy of line in the furnishings and in the circular staircase that linked the levels above and below. Space, airiness and, one might say, a monastic silence, was the dominant impression.

It's often a defence of great wealth that it bequeaths wonderful objects to posterity, offering challenges to artists and artisans in realising the grandiose dreams of kings, popes and nobility, creating drama in the lives of the ordinary people. However, it takes little imagination to consider also that well designed public schools for every parish, hospitals, public libraries, community buildings, beautiful spaces with public parks and gardens, houses that are light and airy, with sanitation, fuel and a division between sleeping and eating quarters and with separate realms for the animals, might just as readily attract the wonder and admiration of posterity which would be impressed by what must have been clearly enlightened government. Certainly, where circumstances allow it, artists have never turned their backs on such subjects.

When I see those tiny little hovels from the past that some of Italy's poor still occupy, where one can't stand up inside, where there is no window, only a door, shut in winter, with smoke from the fire suffocating the inhabitants, and I imagine the animals sleeping inside with the humans, then I think of the splendour of projects like Catania's Benedictine monastery, set up to house a few score monks along with ancillaries to serve them, and I really wonder how it is possible to deceive oneself into thinking that such a discrepancy between the haves and the have-nots reflects the values of Jesus Christ.

24

Detesting anything that glorifies war, I left until the day I was departing Catania a visit to *The Museum of the Allied Landing in Sicily, 1943,* one of the permanent exhibits at Le Ciminiere, The Chimneys, a huge cultural complex fashioned out of Catania's ancient sulphur refineries.

A scatter of squat refinery buildings looking a bit like hotels in a Monopoly game, the complex is well supplied with the eponymous chimneys, varied in height but far too low in public health terms, the area rimmed round by metal galleries and pipes, dotted with trees and shrubs, and at the rear, separating the centre from the sea, a long and intricate spray of railway tracks merging into one another with all the energy and drama of art. But perish the thought of a busker or a juggler working the crowds the way they do out front of the Pompidou Centre in Paris. It's monastic quiet at the Chimneys of Catania.

US engineers cooperated with the Regional Parliament to build the Allied invasion museum. A bemusing concept. Why would a belligerent that invaded Sicily and bombed it to bits want to build a war museum showing that destruction? To remind Italians of what might happen to them should they follow another dictator into war? Why, Italians already know more about that than most other people on the planet. They've been ruled by many dictators, invariably live under authoritarian regimes and, unlike the British and Americans, have been invaded more times than they can count. Why would Italians themselves want a permanent reminder on their land of defeat by an enemy?

Could it be that the Allied Landing Museum was sponsored by the mafia, who, along with Lucky Luciano were prominent beneficiaries of the invasion, more precisely, of the American landing in western Sicily? Or, gratitude not yet on the public record as a mafia virtue, perhaps it was just the usual story of a privileged few on all sides having seen an opportunity to make money?

American bases in Sicily have been a constant since the War. It has been argued that they add little to the economy, all their goods and services coming from the US, and that heavy drug use among personnel has drawn the mafia into towns hitherto mafia-free, the two developments heavily impacting on unemployed youth.

NAS Sigonella, a major US complex, is only eleven kilometres from Catania. Though theoretically a 'tenant' of the Italian military, Americans speak of it as 'landlord' to more than forty other US units in the area. Protests directed at the base were made against the US intervention in Iraq. Perhaps the Museum is a useful reminder of US power to restive dissidents.

The project's official justification is the usual gobbledygook: the Museum was set up to give people 'a deep awareness of a historical event – the Battle of Sicily – which started the new democratic course of our country.' (Which democratic course was that?) It was promoted by the province of Catania, and put up thanks to the enthusiastic collaboration of people fond of this subject.

That's about as much clarity as you will get in Sicily for the provenance of any project and it generates more questions than answers.

The Museum, open since 2001, has apparently proven popular with visitors to Le Ciminiere. 'Finally we can say it achieved its aims, which were to deliver a peace message to young generations and to underline the importance of civil and democratic values. We can learn peace from war events.'

This twaddle, it may be noted, was composed nearly six decades after the Allied invasion, at the end of a period commonly viewed as one of the most tumultuous in the history of modern Italy, when terrorist bomb attacks for several years destabilised the whole nation, bringing it to the brink of civil war.

As a prelude to a severely abridged tour, lunchtime being only an hour away, the Museum guide led me into a little cinema and I watched a short documentary on Italy in the War. Sicily was the worst hit region, being pulverised for thirty-eight days. The authorities urged people to flee to the country where they hid in caves and grottos as they had done centuries before, in flight from invaders. Catanese crowded into lava caves and the Benedictine Monastery cellars, even tucking themselves into the recesses of the Roman amphitheatre in the city centre, itself a ruin but usefully deep, dank and dark.

The eastern part of Sicily was bombed to bits, Messina twice: poor Messina, because, although thousands of people had been injured or killed during the first onslaught, the earthquake-strengthened buildings were left standing and the Americans mistakenly thought they had missed their target. They tried again. Messina suffered fifty-eight bombing raids and Catania eighty-seven. Nor did western Sicily escape unscathed, even after the mafia/US deal. Agrigento and its port were bombed thirty-eight times, Sciacca ten, Trapani forty-one and Marsala sixteen.

Looking at the wrinkled faces of Sicilian farmers in their fields seemingly indifferent to the mountains of rubble transforming their landscape, still going about their labours, stoic like oxen, taking whatever comes because they don't know what is coming or from where or why, it would be easy to think peasants are a special breed, it is their nature to be like that. But now I know the stereotypical peasant is an artificial construction, shaped by others to fulfil a serving role against their will and their natural inclinations.

In the propaganda that states routinely produce during war Roosevelt and Churchill were introduced to Sicilians as 'the cat and the fox' in *Pinocchio*, very different from the waxed figures I saw in Madame Tussaud's, both leaders posed in homely environments, looking strong and decisive but also benign. The two greatest dangers facing Italy, according to its own propaganda units, were damage to its masterpieces and rape by black American soldiers. After the War, so I recollect from the Italian film, *Two Women*, the black villains were reconfigured as Moors from North Africa.

Among the introductory exhibits at the Museum was a reconstruction of a typical Sicilian piazza of the time with stables, a tailor's shop, a grocery store and, of course, the church. Compellingly real. What I did not realise was that this piazza was only the entrance to a replication of an entire small town with streets and houses whose interiors conveyed how the inhabitants lived. And at the end of the tour, the town was shown after being bombed.

However, the guide bypassed the rest of the town, crossed the piazza and led me into a small dark windowless room where she directed me to sit on a bench.

'This is a real air raid shelter,' she said. 'You will get a surprise. Don't be frightened.'

Left alone in what felt like a thick padded darkness, I waited, curious to learn what might happen, and a few seconds later the whole room started lurching, forward and back and sideways, so that I was thrown about, not too ruggedly, but disorienting me a little, with sirens screaming, people shrieking and the sound of bombs falling. Cleverly scary simulation.

Other exhibits were equally impressive. For a second or so when I came across an Italian soldier in a bunker firing at the enemy through a slot in the wall while his comrade was handling munitions I thought they were real. They were lifesize and actually moving in a thoroughly realistic way.

Little boys on a school excursion were hypnotised by the war materiel. I saw one about nine years old, tenderly caressing a great torpedo that filled an entire room and murmuring '*che bello, che bello.*'

At the very end of the tour, we came back upon the piazza we had entered at the beginning, and saw that it had been smashed to bits. Nothing but wood and debris scattered over the ground. I would have been curious to see the little boy's reaction to this outcome of war, but neither he nor any of his fellows was anywhere on the horizon.

I think I missed out on far more than I saw in the Museum, but what I did see, made me despair. There's just no way to make war dull. That's the problem. People who think war memorials engender peace are romancing. War makes many ordinary people feel more intensely alive than they have ever felt before or will feel again. Australian soldiers' diaries I have reviewed in the past show that some acknowledge dreading a return to the boring routines of peace. Catania's museum of the military landing was created, according to the Regional President, "Thanks to the enthusiastic collaboration of people *fond of this subject*." Enough said.

Syracuse

It doesn't do to arrive in Syracuse by coach with the head full of things Hellenic only to have the eyes alight on a foreshore dominated by the Esso Oil refinery and its candy-striped chimneys lined up like sticks of Edinburgh rock. Every trip I counted them, always arriving at a different total, though never fewer than thirty-two. I also cogitated on the origins, ownership and function of this refinery, later meeting one of its Sicilian engineers who dressed like an American and spoke excellent English with an American accent.

He had set up the first branch of Amnesty International in Palermo and I met him in a Syracusan apartment where he was helping locals to establish a branch in their city. I agreed to hand out brochures for his little group late one moonlit night in the Piazza del Duomo, recollecting that not very far away the Ulysses Irish pub had been twice burned down by the mafia because its owner refused to pay the pizzo. *But I suppose there's nothing to stop two dysfunctional societies from trying to help one another.*

Nonetheless I loved Syracuse. At least, Ortygia, the islet the Greeks named for its 'quail' shape and that hosts the old city with all the most important ancient monuments. The island is connected to the mainland, to New Syracuse, by bridges. It was weeks before I crossed a bridge to visit the archaeological park with the Greek theatre and the Roman amphitheatre. From a distance and from riding through it in a taxi or on a bus, I didn't like the new town. Too modern, lots of family-sized light industry.

But I could gush for hours over the old city's Cathedral Square, perhaps because B and B Oikos where I stayed happily for six weeks is at the back of it, on the side opposite the church itself and I spent a lot of time there and close by. It's an enchanting, immensely hospitable public space, huge but not dwarfing. Not really a square at all, being very wide in proportion to its depth, shaped like a trapezium with the top and bottom sides curving in towards each other. Some major streets feed into it from both sides and its huge area allows it to accommodate the Council Chambers and the Cathedral as well as a contemporary art gallery that is pretty impoverished, content wise.

All this space is domesticated, giving rise to natural precincts. Children and their dads often kick a ball about: Couples can take a passeggiata *or pass through on a bike ride, organizations have pitches where they promote themselves through their stands and a brass band regularly delivers a concert. There's an open air café serving scores or more of tourists and locals – and everything can go on at the same time if necessary.*

'Oikos' the name of my B and B means 'sacred residence', the Greek definition of a temple. And the Greek heritage is never far from the minds of contemporary Syracusans.

25

I had the most elegant, comforting room at B and B Oikos in Via delle Carceri Vecchie, the Street of the Old Prisons behind the far side of Cathedral Square. To judge by the street-level grids at the base of buildings now largely converted to government offices, the prisons might have been more like dungeons.

Maria, the B and B owner, gave me the room at a cheap price because it overlooked the street which is properly a lane and was the only room in the *pensione* without its own bathroom. But an external bathroom (mine alone) was only two steps away. Other rooms had wonderful sea views, still and spare like an Edward Hopper painting or that famous early one of Salvador Dalí, *Figure at a Window*. I was delighted, however, to be able to watch from my balcony everyone going down the lane and eavesdrop on their conversations.

Not that I needed to eavesdrop. The acoustics were amazing. One night about three a.m. I became fed up with the laughter and chat of some young people in the lane, and crept out onto the balcony to glare at them. They were about fifty metres away and their voices rose very clearly to my ears. On impulse I picked up a ripe banana from my fruit bowl and broke it into three pieces, one of which I threw towards them. It landed with a soggy little 'plop', louder than I could have imagined. They paused for a second and then resumed their conversation. I threw another piece and quickly retreated behind a shutter. This time they stopped talking and glanced about them. The third time they saw the tiny missile coming and bent over to examine it, then broke into laughter before running off down the lane.

I loved that B and B at Syracuse, where Maria served fruits and other products from her own orchard and farm at breakfast, gave me free access to a little room where I could enjoy broadband Internet undisturbed, wrote a proper condolences letter for me and introduced me to a brilliant professor of English at Naples University, an open-hearted woman who insisted I visit her holiday flat in Capri and, the following year, spend a week at her luxurious apartment in Naples.

On the eve of my departure from the B and B, when the low sum on the bill drew a puzzled enquiry from me, Maria swore she had mistakenly quoted me a price that had been too high. She had obviously confused my booking with someone else's, she said. The old story, I thought. Sicilians love giving you unexpected discounts.

In that lane I bought a beautiful long kaftan of heavy silk and linen from two sisters who had a workshop next to a cabinetmaker. One designed garments and furnishings, the other cut and sewed them, many of the seams by hand, and passed them back to the designer for painting. The kaftan was closely fitted on the inside while the outside swished. Not a tent at all and very comfortable.

The sisters belonged to a craft guild in Syracuse, a kind of cooperative where members helped each other with ideas and marketing. Their shop was a treasure trove vibrant with colour and textures.

Ortygia is the place where I started looking seriously in real estate windows at houses and apartments for sale. It's a lovely city with winding narrow streets, unusual shops and modestly priced eateries that produce simple but sophisticated meals. If it hadn't been for the post office criminals and the torching of the Ulysses Irish pub I might have forgotten all about the mafia.

26

Within a day of my arrival in Syracuse I walked into a government office that had some contact with foreigners and approached a clerk, saying I hadn't come for official assistance but that I was writing a book on Sicily and if she thought she might have something interesting to contribute I'd be happy to offer her lunch so that we could discuss it.

She looked at me impassively for a moment and then asked if I were German. By this time I had learned that for Sicilians all Germans are wealthy, all foreigners indeed are wealthy. Therefore all foreigners are German. Widespread errors of logic are to be expected in a society where rationality is renounced for revelation.

Her face brightened when I said I was from Australia. I knew what was coming.

"They say Australia has lots of jobs."

'Many more than here, certainly. Our governments want people to have jobs. We do not have a fixed twenty-five per cent unemployment rate. There would probably be a revolution if that happened.'

She could not meet me for lunch. Her mother-in-law expected her for a meal on the three mornings that she worked. She job-shared with another woman who put in three afternoons. The office closed on Sundays. She could meet me in a bar for a coffee on a morning that she did not work. That settled, we chatted for five or ten minutes more. It was no surprise to find her a university graduate who had studied economics and English, hoping to become a journalist. But graduation now several years behind her, this meagrely paid lowly work she currently performed was all she could find. Her husband, also a graduate, was similarly under-employed.

Somehow we got talking about Foucault. His name was unknown to her but she reacted keenly to his ideas of power and knowledge and the internalizing of social control that was explored in Jeremy Bentham's Panopticon. We were to meet in three days time. I told her I'd look for a copy of *Discipline and Punish*, or the *Birth of the Clinic* in one of the bookshops. A futile search. The Church closed the Index of banned books in the 1960s but its censorship strategy is simply being modernised, initially by ensuring the bookshops do not stock dangerous content and currently by establishing a controlling presence in the publishing industry, already the biggest publisher in Germany.

One bookshop I entered in Ortygia, near Piazza Archimede had metres of fusty old books in plain identical wrappers, obviously never touched. When I enquired of the bookseller why the shelves were full of these books and asked if there were any demand for them he shrugged apologetically, assuring me that he had nothing to do with the selection. 'That's what they send me.'

In the end I bought the woman an anthology of English poetry.

To my embarrassment, she turned up clutching a book that must have cost her more than she could afford and would have been precious to her. Conceived and executed by a well known French journalist, Marcelle Padovani, who writes for the French press on Italian subjects, especially Sicily and the mafia in Sicily, it is based on twenty interviews the French woman conducted with one of the two Palermo maxi-trial judges, Giovanni Falcone, between March and June 1991, little more than a year before the judges were car-bombed.

Along with the book, the clerk had brought me a cellphone number and a name: Bruno Piazzese. She urged me to speak to him. He had defied the mafia and they had burned down his disco. Now he was fighting them. I tried to explain to her that I find anything associated with criminals intensely boring. But, to please her and perhaps because I was underestimating the significance of Piazzese's resistance, for three days I tried to reach him, leaving a message and asking him to ring me. On the third day, my cellphone rang, and when I answered, a rough voice said in quite an ugly tone: 'Are you a beautiful virgin?' then hung up, cackling.

I visited the clerk again and asked her if she would like to get on to Piazzese herself and suggest he might ring me. Finally he did. He nominated nine thirty p.m. that night at a bar near Ortygia's main esplanade. I arrived fifteen minutes early and found the piazza almost deserted and I the only one sitting at an outside table. The lighting there was dim and half the bar lay in darkness, though I saw waiters moving about inside. Nobody came to take my order. They were obviously closing down. Come half past nine, nobody had shown up. I kept scanning the piazza, hoping to spot a man heading in my direction. At nine forty-five p.m. when I was about to rise and leave, a black car with opaque windows drew up near the bar. Three men got out and began walking towards me. I remembered the rough tones of the voice on the phone and felt my chest go tight.

Then one stepped out in front and strode towards me, hand outstretched and greeting me by name. 'I'm Bruno Piazzese.' And indicating the other two without making introductions, said, 'These are my escorts.'

One was tall and bulky, in an oddly shapeless, deforming kind of coat, very un-Italian style I thought, and the other smaller and slimmer. Piazzese's age was hard to tell. Mid-forties perhaps. He did not have a married look and from the way he talked throughout I doubted he was married but I didn't ask him any personal questions. He and I sat on a stone bench in a poorly lit section of the esplanade. The two escorts hovered about a metre away.

Not to waste time, I invited him: 'Tell me everything. I'm all ears.'

Some years ago he had left Syracuse to go and work in Venezuela, which, of course I would know was an oil rich country and he did in fact do well there. So after a period he decided to return to Syracuse and open a Ulysses Irish pub. Had he read Joyce, I wanted to know, but he laughed and shook his head saying that it was a marketing name. A friend had told him that the Ulysses Irish pub would draw the tourists like iron filings to a magnet.

I had in fact noticed the pub on one of my walks. It was a large structure in a prime position, prominent and close to the water. Piazzese said it offered a complex of services, bistro, bar, disco, restaurant and entertainment.

For the first two years everything went smoothly and the business prospered. Then one day he had a visitor. A stranger. He asked how things were going and Piazzese told him they were coming along nicely. The stranger then said: 'We want our bit.'

But had he not thought about that before he started the pub? I reminded him of the eight or nine Palermitani university graduates who, unable to find work, decided to combine what capital they could and open an Irish pub. One asked the others what they would do when the mafia knocked. Some days later astonished citizens woke to find themselves in a storm of flyers stuck on posts, windows, walls, in foyers and hallways, in parks and schools, in bus stations saying: 'A city where 97 per cent of businesses pay the pizzo is a city without dignity.' Needless to say the students were rounded up by police who suspected them of being terrorists.

'I had a bookshop before I went to Venezuela,' Piazzese told me. 'The mafia never came near me.' I didn't wonder. The cost-benefit would not have been positive.

Piazzese informed the stranger that he was not paying the *pizzo* which, incidentally, is the basis of a support fund mafia use to compensate the families whose breadwinners, generally lower ranking mafia, have gone to gaol for the good of the criminal cause. Without this policy, recruitment to the mafia would plummet. Piazzese said his clients were not the kind of people to smile on poker machines and that he had no plans to install them.

Within another few days, several poker machines arrived at the pub and were installed by the mafia. Piazzese immediately had them covered with black cloths. Nothing more happened for a while. Then one night about two a.m. when he returned to the pub to fetch something he had left behind he noticed a smell of petrol and immediately began to search for the source. It became clear that he had returned just before the mafia were about to torch the pub.

The police, amazingly, found the perpetrators and they were arrested. But the mafia are renowned for their patience and the pub was eventually torched. When the insurance money came through Piazzese had the pub rebuilt. That was the second version I had noticed on my walk. The justice department had agreed to set up a closed circuit camera in the pub and provide other security. However, it was later decided that the CCTV cost too much. What nonsense. The camera was withdrawn and security personnel deployed at night. Remember Pirandello and the value of appearance? The reality was that the CCTV was too effective.

I met up with Piazzese over a year later. The pub had been torched again. This time the justice department had asked him, so he told me, to become a symbol of anti-mafia resistance. The government would pay for the rebuilding of the pub and he must carry on administering it. But, he confessed, construction had halted because the contractors claimed payment had stopped. They were suing the government. 'Everything is expected to be resolved by September,' (six months away) he assured me cheerfully.

He has now had an escort for several years and is President of the Anti-mafia Association. Once I saw him on You-Tube delivering a public speech to a huge gathering of Turin students, assuring them that Italy was one country.

While near to completing this book, I twice contacted the clerk to ask if the Ulysses Irish pub has been completed or is destined to join the graveyard of so many other mafia-involved construction projects in Sicily. She was no longer employed because of the bad economic times, she explained. But she made no reply to my enquiry about the pub and Piazzese, not even though I pressed her a second time.

27

On the eve of my second visit to Syracuse, Saro Portale, hearing that I was returning there for a week, asked if I had visited the Jewish baths in the city. Observing my blank look he urged me to go and visit them.

'They are simply wonderful. They were buried under an old palazzo that a Syracuse widow was in the process of transforming into a hotel and were uncovered only fifteen years ago.'

A foreman working on the conversion had informed the owner he had found a door plastered over in a wall. Did she want the door to stay sealed? Thinking an additional hotel room might be in the offing, the woman instructed him to go ahead and see where the door led to: to the top of a set of steps partially buried in rubble, as it turned out.

In subsequent excavations five baths were unearthed eighteen metres below ground. A local archaeologist called to examine the site said he thought they were a Miqwe, (usually a plural noun) Jewish ritual cleansing baths, probably from the Byzantine era. To be certain, the woman sought confirmation by two rabbis, one from New York and another from Jerusalem. The two rabbis concurred in the archaeologist's opinion. They thought the Miqwe to be probably the oldest ritual baths in Europe, the best preserved and certainly the biggest, some other Miqwe having only one bath. They conjectured that the baths had very likely been covered up at the time of the expulsion of the Jews.

Back in Syracuse I could not find a single person who had heard of the baths or could direct me to them. Not even Maria, the owner of B and B Oikos and she was generally well informed about her city. I tried Google and found the address: Alla Giudecca srl, (limited liability company) Residence Hotel, Via Alagona 52, 96100, Siracusa.

It had earlier occurred to me that Jews might have lived in Syracuse at some stage because the major thoroughfare which gives access to the Puppet Theatre is called La Via della Giudecca, The Jewish Quarter, which also encompasses four adjoining lanes numbered one to four – two of the lanes attractively restored and the other two in great disrepair. *The Masses are Asses,* a Yiddish theatre production I had attended on first arriving in Catania had revealed that Jews lived in Sicily until 1493, a year after Isabella of Spain enforced the expulsion of non-Christians from all Spanish possessions.

I had been along Via Alagona before but not having any notion of a Miqwe thought it pretty nondescript. Searching unsuccessfully for a small hotel made the street seem much longer. I arrived at the sea without detecting the faintest trace of anything but ordinary housing, grumping to myself that I had never before had to peer about me for a hotel, that well behaved hotels tout for business, clamour for attention.

Slowly I retraced my steps, probing the walls with my eyes and ensuring I was examining both sides of the street. About a third of the way up, I noticed a woman emerge from her doorway and seat herself on a chair whose weathered condition suggested it had long been dedicated to street watching. I approached her and asked if she were local. Could she direct me to the Alla Giudecca Hotel in this street? She frowned, concentrating.

'But there is no hotel in this street.'

'This is Via Alagona?'

'Yes.'

Unfortunately I had not thought to record the street number of the hotel which I had imagined would stand out, what with all the pizzazz hotels exhibit today.

'But there is a hotel here built over ancient Jewish baths,' I said.

I was mistaken, she said.

I resumed walking and within two minutes had found the hotel. Running an eye over the entrance to the palazzo I forgave myself for having missed the place. The heavy wooden door, painted an inconspicuous dark green, bore no sign of its identity. What had caught my attention was a minuscule plaque attached to the wall beside the door, identifying the place as the Alla Giudecca Residence Hotel and the site of the Jewish ritual baths.

There was something grudging and unwelcoming about the way the door was barely ajar. I had to push it wider to step into the entry. Straight ahead I saw a meeting room of some kind, filled with neat rows of transparent plastic chairs, all facing a podium. On my left, by craning forward, I made out what seemed to be the reception area. Not a soul in sight. I edged a little further inside the entry and turned round to look more closely at the reception area.

At that moment, the door thrust open behind me and a man bounded up the few steps, pausing when he saw me. '*Buon giorno*,' he said, smiling, and without waiting for my reply entered the reception area, promptly disappearing like the white rabbit down a hole. Where had he gone? There was still nobody about. I sat cross-legged on the ground and waited. Eventually I heard the click click of high heels and a young woman with an Anglo appearance entered the reception area from the back.

She looked at me as if mystified by my presence.

'I'm hoping to find the Jewish ritual baths here.'

Po-faced and with a strong American accent, she said: 'Yes. They're here. But we take tours only on the hour.'

I glanced at my watch. Twenty minutes to six.

'Okay if I'll sit here and read my book until six o'clock?'

She nodded. 'The tour costs five euros and lasts about half an hour.'

Then she retreated to her desk in reception and went on with her work. At six sharp she was standing beside me again with her hand ready to receive the money. No one else was taking the tour.

'This way,' she said, heading towards the back of the building, where the man had disappeared. We walked past the transparent chairs through a door leading into a courtyard. Looking up, I saw at first floor level a surprising number of balconies, French windows opening out onto them. These were the hotel apartments, the guide told me. Twenty-three air-conditioned and furnished, renting for 110 euros a night. The man in a hurry must have been a tenant.

The baths were not exclusively for Jews, the guide informed me. Jews visiting them were mainly Orthodox. Noting that she kept referring to 'they' I asked her if she were Jewish.

'No, I'm a Christian. My parents live in Connecticut. There are no Jews in Syracuse.'

The words tolled like a bell. A tocsin. 'There are no Jews in Syracuse.' Did that mean there were Jews in other parts of Sicily? Or none in Sicily?

'None came back, then, after the expulsion?'

'It seems not,' the guide said, after a moment's thought, 'but I don't really know anything about that.' She was deliberately detached, wary and formal. Possibly a university student, a Connecticut Christian doing penance.

Then she led me to a hole in the ground and pointed eighteen metres down.

I leaned over and peered into scary depths, feeling my heart give a sudden lurch. 'Gosh. It's terribly deep. Like making a journey to the centre of the earth.'

'This hole is a well sunk by the Greeks,' she said. 'When the Jews saw it they would have realized they had found an excellent place to dig the baths.'

The five baths were in a large underground cave hewn out of the rock, the walls a gleaming dark blue, with a multi-vaulted roof, quite high overhead, each vault spread out like a mushroom, supported by massive pillars of rock left standing in the ground as part of the excavation. Three baths were laid out on the ground almost in a triangle, while each of the other two baths was some distance off, on opposite sides. These, the guide said, were likely to have been used by people who, for one reason or another, sought more privacy for their nakedness.

The baths, a metre and a half deep, bore no resemblance to baths as we know them, but were pools, one end roughly arched in the Moorish style, probably not as big as a modern bath and not intended to be used for a good scrub. They were for ritual cleansing after menstruation and parturition, or in the case of men, after ejaculation or before important ceremonies.

Women descended into them through a series of steps and, in the water, adopted the foetal position.

The guide switched on a light. I imagined the bathers and their assistants had used flaming brands.

Looking into the baths, mesmerised by their still, deep water, so cool and sweet, thinking of how fiercely hot it had been outside during the day, and relishing the uncommonly fresh air inside the cave, I felt suddenly peaceful and relaxed, imagining I could hear the low voices of the women murmuring as they prepared to enter the water and then their stillness, in the quietude of their communication with God. It was a domestic, intimate environment, very private and personal, unlike the traditional monuments I had encountered in Sicily till that time.

Temples and cathedrals were hugely public, highly competitive manifestations of wealth and power, of religion organized, collective and intimidating. Here in this underground cave, modesty and humility were the dominant motifs.

The guide had seemed to know very little, reproducing what I discovered later, were the contents of a short brochure. She had said nothing about the background to the excavation or the relationship between the hotel and the baths. Had the Jews bought out the widow and built the hotel themselves, or were they joint partners, and had the widow undertaken to care-take the baths?

I wondered if the widow were still alive. It would have been fascinating to hear her account of the discovery and what transpired afterwards.

While surfing the Net, trying to find something more about Syracuse and the Jewish baths, I came across an article by a Sicilian historian, Gaetano Cipolla, now based in the United States and who, writing in 1994, said that as a child in Sicily, growing up, he had never heard a word of Jews having ever lived in the region, or on Trinacria. He could see countless signs of other groups that had inhabited Sicily, the Phoenicians, Greeks, Romans, Arabs, Normans, Swabians, French, Aragonese, Spaniards and the Americans, the last foreigners to invade Sicily, but there was no synagogue or ghetto.

That suggests to me the street names I saw must have been put up in very recent times, a belated recognition of the Jewish presence. The restoration of houses in two of the lanes is probably also a recent event.

Cipolla thought that the Jews might have been erased from the landscape because they never conquered Sicily, nor did they raise monuments to themselves. But they were there for fourteen centuries living side by side with Christians and Arabs, in relative harmony, as teachers, merchants, doctors, farmers, textile workers, dyers and shoemakers, contributing to Sicily's economic and cultural life.

In fact, Israeli historians of the Diaspora have been digging into Arab accounts and books from the late Middle Ages unearthing documentation that suggests the Jewish presence in Sicily till the expulsion was active and varied but substantially tied to trade and subject to all kinds of vicissitudes related to the numerous wars in the Mediterranean.

Until 1992, however, when a week long convention was held in Trapani to discuss the historical importance of Jews in Sicily, they seemed to have been entirely wiped from the Sicilian consciousness. (No need to guess who monitored the process.) That was the year the baths were uncovered and two years before Cipolla wrote his article.

Mystified, as well he might be, Cipolla searched in the Sicilian archives, discovering vast deposits of information about the region's Jews: more than thirty thousand had been transported to Sicily after the sacking of Jerusalem in 73BCE. In Sicily the Romans sold the Jews as slaves, but over time they became free and enjoyed autonomy as a group.

Whatever anti-Semitism evidenced in Sicily, Cipolla said, was not personal. His generation had never seen a Jew and thought they were mythical figures. Anti-Semitism had to do with the biblical guilt of the Jews as the people who had failed to recognize the divinity of Jesus and had killed him.

'This is what we Catholics were taught through catechism, before the Church became more enlightened.'

Cipolla cites documents composed by high ranking Sicilians and dispatched to the Spanish Crown. They are couched in strong, even outraged terms, protesting that there was absolutely no cause to exile the region's Jews, none of whom engaged in usury or tried to proselytise, as the Crown alleged, and the Sicilians would receive no benefit whatever from the expulsion. On the contrary.

Cipolla says it was Sicily's ill luck so often to have its future determined far away, by persons unknown, to meet exigencies with no relevance to the region. My view is, however, that Sicily's wretched condition has nothing to do with luck, but rather to its domination by a Church hell-bent, if one might use the expression, on eliminating all opposition to its ideology. The Jewish expulsion took place 200 years after the Dominicans began their historic commitment to developing the art and technology of compelling the Church's 'subjects' to think with one mind and, although the expulsion of Spain's Jews and Muslims is always attributed to Isabella of Aragon, she was acting under the guidance of her confessor.

The details of the conditions imposed on the Jews who were to be exiled make for sad reading, being pervaded by rank injustice. After centuries as Sicilians, they departed with only their skills as capital, all their property and cash winkled out of them in one form or another. By various means some managed to prolong their stay in other parts of Italy's south until 1541, moving from one place to another, but after that, the south of Italy's religious cleansing was complete and despite calls from authorities in 1740 and 1747 for Jews to come back to Sicily, they have never done so. Calls? Were there offers of reparations?

According to Cipolla, all that remains of the Jewish presence in Sicily are the names they gave their synagogue communities in other parts of the world where they had had to sink new roots: Puglia, Calabria, Otranto, Ortygia and Messina, all cities in the Italian south.

28

Since the summer arrival in Rome of my old Wollongong friends, the Borghese, I had been trying to cajole them into coming further south to visit me in Syracuse. At first, Andrea would hear none of it. He eventually changed his mind, saying he had been intrigued by the two letters I had written them.

'They are much better than those other things you write,' he told me on the phone. 'They're light and funny. That's what I like to read, not those politicised things you usually go in for. I hope you will write a light book on Sicily.'

'I'd like to think Sicily has a light book in it,' I said, 'and that I will be the one to find it. Certainly I'll be out there in the dark, searching keen as Diogenes was to find an honest man.'

An added inducement for Andrea's visit was a desire to visit his cousin, Prince Camillo Borghese, whom he usually caught up with in Rome but who this year had decided to spend summer on the family estate in Sicily.

'So long as we can go to Catania and spend a bit of time with my cousin.'

When the Borghese arrived Andrea was carrying Ermete's ashes. In all the turmoil of finally securing my husband's mortuary passport right on the eve of my departure in January, I mislaid it, had to leave home without the ashes and then, too late, discovered the passport on the way to the airport. The ashes weighed seven kilos and were to be carried as hand luggage. Andrea had already overshot his hand luggage quota. I knew that without asking. He continually trotted backwards and forwards between Wollongong and Rome, carrying kilos more papers than a prime minister required for top-level talks, but he assured me, 'It's no problem at all to bring Ermete. I'm sure he'll feel more secure with me in any case. I'll certainly feel more secure on his behalf that he's in my hands and not yours. Of course the problem with you, Merovnia, is never your hands but your head.'

Our long friendship was of the kind you might expect to find between two Tasmanian devils. A lot of scratching and biting going on and periodically a band-aid or two required. It's not easy for a Roman aristocrat to make common cause with someone who grew up on the Red Clyde when the Attlee government was about to turn Britain into a welfare state, and it's just as difficult for anyone raised in a society where two industrial classes share the power, with all that implies, to accept that feudal values originating in the Middle Ages are in any way tolerable today.

But there we are – and there we were, Marisa, Andrea and I, climbing into a taxi in Catania, after a fun time on the ferry crossing from Naples where we had arranged to meet. Surprisingly, we had never shared a taxi before. Andrea rode in the front with the driver, Marisa and I in the back. Once on our way to the car hire agency, I swivelled around looking through every window, rejoicing in now familiar landmarks, happy to be back in Catania even if only long enough to pick up the car before we left for Syracuse.

Daydreaming, I paid little attention to the conversation going on in front, taxi drivers in my extensive Sydney experience being mostly obnoxious, resentful people, blistering with prejudice, rabid as medieval dogs and the minute they open their mouths best told to be quiet, that one doesn't want any discourses on ethnicity, multiculturalism, the gospel, or right-wing disc jockeys.

Andrea, however, was twisted sideways in his seat, giving the driver his full attention. 'Have you been driving long?'

That made me sit up. With Andrea, questions are never innocuous. Was the driver giving evidence of incompetence? Not that he knew of, it seemed. His face was wreathed in smiles. 'Over fifty years. I'm seventy-five.'

'*Complimenti*,' said Andrea. 'I imagine it takes that long to master Catania traffic.'

Drawing his head back slightly, the driver turned to give Andrea an appraising look, but answered serenely, 'There's always something new to learn.'

'Yes, indeed,' said Andrea. 'And what do you think of the new mayor? Is he doing a good job?'

The driver beeped his horn. 'Look at that woman. There's a sign there saying no entry into this street. They do what they like here. And get away with it. Well, the last mayor was actually pretty good, I have to say. Even if he was from the Left.'

He was talking about Enzo Bianco, one of those mayoral meteors that occasionally streak across the political firmament in the south, the man whose term of office was said to have ushered in a Renaissance for Catania: street clean-ups, flower plantings, improved services, dramatic events, something new every day, a feeling that everything was possible, an admirer had told me. And where is he now? I had wanted to know. Still alive?

In Rome, where else? Bianco had been made Minister for the Interior in the national government and even though this post ended with a change of government, the Opposition, for want of a better word, had kept him on as undersecretary of the department, a post that ensured his attitude and ideas still counted.

The new mayor was Berlusconi's man, Umberto Scapagnini, a pharmacology professor at the University of Catania. Aside from having demonstrated a reported penchant for Brazilian dancing girls, the mayor's performance was still open to serious appraisal.

The taxi driver had nothing more to say on the new mayor, maybe because Andrea had deftly switched the conversation to War memories. By the time we reached a bar near the car hire agency, the old man and Andrea were engrossed in the subject of Andrea's father, the famous naval commander, Valerio Borghese. Happy recollections lent a glow to the driver's face. Yes, he had fond memories of the 'Black Prince'. What an admirable man. A noble man. Such a wonderful commander. A person of integrity and moral courage. I listened, amazed, to this man's benignity. We should be importing Sicilian taxi drivers to Sydney.

Andrea was beaming. When the driver had exhausted his superlatives and exited from the taxi, intent on removing our suitcases from the boot, Andrea was with him in a minute, poised to make his dramatic announcement:

'Valerio Borghese was my father.' Then he reached for the driver's hand and clasped it. 'Andrea Scire Borghese.'

Shock, disbelief and delight passed fleetingly in turn across the driver's face. His eyes moistening, he reached into his suit pocket for a large handkerchief.

'I can't believe it. You're the son of the Black Prince. Valerio Borghese?'

Andrea was already riffling in his attaché case searching for I knew exactly what. He withdrew one of the stack of postcards he had had printed to celebrate the centenary of his father's birth, showing a head and shoulders silhouette of Valerio Borghese in his Commander of the Decima MAS uniform, and passed it to the driver.

'My father. A little memento.'

The taxi driver pressed it reverently to his lips.

These allusions to past glory had turned our taxi ride into a triumph. And after entering the bar which was large, spacious and offered a lip-smacking array of sweets, pastries and *panini* stuffed with *prosciutto crudo*, tomatoes and buffalo milk mozzarella, with excellent coffee to follow, not to mention an expansive, humorous barista, I knew Andrea was asking himself, can this wonderful place really be Sicily? Afterwards, at the car hire agency, owned by a Dublin-based company we'd found on the Internet, service proved impressively courteous and efficient. The car was not the one we had ordered, they apologised, they would have to give us a larger better model. Same price.

Andrea slipped into Catanese driving mode with the greatest of ease, appearing not to notice the difficulties that normally draw gasps of horror from outsiders, especially aging Sicilian emigrants on holiday, like the pair I had met on Etna. When we succeeding in entering the *autostrada* after only one wrong turn, Andrea exulted that 'this car is wonderful to handle' and went on to enumerate all its virtues. He was really enjoying himself. It was standard Sicilian weather, blue skies, sunny, hotting up as the day advanced but comfortable in the car because of the air-conditioning.

From time to time he and Marisa were drawn to the beauty of some especially lush cultivated landscape we were passing through on the way south to Syracuse. Andrea kept delighting in the high standard of farming everywhere evident.

'I am very happy to see that Sicilians take such good care of their land.'

'The fact is, Andrea, you've never had any positive expectations of Sicilians at all,' I said. 'I don't know why you judged them so harshly. One would imagine common sense must tell you the entire five million people can't all be mafia and that the bulk of the population must be doing normal things at least some of the time.'

On the other hand... I asked them if they would like me to read out a paper that a nurse had presented at the meeting of women activists I had stumbled on in Syracuse.

'Though it will confirm your worst fears, I have to say.'

It did, particularly when I mentioned that at the end of the nurse's address, a woman in the audience had risen to say that the privatisation of Sicily's health system had put it straight into the hands of the mafia, who, she claimed, were making all the job appointments in the health bureaucracy, including those of doctors. Some graduate doctors, she had said, known to be anti-mafia, would never gain a hospital appointment in Sicily. And those who succeeded in being appointed would have difficulty in retaining public confidence in their integrity if their success depended on their willingness to pay graft or return a favour.

The speaker had called for a return to the public health system.

I was surprised to hear Andrea heave a sigh. 'The bastards,' he said. 'We'd better not get sick while we're here, Marisa. If we do, we fly straight back to Sydney.'

In Syracuse, we met up with one of my new best friends, Adriana Canclini, the woman who had 'adopted' me at a Women for Democracy meeting on my first visit to Syracuse. When she learned that B and B Oikos, where I had stayed so happily, was absolutely full for the exact three days the Borghese would be with me in Syracuse, she offered us the use of a little flat she owned in Ortygia. She, a Northerner who had married a Sicilian, the couple now divorced, was in fact departing for Bolzano the day we arrived, but postponed her departure long enough to deposit us at the entrance to the palazzo. She assured us we would find everything in order, handed over the keys, and asked that we give them to the neighbour downstairs when we left.

We had decided two excursions would be enough for a short visit: one to the archaeological park and the museum and the other to the temples of Agrigento, a very long drive. That came second.

After some more shopping at the supermarket, we arrived at the archaeological park an hour after opening time.

Each of the sites on our list was in touching distance of the others, the whole compact like a closed fist, not endlessly strung out like the temples in Agrigento. Having earlier visited the Greek theatre and the Roman amphitheatre with Rita Piana on my first stay in Syracuse, I was planning to stretch out on a bench in a shady spot somewhere, leaving Marisa and Andrea to tramp over the ancient stadiums alone. The fierce heat was unendurable to me.

We agreed to meet up in an hour's time at the limestone cave memorably christened 'Dionysius's Ear' by Caravaggio, the sixteenth-century painter famed as the originator of chiaroscuro. The 'Ear' was quite near the entrance to the park and I had no difficulty locating it. Oddly there wasn't a soul in sight at the time of my arrival and I entered the cave unthinkingly, startled to find myself alone inside, but relieved to escape the sun, to relax my eyelids and feel cool air fanning out towards me.

The cave was not what I had imagined, light streaming in from the enormous opening something like that of a tent with the flaps pinned back and through a sizable gap in the roof, close to twenty metres high. Its walls were that attractive streaky white of limestone, so highly polished, smooth and cool they invited lavish caresses. Located in the huge Quarry of Paradise, it was said to be an outcome of the quarrying industry, the walls having been polished by the quarrymen. Into its vast space that seemed to reduce me to a few centimetres, Dionysius is reputed to have flung hundreds of prisoners of war, plus a few political prisoners, rivals whose plotting he feared. He was supposed to have put his ear to the gap at the top where he could hear everything everybody was saying and was able to sweep off to the necropolis above the cave those who were sounding intolerably dangerous.

On reflection I decided Dionysius had planted a couple of spies among the slaves and they kept him informed. But the legend would enhance his divine status. And Caravaggio's label, a happy marketing device, has buttressed the tale.

I imagined how it might have felt entering the cave at the end of a day's hard labour in the quarries, where, spurred on by whip and baton, the prisoners hewed out huge blocks of limestone, the material most coveted for raising temples.

It was an enormous source of wealth to Syracuse. Not merely the limestone itself, but the springs associated with it. Syracuse has more springs than any other part of Sicily. They are formed from the rainwater that sinks through the porous limestone until it meets an impermeable surface, whereupon it wells upward to the water table.

Originally the limestone had formed in underground caves. Over time the upper surfaces of the caves partially collapsed, subsiding into what became three quarries, one of them was this Quarry of Paradise where I was sitting. In some places about forty-five metres deep, the quarry lodges Dionysius's Ear as well as the lovely Grotto of the Ropemakers, which is almost contiguous with the cave. But since there are no ropes anywhere today or persons affecting to make them, one sees only another pretty grotto, the water deep and still, stalactites, natural sculptures of limestone with infinitely varied shapes, suspended overhead. The two together, the cave and the grotto, are the quintessence of peace and serenity and could induce a feeling of profound reverence in even the most insensate of souls.

After twenty minutes or so the Borghese appeared beside me, all smiles. Andrea, it seemed, had been less impressed by the Roman amphitheatre than by the stone sarcophagi lining the road to the theatre, and finding the entire structure surrounded by beautiful trees and shrubs. As usual, the Spanish had dismantled much of the original edifice to build fortifications and the near perfect appearance of the amphitheatre today is the result of massive restoration work, most likely funded by overseas sources, Swedes in particular.

While we headed for the 'Ear' together, without warning, a legion of school children suddenly rounded the path leading up to the cave and rushed us inside, treading on our heels.

They could hardly wait to start experimenting with sound effects, unloosing screams and whistles, exaggerating whispers, the nerve-rending cacophony rewarded with exhilarating multiple echoes as if the original sounds were ricocheting all about the cave.

'*Favoloso*,' Andrea kept saying, trying out a few sounds of his own invention in basso profondo, and we exited, wound up and laughing, just like the kids.

The three of us then spent an hour revelling in the beauty of the Quarry of Paradise. I learned from Andrea who had studied architecture for a year at the University of Rome, that acanthus grows everywhere in Greek and Roman ruins and the curling leaves are represented on the capitals of the three types of Greek columns, especially the Corinthian. He recalled the legend supposed to explain what inspired the bronze sculptor and architect, Callimachus, a fifth-century BC Athenian, to conceive the Corinthian capital. Callimachus was said to have been out for a walk in a wood when he came upon the abandoned grave of a young girl. On top of the grave was a closed basket covered with a large terracotta tile and containing the remains of things the girl must have valued when alive.

Since the burial, an acanthus plant had sprouted beneath the basket, its strong stalks and leaves, in seeking to reach their natural height, growing up the sides of the basket till they reached the edges of the tile whose weight pressed on them, causing them to curl to the ground in graceful whorls. From this image came the Corinthian capital.

The bracts of flowers on acanthus are famously tall, and in this limestone park, they were nearly two metres high, projecting from their rich, dark, foliage like feminised spears in pale lilac. This vegetation and the extraordinary shapes and masses of the limestone worked on by nature and the quarrying, have created gardens of immense beauty.

We had intended to visit the other two quarries, but Andrea muttered that his feet were hurting again, and he, a stoic half-Russian joined to a long strain of stoic Romans, not wont to complain of pain, we commiserated with him, deciding to take a break, sit in the Park and stretch our legs, discussing what we had seen.

Then it was time for a quick snack, that is, a pizza and a bottle of water from the kiosk, and we were ready to visit the Paolo Orsi Regional Archaeological Museum, within easy walking distance though further walking was out for us. By car it was mere minutes away.

29

Orsi was a great archaeologist from Trento in the North. He specialised in the Hellenic civilisations, working for many years in Sicily until his death in 1935. The first archaeological museum was apparently lodged in Ortygia, in Cathedral Square, about fifty metres from my B and B, but in 1927, a new museum designed by Orsi's great successor, Bernabo Brea, was built in the park of Villa Landolina, itself the work of another famous architect, Franco Menissi.

The museum is said to be one of the foremost in Europe, something I wouldn't doubt for a minute. It's literally enchanting. When I return to Syracuse I would like to camp in the museum for a month, filling my head with it. It's a multi-disciplinary conception, a veritable oasis of reason in Sicily, intellectually exciting, bent on exposition of problems, using empirical method and logic, offering hypotheses and conclusions or non-conclusions, raising new problems for reflection, conjecture and further investigation. A triumph of science in an anti-science culture.

Mysteries in the Museum are cast as problems, not 'revealed' truths, and solutions always await discovery. In this ancient environment, modernity transforms relics into talebearers and witnesses. The 18,000 artefacts sing, they dance, they give evidence.

Slabs of small print ground me at the entry, with photos and diagrams and maps illustrating the prehistory and history of nearly all the main archaeological sites in the central and eastern sections of Sicily, especially Syracuse, to the end of the Greco-Roman period. I stand reading the texts, amazed. Could Sicily really have had dwarf elephants in prehistoric times?

Marisa and Andrea had gone ahead. Schoolchildren, unleashed, tucked themselves away from their teachers, slipping behind pillars or blending with the artworks on the far sides of glass cases, their teachers left with little groups of the faithful. They marvelled at some of the figures: the fanged Gorgon sticking out his tongue, and more like a jovial Buddha than a creature bent on petrifying the world; the ravishing Venus Anadiomene, risen from the sea, a marble figure who, lacking her head, yet smiles with her lissom body, her inner suppleness seeming to melt the most solid of rocks, not to mention the heart of Guy de Maupassant. Headless women are not an uncommon sight among these Hellenic and Roman sculptures. But their personalities survive decapitation. A headless goddess breast-feeding twins with adult faces had many student admirers who found much to discuss in her.

It's easy to become bemused in this vast museum, however symmetrical and hexagonal it looks from aerial maps. When one's unaware of the shape, or even when aware, one can wander around almost blindly among the different sections, so drawn to the beauty of a bronze male figure here, or there, cases and cases of eye-catching plates, vases and amphorae, that the divisions become irrelevant. Each new room is an Aladdin's cave.

Marisa, Andrea and I eventually caught up with one another in front of an exhibit featuring a large number of smaller female figures, fully dressed in the costumes of their days.

"Look at their bearing and the vigour of their poses," I say, nudging Andrea. 'They're strong women, like Antigone and Hecuba.'

In one plexiglass case, the most striking attribute of the exhibits, all figures, was the widely varied ethnicity evident in the faces, not their dress. The features and colouring ranged from Nordic to African, Iberian to Mongolian. Sicily's multiculturalism is deep-rooted. The history texts say so, and the ceramics, with their accompanying data on the excavations, confirm it.

After three hours, our legs felt like wet sandbags. There was no point lamenting what had to be left unseen. So we gave up, and while Marisa and Andrea ambled off to collect some brochures I went outside and threw myself down on the soft and springy lawn fronting the museum, a delightful rarity in Sicily, vibrant green and every blade of grass pulsing with health. I rubbed my nose in the sweet fragrance, breathing deeply before turning onto my back, stretching out my arms and shoulders in near abandon, ignoring notices forbidding me to do any of those things. Squinting up at the sky through my lashes, relieved that the sun had gone elsewhere, I felt my whole body slacken and sink deeper and deeper into the earth, suddenly overwhelmed by desire for a long, long sleep. In fact, when I awoke, the sun was low in the sky.

'Sit up, Merovnia.'

Andrea was brandishing his camera over me. 'You've been sleeping for ages. We went for a look at the other quarries. I'll take a photo. Then we'll go back and eat, and I'll be the one having a long, long nap.'

30

Agrigento, where we were bound early the next morning, is not easy to get to from Syracuse being right down south and over to the west, across a very rough interior, and if you become lost, it's far from every other place that matters in Sicily: Messina, Catania and Syracuse on the east coast, or Palermo on the north-west. Far even from Gela that spawned Agrigento as an infant colony 200 years after its own foundation by the Greeks.

This was to be my second trip there but Andrea had named it a primary interest – other than visiting his cousin. In early summer 'doing the temples' would be a long hot trek and I had made up my mind I would let Marisa and Andrea do that part on their own.

It was early summer when we were making that trip to the Valley of the Temples. The Borghese's son, Valerio, born in Australia and named after his grandfather, now resident with his beautiful Russian wife and two small children in Artena, close to Rome, had phoned me the previous day on my cellphone when I was waiting for his parents to return from the Roman amphitheatre. He was speaking from Siena where the local guide had taken over his tour group, leaving him free for a few hours. He wanted to know how Marisa and Andrea were reacting to Sicily. To my surprise, when he heard we were driving to Agrigento his voice rose in alarm.

'Oh, you mustn't do that.'

'Why ever not?

'It could be dangerous,' he said. 'Driving over the mountains. Yobbos. They could come after you.' Had I not heard what happened to the couple driving with their child to Palermo when their car broke down? Just recently too. I put my fingers in my ears when he insisted on recounting the details, which would have headlined as murder, rape and robbery.

'Valerio,' I said when he'd finished, 'this has all the characteristics of an urban myth. Probably peddled by the mafia's public relations machine. Have you ever been to Agrigento?'

Yes, he himself had been there, but he didn't include the tour groups. In any case the Sicilian tours weren't long enough to take in cities outside the big four: Palermo, Catania, Syracuse and Messina.

I felt bound to report to Marisa and Andrea what Valerio had said, but they were happy to be persuaded by me that he had been peddling a romance. Andrea was really keen to see the temples and also the museum.

For myself, I was more excited to be in the company of the Borghese than to see Agrigento again, though I did think that the proverbial half-day tour visitors were encouraged to allocate to the city was completely inadequate. The temples are only a part of the Agrigento story.

Andrea had bought a map and we worked on a route: go due east from Syracuse straight across to Gela, from the heads of whose founders Agrigento had sprung, or take a gradual north-east direction from Syracuse, that is, sloping gently up to the left on the map, for Caltagirone, whose name meant absolutely nothing to us, except that I knew *calta* was Arabic in origin and was roughly equivalent to castle, fort or hill. So tentatively, 'big round hill' could be the meaning of Caltagirone, incidentally the birth place of Luigi Sturzo, the beatified philosopher priest whose ideas I encountered in the Palermo monastery when resident there.

Caltagirone's claim to our attention was that it lay almost on a straight line with Agrigento, a very pleasing geometry. Travelling via Ragusa which is the third point of an almost equilateral triangle formed with Caltagirone and Syracuse, that is, driving south-west instead of north-west, didn't rate a single thought. Sadly, as events transpired.

Of course, the idea of making a straight line between any two points on the map of Sicily is laughable. We would in fact be travelling through mountains that can rise to 700 metres. No straight lines. Hills, mountains and plateaus riven by great gorges are the predominant landscape of Sicily, except around Catania whose good fortune it is to enjoy two extremes: Mt Etna, its mass and elevation continually altered by volcanic eruptions, but generally thought to be around 3,300 metres high, and the vast alluvial plain to the south of Etna, stretching to the east coast.

We never tired of looking at and exclaiming over the countryside. Then a thought struck me. 'If you were blindfolded and dropped right here where we are driving, Andrea, could you say where you were, or even in which hemisphere? If you were told you were in the Australian outback would you believe it?'

'Not in the Northern Territory,' he answered promptly. 'But maybe in the Central West Tablelands of New South Wales. Not in England. Not lush enough. Too wild. Too undomesticated, but perhaps France. It could be tricky.'

'Amazing, isn't it,' I said. 'You couldn't say definitively that this is Sicily, that it could only be Sicily, it must be Sicily. And the funny thing is, Sicilians will tell you that everything about them is so extraordinary nobody can understand them or their condition.'

'What condition?' Marisa asked.

'All the things they complain about. But we, above all, in Australia know just how people can change their environment and their perceptions of what they stand for. Look at Wollongong: once decried by outsiders and residents as a monocultural steel town and now seen as a blessed multicultural university city exporting education almost as much as raw materials. And the nation as a whole, gradually viewing itself as part of Asia – with a prime minister who speaks Mandarin. That would have been totally impossible during the period of the White Australia Policy.'

'You keep forgetting Italians are not like the British,' Marisa said. (She was always bringing that up). 'In Australia you can advertise a meeting at your place if you want to organise to change something and forty people might turn up, and you create the officers of the organisation and discuss goals and processes, and then do it. Make the change. But if you tried to do that in Italy, let alone Sicily, not a soul would dare come to your meeting. They would be too scared.'

I didn't believe that and thought it might be an interesting thing to try.

We arrived at Caltagirone about noon. It was overwhelmingly baroque, another city risen from the rubble of the 1699 earthquake. Andrea began lavishing praise on it even before he had alighted from the car in the city centre to ask two businessmen in conversation if they could direct us to a good but modestly priced eatery.

It was surprisingly bourgeois, this town, impossibly bourgeois for Sicily. Like Parma, somehow, pervaded by a sense of industry, order, cleanliness, solid savings accounts and paeans of praise for rare dishes on the tables at home. Attractive shops. Well preserved mansions.

'How can you find a place like this, high on a hill, in the interior of Sicily?' we asked each other, spinning around, for a wider view.

Andrea thought it might be his kind of place.

By the time his long chat with the locals was over, he had logged practically the entire history of Caltagirone, its numerous splendiferous churches – the biggest annual religious event celebrates the arrival of the Normans who installed Roman Christianity and spelled the end of Arab dominion – its renowned La Scala, the steep street of 142 steps cut right up a hill to connect the cathedral to the town centre. Each of the risers between the steps is covered with a ceramic pattern, no two the same. On the second last Sunday in May, a picture is created on the steps from strategically placed vases of flowers. These steps, along with the Ponte San Francesco, which we had seen on our way in, flanked on both sides by ceramic flowers and emblems, are compelling advertisements for the city's position as the centre of a widespread ceramic industry.

Andrea's enjoyment of the place knew no limits when we found ourselves eating in a restaurant offering not only excellent food at a very reasonable cost, but also a large framed photograph, removed from the wall and fondly tendered to Andrea by a waiter expecting his approval. In the centre of the photo was the tightly zipped face of billionaire magnate-cum-Prime Minister, Silvio Berlusconi, surrounded by the restaurant staff and management.

After lunch, when certain members of the right-wing persuasion, waiters and several diners, were farewelling Andrea affectionately and rejoicing in their solidarity, we were all three excited anew to discover in our postprandial stroll, meant to ward off the need for a nap, a huge display centre as big as a department store for the region's ceramics.

Having in my role as an honorary Tuscan been raised to admire Faentina pottery, it had taken me quite some time to accustom myself to the Sicilian product which, at first, I thought horribly kitsch. Thick clay, with too much searing yellow and bright green. Potholders with moustaches extending beyond each cheek had brought on ughs of horror in the early stages of my arrival in Sicily but gradually I came to like the boldness of the ceramic, its 'anything goes' attitude to subject, and what I later saw to be clear differences in the palettes favoured by the artists.

Now I rejoiced in a dazzling emporium of infinitely diverse pots, vases, amphorae, round plant pot holders like heads looking at you with the wide-eyed faces of moustachioed men and sturdy women in Arabic head coverings, jugs, sauce boats, giant serving plates, spoon rests, clocks, soap dishes, in oily yellows and greens, violent blues or magenta, or delicate and subtle pastels, soft blues, greys and pinks – we couldn't get around to see them all – delivered to the centre by the potters from even the tiniest villages in the area. This shop offered a splendid window onto the ceramic artistry of a province and I regarded the work with affection, regretting only that the best were a bit beyond my purse.

My change in attitude has arisen, I think, because I've assimilated the growing Sicilian regard for their Arab heritage, which to some extent is displacing the Hellenic connection from centre stage. Not into the wings, of course, but sharing the spotlight.

And why not? These glamorous men in colourful headgear and silk pyjamas, wearing gaudy pointy toed shoes, and glittering jewels that brought a sparkle to Sicilian eyes, hit the west coast like an army of Armani models, signalling the end of 300 years of stagnation and boredom. Ten thousand of them, Berbers from North Africa, Arabs from Mesopotamia, the Yemen and other parts of the Arabian peninsula, all newish Mohammedans, landed at Mazzara in 827 AD and everyone knew the good times were come again.

We each bought some presents to take back to Australia. Alas, although Andrea wrapped up my twelve pieces for postage as if they were the crown jewels – or perhaps even for that very reason – the package never made it through the Sicilian postal service. Nor did the cashmere jumper, a high fashion quilted jacket and an expensive bag I bought as presents for my brother and two daughters. The two packages, despatched from two separate city post offices obviously never made it into the out mail. When I wrote to the postmasters of each city asking only to hear them express concern, not a word came in reply from either. I've really got it in for that institution. Its reform is at the very heart of any effective modernisation of Sicilian society.

31

It was after four o'clock when we finally reached Agrigento and still fiercely hot. I felt sodden with the humidity, waterlogged in every pore. Feet like frogmen's flippers. Not walking them. Planting them. It was an effort to lift my chest to breathe, sweat streamed down both sides of my nose. I'd never been so liquid before. I just wanted to let my knees bend and topple over in slow motion, lie down where I fell.

I apologised to the Borghese. "I'm so tired. I can't face the temples again in this heat. You go, and I'll find a place to sit in the shade and wait for you. It's roughly a mile and takes about two hours to see everything. Don't hurry. I'll be happy as a log."

I took the measure of a few spots of shade eked out by scanty scrub on the road, opposite Hera's temple and found one about the size of an opened-out umbrella. Then I sat there compacting myself on a rock that might have been from the necropolis, till I cooled off.

The road in front of the temples was wide, but unsealed, pebbly, uneven, bound to fill sandals with grit, a reddish yellow dirt track, and no doubt a quagmire in the rain. A steady traffic of men, women and youths passed before me, speaking in a variety of tongues, French, German, Dutch, Spanish, Greek, the Frenchwomen expensively casual, indifferent to the battering the two-hour walk would be giving their stiletto heeled, backless sandals, strolling casually, as if in the Luxembourg Gardens.

But there were no seats on the route, and only one pay station to provide a drink. If this had been Naples, entrepreneurial types would have been offering ice cold water, *gelati*, and if they thought there was a euro in it, portable seats, or bicycle rickshaws.

I had to move continually from bush to bush to keep out of the sun. Finally I crossed the road and sat on one of the steps leading up to the temple base, brushing away an occasional low energy thought that threatened to stir my torpor. The scaffolding on the columns hardly seemed to have moved since Gaby and I were here four months earlier. This valley is a world heritage site that attracts funds for the maintenance and restoration of the monuments, but to whom does the money go? And to whom is its deployment accountable? Everybody thinks they know in general terms, but as Sciascia says, 'without a name, a date and a time, everything is fiction.'

When the Borghese got back, Andrea was done in. Arthritis pains compounded his discomfort. He launched into a long list of services that should be provided to entertain people while they're on the move: little easy-on easy-off motors, kiosks at every temple – a reward for having reached it – parasols and bikes, the three-wheeled ones as well as the usual sort, to hire.

Marisa wanted to find a place to bathe. We were hot, sticky and fed up. Bugger the temples. Why couldn't they have been on the beach? So we got the car and headed down to the city, where we found signs directing us to the water. On the way we drove through some surprisingly attractive and tranquil streets and lanes, lined with palms and flowering trees, with the upper storeys of comfortable family homes rising above high moss-covered walls. If only we lived here. Just for the night. But in a thankfully short time we were parked a very few metres from a small bay where quite a number of people, young and old were swimming or just floating idly. Naturally, we grimaced at the absence of facilities, having to undress in the car, with no stainless steel showers, no tables and chairs to ease the discomfort. And no bath towels to hire.

Andrea was looking about him. He shook his head. 'Look at this. We're so lucky in Wollongong. Wonderful public facilities. Free. The Council really does a good job.'

'We don't have a towel between us,' I said gloomily, wondering what kind of miracle had been invoked to make me pack my swimming costume, bone dry for decades. Andrea's urgings, thankfully, that we should all three bring our bathing gear. But wiggling and scrabbling and turning somersaults to get out of our clothes and into our swimsuits without exposing ourselves to charges of indecency, changed everything. We exploded with laughter, and our cries of delight turned heads when we rushed into the water, and submerged, sinking down on the sandy seabed. Then we went a little crazy and started splashing each other. All our weariness vanished.

After a while I just lay floating, staring at the sky, the water so buoyant, warmly supportive, I wondered if this part of the coast were like the Dead Sea. Turning my head, I saw the sun lowering in the western sky. A half-hour at the most before it set. But the seashore was well lit up from the apartment buildings and shops lining the waterfront. We kept raising sighs and smiles of relief and pleasure, ecstatic to feel cool and relaxed in salt water, just the littlest bit murky, I cooing to myself like a pigeon.

Almost an hour later we were back in the car, not as clean as we would have liked, since, in the absence of tap water, we had nothing to rinse off the sand and stickiness but the contents of six bottles of water bought from a kiosk. Dressed and tidy, with no food, not even a snack, we decided we were hungry. Not just hungry, starving.

'It's six hours since we've eaten, Mamma,' Andrea groaned, piteously. 'It'll be eight before we find a place and are sitting down to a meal.'

So he hoped. On the way out of Agrigento we found an amazing pizzeria at the back of an ordinary bar-cum-convenience store, a barn of a place, beautifully appointed from ceiling to floor, good quality linen on the tables, linen napkins, and a surfeit of table service. By then it was past ten o'clock. In this vast room there were we three and a group of three couples, with almost as many waiters keen to serve our smallest need.

'Odd,' Marisa said. 'To find a place like this at the back of a bar with a few fridges storing milk and soft drinks.'

Two televisions were mounted on the walls, one on RAI 3 and the other showing soccer on a private channel. We wolfed down some tasty little antipasto items we'd ordered to eat with the bottle of Nero d'Avola we'd asked for, while we waited for the pizzas. Was it that we were hungry and grateful for the ambiance, spacious, tranquil and cool, or that the pizzas themselves were truly special, with no stinting of oil below the base, which was thickish, the way I liked it, whatever the reason, it was the most appetising meal I'd eaten in an age. In fact, I was eating only the second pizza I'd had in a year.

'You'd wonder how they can keep a place this size going, when they have so few diners,' Andrea mused.

'Maybe they don't care whether it goes or not,' I said. 'Maybe it's just a front for money laundering. Or maybe this is the wrong time and the wrong night. But let's enjoy it, anyway, because it's a great end to our day. With that Napolitana and after our marvellous bathe, I'm ready for anything.'

Whatever made me say that?

We ordered coffees at the bar on the way out and selected some boiled sweets to sustain us on the drive back to Syracuse. While the *barista* was ringing up the bill, the owner wandered in and Andrea congratulated him on the decor and the food.

'But for sure this must have been one of your quietest nights, 'Andrea said, cocking his head quizzically. 'I think people must come from far and wide to taste your pizzas.

'Oh, yes.' The owner smiled happily as if a thousand people might have passed through just before we arrived. 'We have our busy moments.'

At the car, climbing into the passenger seat, I asked Andrea, 'Will you be all right to drive, Andrea? A huge pizza and a glass of wine can make a person sleepy.'

'Don't worry,' he said. 'If I don't feel up to it I'll let you know and you can take over.'

Then he and Marisa chortled together. Even I had to smile. I am widely known as one of the world's worst drivers. Marisa, on the other hand, is an excellent driver: I feel safer in a car with her than with many another person, but it makes no difference – Andrea never lets her take the wheel when he is in the car. Normally he is happy to have her wait on him as if he were an oriental potentate, but no matter how tired he is, he won't surrender the keys to the car.

'Do you want to swap seats, Marisa?'

She gave me her usual response. A look of long suffering. 'You know he'll just turn round and talk to you if you sit in the back, and he'll forget to keep his eyes on the road. Keep him talking, darling. That's all I ask.'

I sensed her nestling down in the back seat for a quiet time, and mentally tautened myself, alert to ensure that Andrea didn't give signs of nodding off.

This part of the Sicilian world was eerily quiet. Hardly a car on the road, even so early, not quite midnight. In Catania, people would hardly have started dinner and the eateries round the university would be packed. Crowds six deep would be encircling the two juice kiosks in the piazza near Silvana's B and B.

Andrea figured we would probably make it back to Syracuse just after three o'clock. I felt weary. It was going to be an effort to keep him talking. But then I realised he was in a quiet mood, himself. Happy enough when I suggested turning on the radio, but cautioning me that it should not be Radio Maria.

We were on a good road, driving smoothly, following the signs that periodically appeared, pointing to Syracuse. Then, somehow, Syracuse vanished from the signboards and instead Ragusa began to appear at all the roundabouts.

'Check the map,' Andrea said, handing me his copy. 'See where this Ragusa leads to.' On a small map, Ragusa seemed to be very close to the freeway leading to Catania. We didn't want to go to Catania.

'Ragusa's not on our way,' I said. 'We have to go south to Modica and Ispica and then turn up north towards Syracuse. Let's just keep on this road for the time being.'

Keeping on that road was no easy matter, though. Every intersection we came to had three or four signs, pointing in every direction, one inevitably Ragusa, and we had no idea where the places were. Tourists often complain of bad road signage in Sicily.

Eventually, after driving for half an hour, Andrea, with a hint of exasperation, but quietly, informed us: 'We're going round in circles. We've already been through this roundabout. I recognise it.'

So did Marisa and I when we looked closely at the signs.

'Better go a different way from the last time, then,' we said.

Andrea drove on. After another half-hour, there we were again, back at the same roundabout. Andrea was now looking vexed.

We were mystified that they had stopped signing us to Syracuse. It was not as if we had already arrived there. Why would they sign it so far back, and then stop when there was still a long way to go? If this kept happening, we might be better to sleep in the car and wait till daylight.

Andrea unconsciously straightened his shoulders and we set off again.

About one o'clock we found ourselves entering a small town, the first since leaving Agrigento. At least we'd stopped going round in a circle. Everything was dead quiet. We scanned the buildings quickly, seeking a name for the place, but town names often don't appear till you are leaving. Suddenly, a piazza loomed up, and to our astonishment, we saw three youngish men standing in a quiet huddle, close to the street. They broke off their conversation at the sound of the car and watched while Andrea pulled to a stop two or three metres from them. He lowered the window on my side and leaned across me to call out to them in English, 'Good evening, are we on the right road to Syracuse?' And then, realising his mistake, repeated the question in Italian.

One came quickly to the window. We were in Comiso, he said.

I knew that name. Comiso had been a US base at some stage. Might still be. Once a mafia-free town, I'd heard, until the Americans arrived and the mafia turned up, confident of a welcome after the assistance they had given the Americans during the Allied landing in Sicily in July 1943. With the mafia came the drug trade which the young took to with enthusiasm.

At the same time since the US imported from home every single item they needed in their bases. Comiso didn't even benefit economically from the American presence.

The youth began giving Andrea lengthy directions, bending down, leaning into the car, his head close to mine. A quick glance at his expression reassured me – pleasant, open, good-looking, like many young Sicilians. But less happily I became aware another member of the trio had edged closer, and positioned himself in front of and to the side of the car bonnet, looking through the windscreen at a slight angle, first at me and then trying to get a focus on Marisa behind Andrea. Tall and solidly built with red hair cut short. For a second his eyes, pale blue, bleak and unfriendly, met mine and I knew immediately he and his friend were cut from different cloth. Not a nice type at all. Then I realised the whites of his eyes were red as a ferret's. He was stoned. The three must have been sharing a quiet joint.

Valerio's story of rape and murder on the road to Palermo sprang to my mind. Maybe I had been too ready to dismiss it as an urban myth. Andrea kept chatting on, aglow with bonhomie, more than willing to prolong the conversation, while I, pretending to be looking around the piazza, kept my eye on the redhead whose hard blue gaze hadn't moved from Marisa and me. When she pinched the back of my neck I knew she too was apprehensive.

In the barest whisper, she said, 'Tell Andrea to shut the window and start moving.'

So I muttered under my breath, 'Andrea, close the window. Now. Hurry. It's dangerous. Hurry up.'

And I jabbed him in the ribs with my elbow, whispering in the back of my throat: 'Let's go, let's go.'

Marisa murmured again from the back seat. 'Move, Andrea.'

He hesitated, perplexed and vaguely annoyed, and then while I pinched his arm, muttered 'A thousand thanks' to our informant, and wound the window up. Thank God for that. The redhead hadn't blinked or moved while his friend stepped back, ready to wave us on. He was still standing, concentrating, as we drove past.

Andrea was completely bemused. 'What were you panicking about?' he said to me. 'Why were you pushing me to leave in such a hurry, shut the window and all that silly drama!'

Marisa spoke up in the back: 'You remember what Valerio said, Andrea. He warned us not to stop the car anywhere in the night. To be very careful of any groups of men.'

Andrea was watching the road. 'I think I know where to go now,' he said.

I sank down into my seat, wrung out with tension, immensely relieved to be away from that little town. The bad vibes I'd felt from the redhead had been really disturbing. I was surprised and worried that Andrea had been unaware of the menace in the air. Ermete was much more alert to danger.

Nobody was talking anymore and Andrea had turned off the radio. He was concentrating on the route. We'd been driving for about twenty minutes when he slapped his hand to his head.

'*Porca miseria.*'

We were back at the town again. Not in the centre but at an intersection on the periphery. Ragusa was dominant on the signboards as usual.

'Oh I'll try this way,' he said, barely glancing at the sign board and turning into the nearest road. 'We must eventually get on to the freeway.'

'But I thought the chap gave us clear directions,' I said. 'He was talking long enough.'

Andrea made no reply. About ten or fifteen minutes later, he said abruptly. 'I think we're being followed.'

My eyes widened in the dark and I felt a pulse start beating in my throat. I was scared to look back in case I saw the redhead.

'Oh my God. What makes you think they're following? When did it start? We've been driving about half an hour. Are they behind us now?'

'Yes,' he said.

'Oh no! Can you see that redhead? Imagine it. They must have gone and fetched their car. Or perhaps it was parked by the piazza. What would they have said to each other? 'Let's get after them. They're probably loaded. Two women, just one bloke. Three of us. And more waiting by their cellphones. Easy pickings."

If the one bloke had been Ermete, I thought, it would have been a different story. I wouldn't have been afraid. I would have asked Ermete what we would do and he would have known. After all, he had been a technician in the Decima MAS. Andrea's father was his commander. After Italy withdrew from the War he had been seized by the Germans three times and escaped, so the villagers had told me, and I knew he would have defended me to his last breath. With Andrea, who knew his mettle? His sense of the absurd often turned serious situations into high comedy, when he could make people start laughing through their tears. But that redhead was not looking for a laugh.

'Too far away to see who's driving,' Andrea said, 'and the windows are dark.'

My breathing was getting away from me. I mustn't hyperventilate. I started rocking, surreptitiously, muttering disjointed imprecations liberally laced with swear words and projecting them at the heads of those following us. Andrea suddenly folded up laughing. My blood chilled. God, cracking up so soon! Some Roman.

'But why are you acting like that?' he said, trying to catch his breath. And laughing yet again when he saw my incredulous expression. 'You're so funny. It mightn't be them at all. Could be just somebody who can't find the way the same as us and is hoping we know where to go.'

'But what if it's not?' I snapped. 'You have to be prepared. And there isn't much time. What will we do? Do you have a plan?'

Off he went again, cackling, wiping his eyes on his sleeve. I thought he was going to lose control of the car.

'I've never had such a good laugh in all my life,' he said, tears rolling down his cheeks. 'Have I got a plan? What kind of plan would I have, silly? There's only the road ahead.'

He told us afterwards that at that point a thought had flashed through his mind: 'Soon, maybe, I'll be killed, and the two of you will luckily only be raped.'

Though blissfully ignorant of such fatalism, I was staring at him in horror. Ermete would have already settled on a plan.

'Oh you're such an idiot,' I said between my teeth, glaring at him. 'This isn't the time for playing the big kid. Our lives could be in danger. What will you do if they drive alongside us and try to push us off the road? Huh? Can you envisage that? What will you do?'

All he could do in the circumstances was continue to laugh. I thought, perhaps he's so terrified, he's having a nervous breakdown. My brain was racing. Nowhere useful, though.

'Is there an iron bar under the seat? Ermete always had one there.'

That set him off cackling again. 'Merovnia,' he said, addressing me during his gasps for breath, and in quite a kindly tone, "This is a hire car. Where would we get an iron bar?"

Still mentally scouting around for a weapon, I remembered there was a small cosmetic purse in the bag at my feet. It had a little mirror and nail scissors inside. Maybe I could break the mirror in two pieces. On the steering wheel or something. There would be sharp edges and with a bit of luck sharp points. To jab in an eye. I'd give the scissors to Marisa. At the pistol club she had been a better shot than Andrea. And she was cool. She wasn't making a sound in the back. Probably thinking. Certainly not laughing.

Andrea, I noticed, was now driving at a much faster speed than previously. He could be an expert driver when the occasion demanded it. His brother had once raced cars in Australia and Hong Kong and Ermete told me he thought Andrea good enough to have been a professional racing driver if he had had the interest and the discipline. Perhaps this skill was what he was going to rely on now. In this situation flight might be better than fight. Good if you could get away with it. Anyway now that I had a plan of my own, my breathing had quietened down and I'd stopped ranting. Andrea had also stopped laughing.

Every so often, I'd ask, 'Is the car still behind us?' and he'd nod. It was strange. Difficult to imagine Redhead and his mates following us all the way to Syracuse. Maybe they were too stoned to have a plan themselves. Just following their primeval instincts. Puzzling, though, that they hadn't drawn alongside or attempted to pass us. Then, a few minutes later, I heard Andrea say, his voice tense for the first time, 'They're coming up.'

A flash past. Quick as a blink. Too fast to see into the car. I looked way up ahead for evidence reinforcements might be engaged in blocking the road or something. No other car was in sight, but a *cavalcavia* was very close, one of those humped little bridges that make up a traffic intersection operating on two levels. Then we all three sat up dead straight. Bloody hell. The car had drawn to a halt at the side of the *cavalcavia*. Almost immediately the lights went off. At that very minute I spied a sign a few metres before the *cavalcavia*, pointing right: 'Syracuse,' it said. What joy. What joy. No more Ragusa.

'Right, right, turn right, Andrea,' I yelled at him, grabbing his arm. 'There's a road on the right. Syracuse.'

Without slowing, he veered sharply right and sped even faster along what turned out to be an entry to the freeway, to Syracuse. Hurrah! We were jubilant. Hurrah. Then, just when I was on the point of letting go, of collapsing with exhaustion, I heard him say, 'They're back.' But by this time we were in a major traffic flow and I was too drained to rise to the bait. If that's what it was.

We reached Syracuse about four a.m. On the way, Andrea suddenly said that we hadn't been followed from the *cavalcavia*. The expression on his face made me begin to doubt we had ever been followed at all.

'If you made all that up, Andrea,' I said, 'You are a prime sadist.'

It wouldn't have been uncharacteristic of him to do it, for the drama, and to see my reaction. Like a character out of Pirandello. One mask and then another. Marisa was now adopting a casual air of never having been concerned, saying she had stopped believing we were being followed after we had returned to Comiso by mistake.

'I was surprised you kept believing Andrea,' she said. 'You know what he's like.'

But then who had stopped at the *cavalcavia* – and why did they switch the lights off? That was the mystery.

'If we'd continued we'd have had to slow down at the bridge,' Marisa mused. 'They might have already jumped out of the car and been waiting with guns. They could even have had others waiting at the far side of the bridge. But there's no point speculating,' she concluded. 'We'll never know.'

Messina, a city that must exist

On 16 October 2006 barely two weeks before I arrived in Messina a ten year old boy swam the Strait, starting from the Torre Faro, one of two now decommissioned electricity pylons, each 232 metres high, that used to transmit electricity between the mainland and Sicily. This departure point added 500 metres to the shortest route across the Strait, a distance of 3.8 kilometres, in order to avoid the most dangerous currents. The boy swam almost as fast as the ferry, reaching the far side after fifty-five minutes thirty seconds. Although the currents and the schools of jellyfish had still been a challenge to him, the little Sicilian was unfazed by the monsters of myth.

I tend to associate Messina with rubble and grief. Ravaged by earthquakes, swamped by tsunamis and wasted by war. All three sometimes in quick succession. I remember reading an eye-witness account of a man crying out to the heavens after the 1908 earthquake, wandering a surviving street and lamenting the loss of all his relatives. He was now entirely alone in the world. I felt rent by his anguish.

Yet when I arrived in Messina two years before the centenary of the 1908 disaster, not a stone seemed to be out of place and the locals were moving about with vigour and purpose. Like Agrigento, Messina has been savaged many times. A reported 293 aftershocks were experienced by the city in the days and weeks following the major 1908 earthquake and ninety-one per cent of the buildings were destroyed. Two thirds of the people died and the survivors fled, thousands queuing to emigrate overseas.

Picture postcards made from photos of the event show how the city's two main thoroughfares were unrecognizable, humped up like great slag heaps said to be up to five metres thick. In one postcard soldiers and medical personnel from the Russian Fleet are seen turning over rubble, seeking to recover the dead and wounded. The whole world was shocked by the scale of the destruction.

'There wasn't a Messinese left in town,' a professor of architecture at the University told me, she herself from Calabria. 'The city began again with new people who poured in from all over Italy to rebuild it. Messina, already named 'The City of the Dead' became 'The City that Lost its Memory.'

Yet despite subsequent earthquakes and two world wars it now has a population sixty per cent greater than in 1908. This suggests that Messina is a response to necessity. It must exist – at least while the movement of people, merchandise and invading armies from the mainland to Sicily and thence to the rest of the Mediterranean and further afield depends on crossing the Strait.

It's impossible to imagine a more precise balance between riches and terror than that offered by this narrow stretch of water whose eccentric configuration of land and opposing currents in collusion for centuries offers sea captains a choice between 'a rock and a hard place': either to be smashed by a powerful current against a massive rock 200ft high or, if a captain were clever enough to avoid that fate, be drawn inexorably into the vortex of any one of a number of whirlpools. Those who triumphed knew that they had gained entry to the scythe-shaped port of Messina, one of the safest, best-served ports on world trading routes. Their failure, however, would send horror rippling out far beyond the port: for great riches would go down with the ships and the merchants awaiting the arrival of goods now sunk might well be plunging into bankruptcy.

In 1770 Patrick Brydone suspected the horrors might have been inflated. Not so, he reported. 'Whilst we were still some miles distant from the entry of the strait, we heard the roaring of the current, like the noise of some large impetuous river betwixt narrow banks. This increased in proportion as we advanced, till we saw the water in many places raised to a considerable height, and forming large eddies or whirlpools. The sea in every other place was as smooth as glass. Our old pilot told us... there were five ships wrecked in this spot last winter. We observed that the current set exactly for the rock of Scylla and would infallibly have carried anything thrown into it against that point. So it was not without reason the ancients have painted it as an object of such terror.'

Little wonder that the myth of Scylla and Charybdis is the most famous in the Greek canon, offering a testing ground for the bravest of the Greek heroes and for Homer, their greatest poet. I like this recent translation by A. S. Kline as poetic prose rather than verse.

Being blind, Homer writes from hearsay and has Circe tell the tale:

'In the centre of this cliff-face is a dark cave, facing west towards Erebus, on the path your hollow ship will take, glorious Odysseus, if you listen to my advice. Even a man of great strength could not shoot an arrow from your vessel as far as that arching cavern. Scylla lives there, whose yelp it is true is only that of a new-born whelp, yet she is a foul monster whom not even a god could gaze at with pleasure. She has twelve flailing legs and six long thin necks, each ending in a savage head with a triple row of close-set teeth masking death's black void. She is sunk to her waist in the echoing cave, but extends her jaws from that menacing chasm, and there she fishes, groping eagerly round the cliff for her catch, dolphins and seals or one of the greater creatures that Amphitrite breeds in countless numbers in the moaning depths. No crew passing by in their ship can boast it has ever escaped her unscathed, since each head snatches a man, lifting him from his dark-prowed vessel.

'Odysseus, you will notice the other cliff is lower, only a bow-shot away, and a great fig-tree with dense leaves grows there. Under it divine Charybdis swallows the black waters. Three times a day, she spews them out, and three times darkly sucks them back again. No one, not even Poseidon, could save you from destruction if you are there when she swallows. Hug Scylla's cliff instead, and row your ship past swiftly, since it it's better to mourn six men than your whole crew.'

So she spoke, but Odysseus replied, 'Goddess, I beg you to tell me truly why I cannot both escape deadly Charybdis and yet defeat Scylla when she tries to attack my crew?'

To this the Goddess answered, 'Resolute man is your heart set again on the toils of battle? Will you not even bow to the deathless gods? Scylla is not mortal. She is immortal evil: a dire, ferocious thing of dread. You cannot fight her, there is no defence: the only course is flight. If you pause by the rock to arm yourselves, I fear she will dart out and strike you with all six heads again, and seize as many men as at first. Row past at full speed instead, and call to Cratais, Scylla's mother, who bore her to be the bane of mortal men. She might keep her from darting out once more.'

Six of Odysseus's crew were ultimately seized by Scylla and borne away shrieking in terror.

32

Messina's being so prone to catastrophe and war, yet impelled to rise again however often its population is decimated, it should come as no great surprise to learn that the scale used to measure its earthquakes predates and differs from the Richter scale, the one best known nowadays.

In my pre-Sicilian condition, I had little interest in how to measure earthquakes, but eavesdropping on a conversation between two women in the train bringing me to Messina from Catania started me thinking. One, a Roman, asked the other, a Catanese, if she ever felt afraid of being caught up in an earthquake, observing that, after all, they weren't like volcanic eruptions which nowadays could be detected in advance. And a century had passed since the big Messina quake in 1908. The Roman imagined that another earthquake might be close and wondered whether it was wise to continue making regular visits to her son in Sicily.

Oddly, this was the first time I had heard anyone in Sicily raise the subject of how they felt about living in such a cataclysmic region. Of course the person expressing concern was a Roman, not a Sicilian.

To my surprise, the Catanese said that she went to bed every night fearing that she might wake up under rubble, and that she had a packed suitcase under the bed, ready to flee if she should be able to. In the course of the conversation she revealed that practically nobody in Sicily insured anything, that insurers were not keen to offer the service in any case, except to some businesses.

"So we have to look to the government to help us rebuild our houses," she said. "Imagine how long that takes."

My immediate thought was that bribing would cover the impacted areas like a tsunami.

Later, after Googling the 1908 earthquake in Messina I was intrigued by the reference to its intensity as measured on the 'Mercalli' scale. Why not the Richter scale? For the simple reason that when the earth convulsed in Messina in 1908, Charles Francis Richter was only eight years old and his instrumental system of measuring magnitude was more than twenty years away.

Don Giuseppe Mercalli, the scientist-priest from Milan, creator of the Mercalli Scale was fifty-eight years old and had been studying volcanoes and earthquakes since his mid-twenties. Though he invented his scale late in the nineteenth century it attracted world attention only after being employed on those sites sensationally damaged by the 1908 earthquake, that is, Messina and Reggio Calabria.

The Mercalli scale records in Roman numerals from I to XII key responses to earth movement, in rough order, starting with disturbance felt only by very few people, then by many people, by everyone at specific sites, shifting then to observations indoors of moving objects, slight movement, movement of heavy objects, of delicate items suspended from ceilings, then on to outdoors, with the last six grades focused on degrees of damage to buildings, to those of good design and construction, to well built ordinary structures, to poorly built or badly designed structures, the damage ranging from slight to moderate, considerable, great, buildings moved from foundations, most masonry and structures destroyed, few buildings left standing, bridges destroyed, objects thrown into the air, and at every level the numbers of people feeling afraid, feeling terrified, driven by panic. Level XII describes damage as 'total', with lines of sight and level distorted. It is a relative measurement: every earthquake can yield different levels of intensity and the scale is effective only where there are witnesses to the upheaval. Even the hugest of earthquakes in uninhabited areas are outside its compass.

Richter, a geologist working in California took Mercalli's scale and tried to add a 'scientific' measurement that could record vibrations regardless of their location. To reflect the magnitude of the shock, he chose to measure the acceleration of the ground when it suddenly moves. His scale is logarithmic, and on it a magnitude of seven is ten times larger than a six and 100 times larger than a five. The worst earthquake ever recorded reached 8.9 on the Richter Scale, roughly equivalent to XII on the Mercalli scale.

Although the latter is viewed as non-scientific, depending as it does on hearsay, it calls, in fact, for the use of empirical methods to examine the composition and design of properties seen to have been damaged least or most by an earthquake relative to their distance from the epicentre. Such assessments have enabled significant advances to be made in quake-proofing buildings.

An unexpected, and for many individuals and institutions, highly unwelcome outcome of using the Mercalli scale is that it can unearth evidence of corruption in the construction and maintenance industries by revealing breaches of the 1909 Italian building code for earthquake-prone regions, though this label reflects only differences in degree in Italy since the entire country at some time or another experiences significant earth movement. Shoddy workmanship, failure by contractors to meet contractual specifications and the failure by bureaucrats to ensure quality control inspections, all are revealed by Mercalli's scale. This can open the way to costly litigation.

Mercalli appears to have demonstrated an early vocation for the priesthood. Odd, that children in secular states don't seem to reveal such a vocation. It must be a cultural response. Of five children in one family, three, Mercalli, his brother and his sister went into the Church. In Milan this would signify a conspicuously devout family.

Having created something of a seminary record by his excellent conduct and vigorous application to his studies Mercalli became an ordained priest eighteen months sooner than the norm. At twenty-four he followed up his theological training with courses leading to a diploma in Natural Science. This launched him on a thirty-seven-year long career as a high-school teacher.

Like every other volcano-mad scientist, he was never happier than when out in the field with colleagues, climbing towards the latest eruption on Etna, Stromboli or Vulcano, even on Vesuvius, always venturing into no-go zones, filling his pockets with ores still smouldering, taking enough samples to give to museums and schools. He is said to have written 150 books on seismology, some translated into twenty-eight languages and some still in use today.

One imagines he must have spent little time on his students, but he was known to sit up half the night working, so absorbed, report has it, that on one occasion when an associate called to find out why he had not turned up to supervise an examination set to start at eleven o'clock, the startled priest asked, 'But it can't be daylight already?'

As a scientist-priest, Mercalli inevitably found himself in conflict with the Church. Like Patrick Brydone's fondly regarded Recupero, the priest and volcanologist whom the British scientist met in Catania in 1770, Mercalli was well aware that the earth was far older than the Bible would indicate, and by viewing it as a ballerina whose 'dancing' should be taken into account and prepared for by civil authorities, he was entirely receptive to theories of evolution. Openly so, bringing on himself the hostility of a Jesuit who felt moved to produce a brochure headed 'Six days of the Bible and the Flood' and call on all 'good Christians' to accept the Bible as literal truth.

One wonders at what age or stage of his scientific career Mercalli began demonstrating a degree of non-conformity in his religious behaviour, sufficient to give an impression to some others of being '*tutto laico*', thoroughly secular, often wearing a beret, jacket and trousers and drawing on a cigar. Sometimes even donning an Anglican cassock.

The only portrait I have seen of him shows a long narrow, weather-beaten, ascetic looking face, the eyes deep set and glowing with formidable intensity, a kind of rigid angularity in the posture. Strong and resilient looking. But nervy, not relaxed, as if about to pat his pockets on both sides for his cigar.

Mercalli was originally based in the North in the bleak outpost of Domodossola on the Swiss-Italian border where he taught at a Rosmini College. The philosopher-priest, Antonio Rosmini 1797–1855, now beatified at the behest of John Paul II and awaiting canonization, espoused a form of liberalism influenced by Alexis de Tocqueville's report on America as a nation where liberalism and religion worked together for the spiritual and material good of all. Support for Rosmini was seen by the papacy in Mercalli's time as dangerously liberal.

When in 1887 the priest-geophysicist contributed a small sum to raise a monument commemorating Rosmini, pressure was put on him to leave his post. No doubt the Church was further chagrined to find its errant priest immediately offered a position by the infant Italian state whose coffers were bulging from the expropriation of Church properties, Henry VIII of England having inspired so many secular authorities to follow his example. Mercalli brushed the snow from his boots and moved to southern Italy, first to Acireale, then to Reggio Calabria and finally to Naples, where he ultimately became the Director of the Vesuvian Observatory.

I imagine him, still in his prime, as blissfully happy, probing the mysteries of geophysics and enthusing his students with the desire to unravel the mysteries of the 'dancing' earth.

Thirty-seven when forced to quit his northern post, he had lived and worked in southern Italy for nearly thirty years before dying most horribly, in March 1914. As usual in any case dealing however remotely with the Church or its officers or associates, a forensic clean-up of any potential crime scene is conducted before the event is revealed and a barely plausible story handed out.

The only fact to seem incontrovertible is that his body was carbonised when found. A story wired to the New York Times on March 19 said the death was attributed to his having knocked over a paraffin lamp and set himself alight. A blanket in the room suggested he had attempted unsuccessfully to smother the flames.

A few days later however authorities alleged that it was possible he had been strangled first then petrol poured over his body and set alight. Theft could have been the motive as some money, a fairly modest amount, had been taken. It's a scenario open to many speculations. But let no one shrink from wondering if the Church were directly or indirectly involved in Mercalli's death. In its long and lurid history the Church hierarchy has shrunk from nothing, absolutely nothing, to preserve its interests. Of course it's perfectly possible that it might not have had anything whatever to do with the matter.

Why has no biography been written of Mercalli? There must be substantial archives on him and his work. His relatives might have views on his death. He is, after all, a significant figure in international seismology and the Church could easily have commissioned a work on him. He doesn't even warrant an entry in the massive *New Advent Catholic Encyclopaedia*. Nor has anyone taken up his terrible ending as a 'cold case' worth re-investigating.

But then, the centuries-long war waged against physics and physicists in Italy never lets up.

33

Messina and earthquakes being linked in my mind, my visit to the city was made with low expectations. I was so little engaged by prospects that I made no effort to book accommodation in advance, perhaps thinking none might be available and I could rush north to Florence which in mid-November would be in my favourite mode – fresh *porcini* piled up on counters in the San Lorenzo market and street sellers reaching out to passers-by with paper cones rolled around fragrant roasted chestnuts, split down the middle, drifts of steam escaping from their innards.

My mood got blacker when I trundled my monster suitcase over the station's wide concourse and found the *bagaglio* locked for siesta. Three and a half hours till it re-opened.

"Trains don't *have* a siesta," I growled at the clerk in the main office, lead-bottomed, thick and insolent, a flourishing product of clientelism. She didn't even bother to curl her lip or shrug her shoulders. Just stared at me, her expression radiating such hostility, I had a vision of Sicilians over centuries facing up to their many persecutors, home-grown and foreign, powerless, with nothing but their eyes to convey their contempt and their resistance.

Nothing to do but take a seat in the concourse, mentally manacled to my luggage. I lamented my inability to drag everything inside the bar for a coffee and *panino*. And how was I to roam the streets looking for an information booth let alone check out the accommodation? Arms folded, I sat glaring, savouring every enfeebling moment of my misery.

An hour into the tedium, a woman came through a nearby entry and seated herself beside me. After five minutes I discovered she was waiting for a coach that would not arrive till half past six and would chute her non-stop to Poland. At a speed seemingly faster than light. People slept most of the time, she told me. So one hardly needed to eat.

She had been away from Poland for six months working as a chambermaid in a hotel on Salina, the biggest island in the Aeolian archipelago, and was returning home to spend some time with her husband and two children. After one month, her husband would leave Poland to replace her in Salina and she would stay with the children. This was the best way for them to acquire money to start a small business in Poland. To think what a difference a Pope's nationality can make to his compatriots!

I knew instinctively my suitcase would be safe with her and when she agreed to keep an eye on it I rushed off to the bar. Half-way there, I wheeled round and plodded back, ashamed.

'Sorry. That was so rude of me. Can I offer you a cappuccino and a *panino*? Please?'

No. She was adamant. Her food was divided and packaged for the coach and she would not eat till breakfast the next day. My God.

After I'd returned and we'd made more exchanges of the sort common between people on the move, I broached the subject of her looking after my luggage for an hour or so. 'There's a queue at the luggage room but it's still not open. I can't wait much longer to try finding a place for the night.'

She shooed me away. Yes, yes. Till half past six she would be there. My computer and suitcase she would keep secure. If I should be late back she would put it in the luggage office. It would be open by then.

Outside the station, I recognized an information booth only a few metres away. Open. Gosh, how useful. How abnormal. Within minutes the attendant had given me two phone numbers. She poked her finger out the window and jerked it sideways up the street. 'You can walk to the first. It's under the bridge. The second is about a fifteen-minute walk from here.'

I couldn't believe my luck. In walking distance of the station. I rang the first number and the male who answered told me to come whenever I liked. Even straightaway. The heavy wooden entry door to his palazzo was ajar when I reached it, pushing it open to find myself in a dimly lit hall where the blue rays of a television were streaming out from a sitting room-cum-reception on the right. At my '*Buona sera*' a hugely wide fat man engrossed in watching a soccer game levered himself out of the armchair and waddled towards me, rolling sideways like a boat, appraising me unblinkingly from top to toe. He was decidedly not impressed. A mutual feeling.

'It was you who rang a minute ago?'

'Yes.'

Without another word, he headed for the staircase – no lift, apparently – and pressing one palm flat against the wall for support, panting a little, began to heave himself up the steps with me tripping on his heels. At the landing, on the left, a long passageway with doors aligned on both sides suggested some kind of converted boarding house or hotel. He passed two doors and opened the next, holding it back for me to enter. What a stench. The windows were closed and heavy dark red curtains drawn. A king-size bed dominated the room. God knows how many hundreds of people had performed between its grimy sheets. This was obviously a brothel, or at least a place where prostitutes hired a room by the hour.

I'd rather have slept under the bridge.

'How much per night?'

'Seventy euros.'

My jaw dropped. 'People actually pay you that much for this room?'

'Certainly.'

No wonder he'd been viewing me with skepticism. Probably wondered if I could earn the payment. Hiding a shudder I muttered 'thank you, but it doesn't suit' and scuttled down the stairs, holding my breath till I was out in the street where the air was sweet by comparison.

Back at the railway station I stayed outside near the taxi rank and rang the other number. A male voice again. Everywhere else in Sicily women run the B and Bs. The room was vacant? Yes. He was a little startled to hear I wanted to look at it immediately, but agreed. I could imagine him running around tidying up.

At the taxi rank I told the driver what I wanted. 'Drive me to this address, then wait. I'll go and look at the room. If it's okay you can drive me back to the station where I'll get my luggage and then you can bring me back to that address.'

'*Va bene, signora.*'

He dropped me outside an apartment block in one of Messina's older, more attractive streets, only minutes from a main shopping strip. The apartment was on the fourth floor. A tall good-looking male with red hair was waiting at the lift, looking a little anxious. 'I need to be quick,' I said. 'I've got a taxi downstairs.' He strode ahead of me into the apartment and straight to a bedroom whose far wall was distinguished by tall wooden shutters opening onto a terrace. Good. I ran my eye around the room, scanning the contents – modern, lightweight furniture in the Scandinavian style – and focusing on the smell: *clean*.

'Very nice.'

Then he opened another door. 'This is the second bathroom. Yours alone if you take the room.'

'Yes.' Nodding my head vigorously. 'I will indeed. I'll fetch my luggage from the station. Won't be long.'

Inside the station I held back a minute, observing the Polish woman sitting with my luggage resting at her feet, her hands folded calmly in her lap, shoulders slumping a little. Anticipating a long rest on the bus. She appeared more like an office worker than a chambermaid, in a neat white blouse, long sleeved and buttoned to the neck, and a black skirt that reached to solid ankle boots, obviously gearing up for the approaching Polish winter.

I was suddenly reminded of a character in one of those war movies of the Hitler period where people always seem to be desperate for chocolate. On impulse I hurried to the bar which doubled as a kind of convenience store and began snatching at random from right and left on the shelves chocolates galore, bars large and small, some with nuts or raisins, boxes of peppermint creams, milk chocolates, chocolate-coated caramels, the more varied the better, and funny chocolate figures for children, chucking them into a carrier bag until it was full.

'For your children,' I told the Polish woman, dropping the bag onto her lap and relieving her of my suitcase and computer. She cast a startled glance at the contents, her eyes widening with surprise and pleasure. 'Signora, you shouldn't …' but I knew that I had gotten her just the thing to arouse cheers when she walked in on her family at home. I assured her I would have been sleeping under the bridge without having had her to guard my luggage, gave her a quick kiss on the cheek and hurried off towards the taxi.

On the way to the apartment the driver said, 'Where did you leave your luggage?'

'With a woman in the waiting room.'

'You knew her?'

'No. She's waiting for a coach to take her to Poland this evening.'

The driver turned round. 'You left your luggage with a foreigner, signora? That was very foolish. You don't know what foreigners are like.'

'Well, I'm a foreigner, myself,' I said. 'And, believe me, I know what I'm like. In any case I can tell whether or not a person is honest. I wouldn't have left my luggage with just anyone.'

'Really. You can tell so quickly? And what do you think of me, then, signora? Am I honest?'

We were drawing up outside the apartment block. He turned off the ignition and composed his expression as if he were about to be photographed. I shook my head. 'I couldn't say with confidence. I talked to the Polish woman for over an hour and I've been talking to you for two minutes. But I think you might be *furbo* [foxy]. I think I would have doubts about leaving my luggage with you.'

He grinned. '*Furbo*, eh?'

The fare was reasonable. When he had deposited my luggage on the pavement I gave him a tip. 'Yes, *furbo*.' Shrewd, at the very least.

He pocketed the money, smiling broadly as he climbed back into his cab. Then poked his head out of the window. 'Yes, I can be *furbo* – but only when there's a full moon.' And with a cheeky wink, '*Ciao, signora.* Enjoy Messina.'

In the lift I felt suddenly euphoric. For sure Messina would be earthquake free while I was there.

34

If Nino my new landlord had told me he had worked as a model in his youth, I would have believed him. Of towering dimensions, way over six feet tall and about a metre across square shoulders, broad-chested, with regular, even features, warm brown eyes, tanned cheeks, wide mouth, cleft chin, he looked what he was – honest and decent. Neat and trim, from a perfectly knotted tie just tipping his waistline to elegantly shod feet and wearing leafy colours attuned to a heavy thatch of sandy hair, he radiated a late autumn warmth.

Dumping my luggage out of the way in a corner of my room, I went to find him in the kitchen, delighted to note a wall of shelves in the long hallway, entirely crammed with books. He was standing at the stove, his back to me, tension in his shoulders clearly visible. On hearing my steps, he drew a breath that coincided with the hiss of the coffee rising in the Mokka before turning his head and gesturing towards a chair at a little square table propped against the wall.

We were in a pretty standard Italian eat-in kitchen, but a bit smaller than that of Grzegorz and Rita, whose table could seat six at a pinch. Four would have been a tight fit at Nino's.

After filling our cups he seemed in no hurry to speak. I sat quietly, focusing on the half-completed crossword lodging beside his caffè latte bowl – from breakfast, most likely while he twisted his little coffee cup round and round in its saucer, staring into space, brows knotted, probably wondering if the room he had given me would be vacated in time before his teenage son came home again.

I was obviously in a boy's bedroom, meant to continue as such, since the drawers and wardrobe were still filled with his belongings. A silver-framed photo of the youth in his soccer gear with an arm slung around his younger sister's shoulder was hanging on the wall above his computer workstation.

'Camping out' is really what one does when temporarily renting a room in a private apartment. I've complained before about not having storage space, wardrobes or drawers. Space under the bed for a suitcase is as much as one can hope for. Once, but in Scotland not Italy, when even under the bed was taken, I had to leave my suitcase in a hallway. And not surprisingly boys are often the ones who vacate their rooms for paying guests, having left home to work or study. In Nino's case his son was at school in Pisa with his mother and sister, not knowing that a foreigner from oceans away might be rummaging among his things.

Not that I did, of course. Perish the thought. Were I accustomed to downloading my venial sins on a priest, I might have indulged my curiosity. Left to my own conscience – never. I am of a mind with Lucy Snowe the Protestant narrator in Charlotte Bronte's brillantissimo *Villette*. A young Englishwoman, teaching at a Belgian boarding school, she is aghast to discover that the private contents of her drawers, including personal letters, have been removed, examined and replaced on two occasions and by two different people and that at confession, lying is considered a mere peccadillo compared to missing attendance at church.

On walks with the girls she tries to persuade them that lying is among the most heinous of human behaviours, far worse than missing out on a mass. The authorities, learning of this, transfer her to other duties. Fits perfectly with the Church mission statement and may well be the reason why Italian criminal law allows a defendant to lie and to say anything he likes to the judge, without any risk of being charged with perjury. Witnesses must, however, tell the truth.

Nino was worrying, I imagined, that expectations and entitlements associated with a paying guest might be more than he could stomach. Emptying his coffee cup at one gulp, he slapped it down on the table and said, 'I haven't done this before. I hope it will be all right. You will have to help me.'

The brothel near the station suddenly popped into my head and I had to restrain a giggle, recommending instead that if we dealt with the money side straightaway that would sort out most problems.

How much was he charging a night? When he told me, I could hardly resist a smile.

'You haven't done any market research, have you?'

Another sharp intake of breath. 'Am I asking too much?'

Too little, I told him saying that I would be happy to pay the going rate, a reduced one due to the length of my stay, and set by those in Catania and Syracuse.

When I named the figure, he stared at me for a second or two and then shattered the room with a yell, throwing his hands up in the air and bringing them down again prayerfully clasped on his chest. 'An angel, an angel has come to my house.' He rose to his feet, throwing his arms wide, and whirling around on his toes. 'Oh, this is a happy day, a happy day.'

Believe me, happy days had been few and far between for this man and had I known the story of his life as it later emerged, I might have offered an even higher rent.

In a smooth flow of beautiful, cultivated Italian he confessed he had dreaded renting out a room, but his financial situation had deteriorated considerably in recent months. Essentially he was unemployed. Finding work in Sicily was difficult and depressing. While he could think of no other option he worried that a terrible person might come into his house. Rob him in the middle of the night. Now here was an angel, and honest – where was I from? How lucky to be from somewhere that was not Sicily. Head-butting the wall several times he cried, 'How I hate this place. I was away twenty years and should never have returned.'

Then, impressing on me that he had an unavoidable appointment, he rose to leave, apologizing that he would not return till late.

'Entertaining me or looking after me is not part of the deal,' I assured him. 'You are simply offering me a room. I am well able to look after myself.'

Again the palms of his hands leapt towards each other, pressing tightly together.

'*Macché*,' he said. 'This is a strange business.'

He laid a set of four keys on the table. I'd soon work out the locks. For *cena* there was a good cheap trattoria just around the corner, opposite the primary school. I should make myself at home. Television was in the sitting room. And there were books in the hall. Had I noticed them? I nodded. Said I thought Sicilian writers marvellous. Verga, Vittorini and Sciascia, especially. He laid a neatly manicured hand on my arm and took another look at me, smiling and shaking his head.

'You are too wonderful. *Buona sera, signora*. I'll see you in the morning at breakfast.'

****

Despite his physical attractions Nino was no womanizer. Rather, the big-brotherly type. He lacked any hint of menace and mystery, that touch of flint in a man, however tender, that women are won to. Spontaneous, candid and warm-hearted, there was something of the mother hen about him and his concerns. I blinked to hear that during his twenty years in the North he had been earning a huge salary as a book salesman. Number one in the force, he assured me, producing a bunch of certificates for my perusal. 'Every year.'

'Encyclopaedias?'

'*Per carità, signora!* Medical textbooks. My clients were the broadest medical population, doctors, nurses, students, health bureaucrats inside and outside hospitals. The books were widely advertised and reviewed in medical journals and were sought after. They covered the entire range of medicine and public health. That's a huge market. We were way ahead of the pack. My value rested in my administrative and communicative skills, meeting orders, getting repeat orders and building up a faithful *clienti* that were happy to keep up with new editions and new titles. And I arranged little treats for clients, rewards for their patronage. We were a big family.'

His eyes glowed in happy remembrance. But something must have gone wrong. He was pushing fifty, I estimated, and back here out of work. It seemed that in his youth, before departing for the North, he had formed an attachment with a Messina student teacher, maintaining it while she completed her training in Sicily and served an obligatory period there before she could transfer to the North.

In the meantime he built his career and took out a mortgage on a large and luxurious apartment in one of Turin's best zones. By the time his new bride arrived the mortgage was substantially reduced. He was already salesman of the year in his company, earning top money and there was his wife's added income as a teacher. They had two children, a boy and a girl.

Listening to what happened after that, I wondered if the woman had suffered post-natal depression. As the years passed, it seemed that she became more and more depressed. He had to care for the children. She lost interest in everything about her. She wanted to return to Sicily, the very last thing he himself desired. But in the end he gave up his wonderful job, sold the luxury apartment and the family returned to the south.

They bought the apartment he was in now, with two bedrooms, two bathrooms, a living room and the eat-in kitchen, but no formal dining room that I recall. His wife recovered somewhat and found a teaching position. He tried to develop an outpost of his company in the south and it limped along for several years but eventually had to be wound up.

In the meantime his wife had obtained a transfer to Pisa. She wanted their son to go to Pisa University, Galilei's alma mater and still with an international reputation for its researches in science and medicine. Now Nino was on the point of selling the apartment, moving to Pisa himself and buying another flat there, optimistic that he might again find well paid employment. 'Then I can be with my children."

****

From time to time Nino took me out and about, once to a rugged mountain area of Messina where we drove to a summit and could look across a massive series of high peaks and gorges, curving away in folds, so high, so thickly forested, so deeply riven, as to make my stomach lurch.

'Nobody can live in those forests, surely? Or maybe descendants of those ancient tribes that first settled Sicily. The Siculi?'

He laughed. 'Them too. But my family used to live there, and,' pointing far, far into the distance, 'I used to walk through those forests to the school where my father taught, high on one of the ridges. You can't see it from here, but there's a small community there, hidden away.

'Hidden away,' he repeated, lips tightening. 'My mother lived on a small farm in one of those valleys. My father was her teacher. She was thirteen and my father forty-five when he got her pregnant.'

I kept on looking out over those stupendous, craggy peaks, staring straight ahead, listening, I imagined, like a priest at the confessional. Nino was born when his mother had just turned fourteen. The teacher married her, but his grandmother raised Nino to believe that his mother was his sister.

'She hated me, my sister as I thought she was. My grandmother died when I was about eleven and then *she* started bossing me, getting me to do all the housework before I went to school. She lay about all day, doing pretty well nothing. My father treated her sympathetically. He adored her. She was passively indifferent to him. He never stopped paying for his sin.

'I was a good student and my father encouraged me to think of going to university. *She* was quite viciously opposed to the prospect. She treated me with scorn and one day when she refused to let me go to school at all, insisting I clean the house, I turned on her and grabbed her, shaking her and told her I was not going to be her slave, that I would not allow her to retard my education and that I would not do any more cleaning. After that I spent every spare moment reading and studying, helping only when I felt like it.

'She never breathed a word to me of what my father had done. It was he who eventually confessed. By then I was old enough to know that a decent man does not abuse young girls.

A mature man should not even think of them as sexual prey. I was shocked. Horrified. Disgusted. I pitied my mother, though she rejected my pity with contempt. When my father hinted that she had seduced him I threatened to knock him down.'

What a life for a little boy, trudging alone through these great forests, making his way up the ridge to where his father was still in a position of trust having taken advantage of a child in his professional care. Left behind at home was a slatternly young girl forced into early motherhood and filled with bile and bitterness.

Nino had tried to make up for his father's betrayal of his mother, to show her that not all men were vile. 'She hates me still,' he said, 'but I do my best not to react to her provocations.'

Then he drove me to the ridge, over rough unsealed roads. In the security of a well maintained car the forests were beautiful, even if shadowy and enclosed, a soft green light penetrating the gloom and the sound of running water occasionally breaking their vast silence. I would have been petrified walking there even with a companion.

Surprisingly, the little community that hosted the school appeared to be securely rooted, to have had a stable existence, strung out for some distance along the ridge, with the streets well lit and the paving in good condition. The houses were solidly built and fairly modern. Probably rebuilt after the Second World War. A sizeable concentration of shops, with a doctor's practice and a pharmacy next door to each other, and a buzz of people and cars, generated an impression of prosperity.

'Could your father have gone to gaol?' I asked.

Nino sniffed. 'Not likely. Of course if he had not offered to marry my mother, he would certainly have imperilled himself. But 'doing the right thing', as they say, that is, satisfying another male's honour with no regard for my mother's well-being, and having gone to confession and performed the required rituals, would have brought forgiveness.

'God's, I take it. Not your mother's?'

He gave a thin smile. 'No, no, no. That is not her nature. She knows only how to hate.'

I got a hint of his mother's lack of charm one day when I was alone in the apartment and the phone rang. There was no acknowledging my '*pronto*', just a snarl and a woman demanding hoarsely to speak to Nino. I knew immediately it was the she-wolf.

'I'm afraid he's not home at the moment,' I said, making faces at the wall. 'Who's calling?'

'His mother. Who else would bother to call him?'

I could hear the spit travelling through the earpiece.

Another snarl. 'Where is he?'

'He's out on business,' I said, putting a bit of a bite in my tone and curling my lip, not to mention looking down my nose. 'Can I take a message?'

'*Non mi far ridere* – Don't make me laugh,' she said, wheezing heavily. Definitely not a well person in any sense of the word. 'He hasn't got any business. Business, indeed. Hah!'

Before she could speak further I interrupted and said I would tell him she had called. And put the phone down very gently, just in case she could cast a spell on him. Poor Nino.

When he arrived home I gave him the bare details, keeping my face and voice carefully neutral. 'Your mother rang.'

He nodded. Enough said.

He never stopped talking about his two children. He had followed his wife to Sicily only to keep close to them. He felt very protective towards his daughter in particular, saying that when she reached thirteen he would look at every man he encountered who seemed about forty-five years old, and the thought that such an aged male might abuse his daughter made him want to throttle his father.

'At that age, a girl's a child. Nothing more. It's not normal to regard her sexually. My father was not normal. And yet in certain respects he was a decent person. Very good to me."

****

Though not a playboy, Nino was in no wise a monk. One afternoon light steps in the hallway had me pop my head out of the kitchen, startled to find a strange woman confronting me, a clutch of keys in her hand. On seeing me she smiled shyly: 'I'm Antonia, Nino's friend. You must be Mary Rose. I've heard so much about you.'

I had heard nothing of her. Shaking hands made me aware of a big basket she had deposited at her feet. 'Some dishes I've brought for him. Just a bit extra I add to the cooking for my children – something for you too,' she added. 'If you like Sicilian cooking.'

What a contrast to Nino's mother and his depressed wife, was his beautiful, sweet and loving companion. The prototype of the Italian Madonna/mamma, gentle and giving, but with a strong sense of *amor proprio*. Quietly assertive, yet tactful and composed in her dealings with others. My heart sank when I heard she was studying theology at some institute or other. Applying herself to the misogynist doctrines of Augustine, no doubt. I nodded without much enthusiasm when she told me her ambition was to teach religious studies in a high school. Wouldn't she rather be Marie Curie?

Her own background was not wanting in bizarre elements. She was a single mother long separated from the Calabrian she had married in her early twenties and who had taken their little boy back to Calabria. The son, last seen as a toddler, was now twenty, a commerce student in Calabria. His first visit ever to his mother and sister was pending, and they were planning a big dinner party to welcome him. His cousins would be coming along and Antonia was insisting I should be there, too.

I told Nino his partner was a jewel. 'She must compensate for the problems you have in Sicily.'

'That's the main problem,' he said. '*In* Sicily. Not elsewhere. She will never leave here. She is Sicilian to the core. Her family have been public figures in the region for many years. There's talk of raising a monument to her late father and she would never abandon even her municipality. I want to live in Pisa. But it will be a long way from Antonia.'

Before departing, he had dug out and left on the table an article for me to read, saying, 'This explains everything.'

It was a newsletter piece written by a religious, a eulogy of Antonia's father, who, it seems, had, in just over two decades, almost single-handedly turned a hamlet without even a little school into a model, award-winning town whose social and economic development had completely transformed the lives of the people and won the admiration of the entire region of Sicily.

Nurseries, kindergartens, primary and junior secondary schools, public housing estates, industrial estates, a town hall and other public buildings, new piazzas and new streets, all built according to modern principles of town planning represented a reformation so radical as to call for amazing human skills: as well as having vision, intelligence and commitment, Antonia's father had to take on the regime, the agribusiness class and property owners who dominate Sicily's Regional Council, coax and cajole them into giving their support, persuade them that making the taxation system more progressive, even excluding very low income receivers from being taxed at all, would ultimately profit them.

And the irrefutable miracle achieved by Vito, Antonia's father, had other fantastic components: he had been born into a poor family rendered destitute when his own father was killed in a work accident and the then seventeen-year-old unemployed youth had striven to create income for his mother and siblings by living in the wild, gathering edible fruit and fibrous plants used by ropemakers, sleeping outdoors away from home to extend his working hours and be one mouth fewer to feed.

Notwithstanding such an inauspicious beginning, by age thirty-one when he began his career in public life, the youth had gained a diploma from a polytechnic. Two years later, he took out a degree in Economics and Commerce from the University of Messina and in that year married a baroness who bore him four children, one of them, Antonia.

Morganatic marriages are not at all uncommon in Sicily. One might say that they are almost essential in stabilizing a society that is socially and economically cruelly divided. The steady uploading of outstanding members of the commons into the aristocracy gives a fillip to the latter, bringing it either great beauty and a weighty dowry from women marketed by their fathers, as described in *The Leopard*, or the power and wealth of an ambitious and successful entrepreneur or one of his descendants, perfectly demonstrated by the Florio family, who were, in addition, outsiders from Calabria. These are marriages of extended families, not just individuals, and the intersecting, however narrowly, of entire familial networks blunts the edge of them-and-us hostility.

But Vito had a fatal flaw. He was a Communist. He had joined the Party. And Party support had gained him election as Mayor, the office that offered a base for his reforms. His wife, the baroness, like so many wives of famous Italian communists was a devout churchgoer, ideologically at a polarity from her husband. Yet she married a man bearing the title 'Secretary of the League of Democratic Communists'. Of course, many women hope to reform errant husbands and no doubt her confessor would have obtained some such promise from her and offered her prayerful support.

In fact, Vito appears to have clashed with the Party over the question of his autonomy. He did not want to adhere to every Party ruling, and certainly, such a dynamic, single-minded individual would not have been a Party hack. In April 1979, he lost the support of the Party and failed to be elected Mayor. His public life came to an end and memories of his massive contribution to his *paese* were already fading when he died in 2005, aged eighty.

Raising a monument to this heroic benefactor would never be a moot point. If not to him, to whom? But imagine a wonderful statue in the middle of the major piazza in his town, the first of the piazzas he had had constructed. Every day passers-by admire it. Tales of his municipal valour are passed from generation to generation of children asking their parents, 'Who is the person of the statue?' And it transpires that all his great work was done under the aegis of the Communist Party. Champion the arch-enemy? In a milieu where lies are little regarded and fakery never out of fashion, a lie is the obvious solution to this problem.

The lie quietly appears at the end of the eulogy. Vito was a closet Catholic. And not just giving the appearance of one.

'What few people know or imagine is that [Vito] despite his original political affiliations was a profoundly religious man. Mass every Sunday and festival, the rosary every day, frequent confession and communion, modest and charitable, more so than anyone could imagine.'

Why would 'few' people know or imagine? Because it was a lie. Would a pious Catholic adopt a hugely Communist persona for his entire public life? Not even in a Catholic Wonderland with all its absurdity. Would any Communist who had drawn on the support of the Party for decades to execute an astonishing transformation in the lives of his *compaesani*, revert to religious superstitions merely because he had fallen out with his former colleagues?

So long as the lie finds space on the monument, like the lie on the monument to the Florios, the Church will be content. Appearance is everything.

I haven't yet been back to Antonia's *paese* to check whether a statue of her father has gone up yet. Perhaps the tribute to Vito will take another, much less visible and more honest form.

****

One day, after venturing to Nino during a quiet chat the opinion that Italian schooling and teacher training – totally dominated by the Church – is not oriented towards teaching empirical modes of inquiry or encouraging analytical thinking in the population at large, I was surprised when he hurried off without a word and returned holding a sheet of paper inside a plastic sheath. It contained a book review written by his son Matteo, now twenty but then seventeen. Nino thought I might find it interesting. The book under consideration was *Why we cannot say we are not Mafiosi,* by Alfio Caruso. No bibliographic details are given by the reviewer, nor any indication as to where or if the review were published.

However, on searching the web, I encountered the author of the book in an interview with Beppe Grillo, Italy's immensely popular comedian who is also a highly vocal political activist. Caruso was discussing another more recent book he has authored, pointing the finger at Milanese businessmen who work in league with the mafia, laundering their money and helping them network. It was Caruso's view that the Palermo judge, Giovanni Falcone, had been assassinated because he had commented publicly that 'the mafia are entering the Stock Exchange' and indicated that Milan stockbrokers were soon to come under his scrutiny.

Personally, I would welcome a book with a title structured like Caruso's *Why we cannot say we are not mafiosi,* suggesting as it does a formal argument with the premises and terms neatly laid out for me to follow with little effort.

In fact, even without reading it, I know that the expectations promised by the title will not be met. Analysis and exposition are ever absent from Italian sociopolitical commentary, supplanted by overloaded descriptions and convoluted narratives that intensify the muddle of living with absurdity on a daily basis.

But here is an edited version of Matteo's review:

More than a book this is an extended essay of the informative kind, a portrait of Sicily together with its inhabitants in the thousand facets that characterize them. Detailed descriptions enrich the portrait but the author errs perhaps in generalizing the behaviour of Sicilians.

The majority of us, even if we live on the island, seem to be in the dark about many happenings, but that is probably only because we refuse to see them.

The author distances himself from this closed mentality, from our failure to make good use of resources, from the corruption of politicians and judges, which persists on a large scale thanks to the omertà *of the citizenry. We take little account of the overwhelming ignorance, spread extensively through illiteracy, that separates us from the rest of the country. We remain trapped in the great tight network of the party in power, yes in power, not government.*

Matteo too is here falling back on description. 'The closed mentality of the Sicilian people, the failure to make good use of resources, corruption..." But how did this mentality become closed? Why is the region so corrupt? Has he ever really looked at Sicilian history to discover how the people have arrived at their present predicament? If not, why not?

I told Nino I doubted any seventeen-year-old Australian could imagine writing about his country in such terms. But they might possibly imagine how to go about changing things.

****

A year after returning to Australia I made another trip to Italy, briefly to Sicily where Nino and Antonia came to Catania and met up with me for a meal at Rita and Grzegorz's place. He was pretty cheerful. His former wife and the children were happily settled in Pisa. He visited regularly but had decided not to move there. His mother had died. That she-wolf. But I offered my condolences because he did have an attachment to her. She had left him a property in a beautiful spot just out of Messina and he was hoping to develop it as a B and B. Maybe I would come and stay when I had written my book. My visit had shown him the possibilities, he said, smiling broadly. Antonia too was excited by the project. He had sold the apartment in Messina because he was obliged by law to stay on the premises of the B and B.

'Everything has taken a turn for the better,' he told me.

'It can happen,' I said. 'Even in Sicily.'

35

Two or three days before leaving Messina, I spent forty euros to go and say hullo to people I didn't really want to meet in a place I didn't want to visit, at a time of the day that made it impossible for me to have a decent meal. No *pranzo*, no *cena*. Just a huge spread of nibbles that were mainly sweet. Things like that can happen if you start chatting to someone on an overnight train from Paris to Rome, as I did, earlier in the year.

The woman sharing my wagon-lit, hearing that I was writing a book on Sicily, pressed me to visit friends of hers in a place not far from Messina. She assured me the couple were cultivated, well educated and 'very, very rich' – they lived in a beautiful castle – and the wife, who spoke excellent English, loved to meet new people, especially if they were English. I thanked her for the contact details she wrote on a piece of notepaper but my heart, for some inexplicable reason, sank with dread.

On the appointed day, the dread returned. To begin with, the couple lived in a hamlet which turned out to be an hour on the train from Messina. Secondly, the "*festa*" which my train companion thought was to be an all day affair and that I must under all circumstances attend, was instead to be strictly from five thirty p.m. till seven thirty p.m. and thirdly, the day of the *festa* was Sunday when, in the entire day, there is usually only one train there and back to little places out of the city.

Sure enough, the train was leaving Messina at three thirty p.m., would arrive at my destination at four thirty-eight p.m. and the only train returning would leave at six thirty p.m. Perhaps if I had rung my hosts to confirm that I was coming, they might have asked how I was placed for transport, but I had lost their telephone number (a Jungian slip) and had almost made up my mind not to go.

In the end, professionalism of a sort won out. Besides, I was reluctant to disappoint my friend on the train. She is, after all, the daughter of a former ambassador to France, she had quizzed me thoroughly about my approach to the book on Sicily, and I figured she expected me to learn something important from getting to know her very, very rich castle dwellers. I rang her, embarrassed, to ask her if she could let me have their number, and she herself enquired about my travel arrangements.

'Are you staying in a hotel in town?'

'For a two-hour visit?' I said. 'Not really.'

She was apologetic. She had thought it an all day affair at the castle. That was why she had asked me to set aside a day.

'Don't worry,' I said. 'I won't end up sleeping on a park bench.'

She texted me the number, but I didn't ring the couple, just kept the number for any emergency after I arrived. Of course, I had spoken with the wife earlier, otherwise I wouldn't have known that the occasion was to last for strictly two hours.

Seated in the train, my usual twenty minutes before departure time, clutching a regrettably small box of *marrons glacés* for my hosts, there being nothing larger available at three bars, I felt my spirits rise. They remained buoyant even though we drew into the hamlet twenty minutes late. The station looked abandoned. Not a person, let alone a taxi, in sight. The worst feature of this excursion was having to wear my best shoes, delicate as they were, and pick my way over humpy pebbles cemented to stone 'bricks', in various patterns, a star or a diamond being popular, forming 'tiles' about two feet square, a combination of beauty and function, being a modified Arab version of the hardwearing Roman road.

I was always coming across these road tile patterns in the older country towns and villages, and stopped to admire them every time. In my boots or walking shoes, however, there was no need to leap from one stone brick to another avoiding the edges of the pebbles where my heels could be caught. Anyone watching me at this place might have been reminded of those high-stepping Spanish horses that make regular appearances on Sunday television programs.

Eventually I reached the central piazza which was surprisingly impressive for such a small community. That kind of discovery in Sicily can sometimes point to the vicissitudes of history, to one or more periods when a hamlet might have been a town or even a modest city. I was relieved to find a cheering level of social activity I had hardly suspected from the station, with people sitting outside the bars eating *gelati* or *brioches* dripping almond *granita*, a favourite Sicilian sweet, the young whizzing about on their *motorini* and clusters of old men talking in shop doorways while their wives, seated on an array of chairs drawn close together in their tiny front gardens, chatted but without neglecting to work, preparing vegetables from big bowls on their laps, or knitting or embroidering.

Observing one such group of women I was captivated by the sight of a tall and narrow window behind them, the wall around which had been framed with a row of majolica tiles, predominantly blue. What a brilliant idea. Worth copying, I thought, but our windows at home were much too big to be tiled all round like these. Still, majolica tiles are continually appearing in new contexts. Four arranged in a diamond shape are sometimes glued to the front door, and a small 'carpet' of tiles may replace a doormat.

Everyone in the piazza gave me the same direction.

'Straight ahead.' And when I asked if it were far to Via Castello, where the couple live, the glee in their expressions answered for them.

'Quite a way.'

'Uphill, too?' They were less positive about that.

'Not too bad.'

They denied any knowledge of the family, something I found incredible and decided must be reflecting the traditional *omertà* country people developed over centuries to protect themselves against foreign rulers and today, of course, against their modern oppressors.

There was nothing to do but keep '*sempre diritto*' and hope for luck. It arrived some hundreds of metres into my uphill walk when I spotted an old Sicilian, gnarled and weather-beaten, emerging from his gate and making ready to climb into his car. He looked like a traditional farm labourer. If anyone knows them, he will, I assured myself. Seeing me hurrying towards him, he paused, smiling, his eyes like two little lumps of shiny coal.

'Take it easy, signora. It's too hot to hurry.' The smile broadened when I mentioned the couple's name.

'The owners of the castle, you mean? Of course I know them. I worked for them for years.'

He swung his arm to the right, in the direction of a dirt track that began behind and parallel to the road, and that I might have walked past had I not seen him, and made snaking movements to indicate I should follow the winding road. When he saw dismay cloud my face, his expression lit up, and he said:

'Don't worry, signora, I can take you there.'

I told him I had been looking for a taxi and that I would be happy to pay him.

'No, no, no. Absolutely not. I'm free, I have time.'

What a relief. And a surprise too, to find that we weren't going to drive along the dirt track. That was a shorter route, he explained, for walkers only, but we would go a little way along the highway and then up the driveway to the castle. In less than five minutes we were there.

He was certainly familiar with the place and with the parking arrangements. When we got out, he briskly negotiated the gates, buzzers and other contemporary entry and exit controls till we arrived at what was in effect a piazza in front of the castle, whose broad steps led up to a heavy double door. Confidently, he pressed the bell.

The owner, Paolina, opened the door herself. She stared at my guide, projecting a restrained amazement. Perhaps he had never before used the front door to come calling. It had been a hot late autumn day, but Paolina was wearing a pale blue cashmere sweater over a classic tweed skirt in blends of soft blue and lavender. The pearls and the low-heeled Italian shoes spelling expensive simplicity, the carefully groomed hair, trim figure and slightly frigid manner, were all caste marks of the "very rich" as my friend on the train had labelled the couple.

I introduced myself, explaining how fortunate I had been to find this man who had helped me so willingly.

'I wanted to pay him,' I told her, 'but he refuses to let me.'

'No, he won't take payment,' she said. 'It's better not to press him.'

He, in the meantime, had launched into an animated if unilateral conversation with her, obviously at his ease, smiling and laughing, and leaning forward, confidentially. By this time, her husband, Anselmo, had arrived and positioned himself at his wife's side, looking from his worker to me and back to the man, with some bemusement. The worker then turned to him and launched into a long story. Beneventi listened politely, like his wife, and in absolute silence, not emitting any of the responses designed to encourage a speaker.

Eventually, without appearing to hurry, he tied up the conversation, I thanked the old man again and he went off, smiling, obviously having enjoyed his brief encounter.

'You were expecting me today?' I said, now having the couple's close attention.

'Yes,' Paolina promptly responded, leading me into the front room. 'But we thought you were going to ring to confirm it.' I explained that I had mislaid their phone number. Adding. 'Look, I must tell you this immediately. I'm afraid I'll have to leave in an hour. There was only one train coming today and the only one going back leaves at six thirty p.m.'

That thawed them. The hint of frigidity in their manner melted away. Action was called for and Paolina was obviously an organizer. Also a woman of few words. She glanced across at her husband and said in pleasantly modulated English: 'Can you find out if there's a train leaving at a different time from another station, maybe Barcellona?'

Still anxious to get out of the place, however, I interposed hurriedly, 'Perhaps it will be enough just to have a look at each other now, see what we think and if the result is promising we might arrange later to meet in Messina at some stage for a coffee.'

They both stared. What? What was she saying? It was not what one was used to. Or at least one did not speak it aloud. But they were people trained not to show what they were thinking. Without further comment the husband disappeared and Paolina led me to a visitors' book opened out on a table. Strange that in this castle there was no entry hall, no place to hang outer garments, place bags. I deposited the *marrons glacés* on the table and wrote my name in the book. It would head the list on the page. Later when they were browsing through their guest books they would say, who on earth was that?

'Come out into the gardens,' Paolina then advised me, 'My friend has arrived with her group.'

We passed through an archway into a courtyard at the top of the drive, and encountered, sitting on a bench at the side, on the fringe of what I could see were extensive formal gardens of the kind commonly associated with English country houses, a woman, over whom a man, her husband I learned, was anxiously hovering, she disporting before the concerned eyes of Beneventi, a thickly stockinged leg and explaining how she had stumbled over an obstacle that day and badly sprained her ankle.

On our being introduced, she immediately announced that she and Paolina were best friends and had known each other from elementary school, something she obviously took pride in. She admired Paolina and adopted the same almost adulatory tones in speaking of her, that the woman on the train had used when urging me to meet the Beneventi.

The friend was half Neapolitan and half Sicilian, so she said, living in Naples but spending much of her time here in Sicily. If she and Paolina were the same age, the latter was certainly wearing better, particularly her face, which demonstrated the pale protected complexion some women choose to live by, while the other had been a proud sunlover and was now suffering the consequences; swarthy, leathery skin with yellow tones, dry, lined and stained. The one was warm and expansive, the other cool, reserved and disciplined. It was easy to see what had brought them together at school.

The friend was now describing what sounded like a ten-course luxurious lunch she had served to her bus group at her house that day. There were forty of them, mainly Neapolitans, whom she had urged to make a three-day visit to Sicily. Some of them were now straggling up the path towards us. The Neapolitan's brow furrowed.

'I hadn't realized the bus couldn't come right up,' she said to Paolina. 'Some people are quite frail and have trouble walking.'

The fact was, buses weren't supposed to be coming up. A notice in the courtyard had said clearly, 'The castle is not open to the public,' meaning that the grounds were, perhaps? So the gardens and the farms were very likely featured sights. Did the Beneventi charge visitors to meet the costs of maintaining the property? But why would they if they were very, *very* rich? Well, pursuing riches is like reaching for the stars. Never an end to it.

Once all the tourists were happily assembled in the courtyard, the air turned mellow and balmy with a profusion of elegantly phrased compliments and courtesies; several men, separately, of course, reached for my right hand and bent over it to within a millimetre and I wondered how they managed to stop with such precision as if they had some sensoring mechanism in their lips.

It wasn't only the Beneventi castle that was attracting compliments. Some late in the day praises were being bestowed on the Neapolitan's house. Several of the bus group had not yet been able to convey their appreciation of the marvellous lunch she had put on for them and the opportunity to visit her in her beautiful home. They were kept busy praising first one house and then the other. The Neapolitan's friends in Naples, it seemed, were distinct from her friends in Sicily. I'm always surprised to see how reluctant Italians are to travel anywhere a little distant to visit friends. Probably organizing a bus and arranging everything herself was the only way the Neapolitan could succeed in her goal which was clearly to bridge a gap between her friends on the island and the others on the mainland.

People made their way into the castle, and wandered around through the rooms closest to the entry, not as a formal tour, just looking idly (or shrewdly in some cases) the way they might on a first visit to any house. There were some gasps over the large expanse of antique majolica tiles covering the floors, faded like washed-out frescoes, but still in excellent condition and more gasps when we encountered two large rooms recently recovered with new majolica tiles, splendidly sumptuous. I was rapidly deciding that this castle was one of the best maintained private dwellings I had seen in Sicily, and by then I'd seen a few. It gave the impression that everything inside worked, that when screws fell out of a door handle they would be immediately replaced. There was a general air of efficiency about the entire environment. I wondered how the Beneventi got to be like that. If I ever meet them again, I shall have to find out.

While people were circulating those inclined would front up to another guest and murmur their surname, receiving the other's in exchange. 'What kind of name is that?' one asked me, when I murmured 'Liverani'.

Clearly not a football fan. An attendant at the Antonello da Messina exhibition in Rome had asked me excitedly if I were related to the champion soccer player of that name.

'Never heard of him,' I'd replied.

One superbly dressed woman astonished me when she added to her name, 'I'm very old.' About eighty, I guessed. She then took me by the elbow and drew my attention to a wall dominated by an acquarello portrait of two women in Edwardian dress, commenting on it in admiring detail. Then she asked me in French if I spoke French and I said to her in French, no I speak English. She unfortunately did not. Her Italian sounded so French that I asked her which was her mother tongue. She was not Neapolitan, but came from Mantua and had had to learn French because she worked for Hermes, the famous French fashion designer, and was in regular communication with the Paris office.

It was turning out to be quite a pleasant evening. The air was cool and fresh, and people were proving interesting in unexpected ways. The Hermes lady introduced me to her brother-in-law, a professor of land management at Naples University, and whose domain covered Sicily. I told him I thought his department must be doing good work because I had never seen agricultural land so well cared for as in Sicily.

'But are you not involved with the management of the foreshores? There are some dreadfully ugly and unsound buildings set up horizontally, almost on the water. Really, they're brutalising some of the most beautiful parts of your urban coastline, and public access is closed off, I've noticed.'

I told him I'd even seen great mansions right here in Messina, built on sand dunes that should be stabilizing the beaches. How can anyone think of building a house on sand? Don't they read the Bible?

'Corruption,' the professor answered tersely. 'Our advice is not always welcome.'

By now, a very long table had been set out in a room next to the kitchen, covered with an overwhelming variety of Sicilian sweets, such a feast to the eye, you hardly needed to eat, plus some nondescript "western style" savouries, the kind bought from the frozen food section of the supermarkets. Jugs of delicious home-made dessert wine and liberal amounts of bottled water were distributed throughout the length of the table. Catering assistants on hand kept the drinks and food moving.

I introduced myself to a woman who turned out to be a librarian at the National Library of Naples. She smilingly made room for a third woman, who was wandering around looking a bit lost. To my surprise they quickly raised the subject of their mafia, the camorra, which has been in the news recently because of its pernicious involvement in waste disposal and in the mountains of waste that had been let block the streets of a certain section of Naples until the public had started protesting. Waste disposal, not surprisingly when one thinks of the numerous bodies they have to get rid of, has traditionally been in the hands of the mafia, along with construction and road transport. Public health problems related to sanitation have in the past led to nightmarish epidemics of typhoid and cholera in both Naples and Sicily.

Naples was in a mess at the moment, the women said. In Sicily the mafia was quiet, and in Naples the camorra were being so disruptive. 'It's always like that,' they agreed in concert. 'When one's up the other's down.'

I told them I had been very impressed by the housing projects I had seen along the railway lines when I was coming into Naples by train. 'They look very bright and attractive,' I said, 'vastly superior to the third world dwellings I've seen along the tracks leading from Stansted airport to London's Liverpool Street Station.'

At precisely seven thirty p.m., people began heading for the front door where the Beneventi were waiting to say goodbye. Beneventi showed me the railway times he had found. A train was leaving Barcellona station for Messina at eight thirty p.m. He would take me but probably earlier than that and would have to leave me there.

'That's fine,' I said. 'I have a book to read.'

The Neapolitan and her husband were staying on with the Beneventi. Paolina asked me if I would like to come back into the house for a drink or something more to eat, but I said I would be happy to go to Barcellona whenever her husband wanted to make the move. She then asked me with a smile if I would like a doggy bag, but I shook my head.

'Not advisable for my waist.'

I overheard the Neapolitan say something about money, that some people had just given her the money now and I decided that everything had been paid for, perhaps to aid a charity.

Beneventi was keen to leave straight away. Perhaps he was tired and wanted a quiet dinner with his wife, or they might even have had another engagement. But I could see he was pleased when I indicated my willingness to go immediately. In the car, he started to chat quite freely. There were lots of questions I could have put to him about his work and lifestyle but I couldn't bring myself to, and I let him shape the conversation.

He was not entirely Sicilian. One of his parents came from the North. And one grandmother was Jewish. He must have been older than he looked, telling me that fifty years ago, before the War, Sicilians had been an ugly lot. The women especially. They were very short, especially in the leg, dumpy and hairy all over. And had bad teeth.

'Really?'

What an extraordinary conversation. I wondered what had triggered his comments. Southern women did tend to be short, though my Calabrese friend in Australia, Pina Molino, was about 1. 74 metres, slim, with a beautiful face, large dark eyes thickly lashed, a wide mouth and strong white teeth.

I couldn't believe in such a wide generalization, even if he were talking about peasant women. Some of their daughters would have been beauties. That's how they married up.

I said, 'Bad teeth would have been the result of poverty, surely. The whole of non-industrialised Europe was incredibly poor before the War, and even the lower classes of the industrialized countries. Southern women also did a lot of heavy labour. That can alter the shape of your body. Broaden your back. Thicken your waist. They wouldn't have had time or energy to shave their legs.'

'They're very different today, though,' he said, his tone rapidly warming. 'Some of the women who turn up to work on our farms look like fashion models, tall, with long legs and wrists that are very… very…'

'Delicate?' I ventured.

Fragile, fine. Yes.

I wondered what had happened to the hairy arms.

The conversation moved into absurdity when we went on to talk about the differing heights of Chinese in the north and south, the increasing height of the Japanese, the improvement of teeth because of greater access to protein and fluoridated water. Then I changed the subject. It was time for a bit of judicious name dropping.

'You must move in circles that bring you into contact with Camillo Borghese, the Prince of Paterno? From the Roman family. Do you know him?'

He thought that one over for a bit and finally conceded, 'Ye-e-s, I know him.'

'He's the cousin of a good friend of mine,' I said. 'Andrea Borghese, the son of Valerio Borghese, the Principe Nero.'

I explained that Andrea had emigrated to Australia in the 1970s and Ermete and I had gotten to know him there, that I'd gone with Andrea and Marisa to Paterno, to the Prince Borghese's for lunch and had visited the Prince again on my own to chat to him at greater length. 'It's necessary when I'm writing about Sicily to give some idea of the social classes. One can't just say Sicilians. Camillo's wife's family was one of the latifondi. Would you be in that category? I believe you're very rich.'

How could I be talking like this? It was appalling. Yet I did it quite deliberately and shamelessly. I felt intuitively that it was the right thing to say to this man.

'We have farms,' he said. 'Gentry, I suppose, you might call us.'

I drew the conversation back to Valerio Borghese and the Decima MAS which served as a model for the US SEALS. Decima MAS (*Mezzi d'Assalto* – assault vehicle) was the first ever unit of frogmen deployed in war, created and commanded by Valerio Borghese who had them trained to fight undercover and underwater, operating midget submarines and assault boats armed with a variety of destructive torpedoes. Beneventi had heard of the unit but knew nothing of the details.

Borghese and the Decima MAS developed covert tactics around small teams armed with explosives carrying out secret night-time operations. When the King of Italy signed an armistice with the Allies on 8 September 1943, groans from the Italian commandos must have been heard by sea life all around the globe. Their plan to blow up New York harbour, just brought to completion and scheduled for execution within a day or two, was to be scotched.

Beneventi's eyes widened when he heard this. 'Blow up New York harbour? Well, I'm glad they did not succeed. I hate to think how the Americans would have responded.'

Andrea himself originally knew nothing of this, or indeed of his father's later involvement in an abortive attempt to overthrow the Italian government. That particular plot, to be launched on 6 December, 1970 was associated with the United States' anti-communist strategies, its success dependent on Valerio Borghese's standing with the Italian military. His own force, the Decima MAS, universally admired him, but relations between Borghese and the military generally had soured when it became obvious to him during the War that information about his planned operations was being leaked. To put a stop to it he broke off contact with his peers in the military at large. His suspicions were confirmed when Decima MAS operations immediately began enjoying formidable successes and inflicting serious losses on Allied shipping in the Mediterranean.

The absence of trust between Borghese and the military, however, saved Italy from the same fate as Chile, where General Pinochet enjoyed the support of all the armed forces. At the crucial moment, on the eve of the plot scheduled for launching at four a.m., when it was planned to seize control of the nation's radio stations and imprison members of the Communist Party, the Italian military, debating into the early hours of the morning, voted to support the elected government. Borghese, hearing of this only at the last moment fled to exile in Spain.

The Italian government, after investigating the plot decided to offer him an amnesty, allowing him to return to Italy in exchange for information on the conspiracy. Borghese agreed. Living on his own, his wife having died in a car accident some years previously, he missed his friends and family. When it became known that he had accepted the government's offer and was returning to Italy, the instigators of the plot would obviously have had cause to be alarmed. It was no surprise to the Italians, therefore, that Borghese failed to make it back to Italy: he was said to have died suddenly of a heart attack in Spain, after having been seen dining at a restaurant in the company of an attractive woman. Those closest to him have no doubt that his lady companion had been hired to administer poison to him at the meal.

Beneventi had listened intently to all this. I could tell he had known nothing of it and was intrigued to know how I knew what I knew.

When we reached the station, he got out, and we shook hands.

'It was good to have a chat with you,' I said, 'even if it were so short.'

'Yes, indeed. When are you leaving Messina?'

'The 14th of November. I'm going back to Florence then, to start writing up my notes.'

'We must try to arrange to meet with you again,' he said.

'That would be lovely.'

But I knew it wouldn't happen. Best not.

Part IV The argument

36

A pre-capitalist absurdity

Every visitor to Sicily enthuses over its glorious past, a past that cloisters the region in mystery, myths and maelstroms so mesmerising, that the present and future can lay no claim to attention. Yet when we're visually and emotionally sated on Trinacria's memorabilia of death and the afterlife, those temples, monasteries, mosques, churches, sanctuaries, tombs, catacombs, sarcophagi and slaughter sites attributable to the Greeks, Romans, Carthaginians, Arabs, Normans, Swabians, Angevins and Aragonese – and exulting over the baroque with its voluptuous excesses, or marvelling at the heart-warming munificence of Etna – if mindful of its tantrums – when we've embraced it all, eating and drinking, laughing and singing, and writing ecstatic cards home, and then pause for a moment to look at the human beings who are the living legacy of this glorious past, what do we find? An enduring twenty-five per cent unemployment rate, higher than the worst recorded in the USA during the Great Depression of 1929.

A 2008 EU report on Sicily spells out the details, testifying to an economy unimaginable for any other place in the developed world, especially an autonomous region of Italy whose Northern quadrilateral is among the most advanced industrial sectors in Europe. That the misery and ignorance of the commons, frequently remarked on by eighteenth-century writers, has endured till the present day obviously did not escape the attention of a European Union Committee on Regional Development whose members visited Sicily and Malta in September 2006. For several days the committee surveyed what the administrators had done with the funds given them by the EU to advance their societies. Sicily had received eight billion euros over the period 2000 to 2006, and Malta, a micro-state and a new member of the EU, a very much smaller sum.

These money transfers are not handouts. They are meant to invigorate the entire European Union economy. For instance, if Sicily decides to expand its railway networks, the rolling stock might be built in Germany and the railway tracks in France.

Each region was examined in turn and though the 2008 report makes no attempt to compare relative efficiencies, merely juxtaposing the accounts forces a contrast which could hardly be more illuminating.

Sicily and Malta have histories that run in tandem to a point. Malta, like Trinacria, is the largest island in an archipelago, but a very much smaller region than Sicily with which for centuries it formed a political unit. Malta, like Sicily, is strongly Catholic, ninety-eight per cent of its population being of that religion. The island, however, was ruled for nearly 300 years by the papacy's military/hospitaller force, the Knights of Malta, and for another 150 years by the English, both powers maintaining strong defence forces in the region, of itself enough to keep the population in contact with developments in the outside world.

Contact with British civil servants and the strong British naval presence on their island exposed the Maltese to modernity through the ideas of the Scottish Enlightenment which, unlike the European Enlightenment, was not anti-clerical. English, however, displaced Italian on the island and was given equal status with Maltese as an official language. So the Maltese, unlike the Sicilians experienced indirectly, if not directly, a high degree of contact with a non-Catholic and religiously tolerant culture. They were also presided over by a strong central state with a commitment to the rule of law. Thus their ruling class had no need of a mafia. Moreover, as a tiny colony of the most advanced industrialised nation on the planet they were made aware of the importance of education and literacy. In stark contrast to the poor showing of pupils in Sicilian schools, their school attendance rate in 2008 was estimated at ninety-seven per cent and literacy at ninety-three per cent.

With a population of only 400,000, Malta is smaller than the city of Catania. A new EU member since May 2004, it was among the few 'new Member States' to have already met its expenditure obligations for 2006, while its structural fund system has successfully passed a number of audits. Its government was to receive eight hundred million euros to cover 2007-2013, ten times as much as it received for the previous period. According to the EU report, achieving a sustainable rate of economic growth while ensuring a high level of employment, a low and stable inflation rate and improvements in the standard of living are the Maltese Government's main priorities. Improving transport, education and employment are also listed.

****

Sicily's European Union report, on the other hand, makes depressing, if essential reading.

'A region whose development is below the European average, Sicily still has a fragile production base, an economic structure featuring low industrial employment compared to agriculture and construction and unemployment of over twenty-five per cent (over thirty-five per cent for women, and over fifty per cent for the under-twenty-fives), with peaks in the province of Enna and the cities of Catania, Palermo and Messina. Real GDP growth has been negative on three occasions since 1992; as a general rule, growth has remained below the national average.

'The region exports a little less than six per cent of its production, in contrast with a national average of twenty per cent. Infrastructure development is well below the national average.'

The report goes on: 'Sicily's remarkable natural environment and cultural heritage are under enhanced. The number of national visitors to the region has grown over the last decade while the number of overseas visitors has declined.'

Given the legendary mafia fixation on 'respect' it was clearly an insult to the EU delegation that Salvatore Cuffaro, President of the Regional Government and kin to a prominent mafia family, despite knowing well in advance of the delegation's visit, had chosen to go to Brussels to attend a meeting on illegal immigration. The report says: 'At the formal meeting with government members, Claudio Fava stressed the gravity of the absence of the Region's President... who *inter alia* is responsible for the management of the structural funds'.

The President was eventually forced to resign after being convicted of associating with the mafia.

An American sourced data bank on the mafia casts some light on the deployment of the EU funds in Sicily. This states that back in 2000, when money allocations from the EU were under discussion, those checking the tape of a mafia phone under surveillance made the following note: 'The European Union "Agenda 2000" is envisaging spending 7,586 billion euros over six years in Sicily – a chosen target of Cosa Nostra. They're (the mafia) advising everyone not to make a noise and attract attention because 'we've got to get our hands on all of this Agenda 2000.'

At meetings with various groups that included a representative of Sicilian 'industry' and some union leaders, the EU delegation were presented with a long list of complaints about how the EU funds had been managed by the authorities. They heard that there was no global view of how development should be implemented or how to overcome the structural weaknesses of the economic and social system. The whole system was weak, were it from the entrepreneurial point of view or that of infrastructure. Problems were exacerbated by continual high unemployment. Resources had been dissipated instead of concentrated on essential targets. There was too much red tape and procedures were very bureaucratic. Then again, the local administration had had insufficient training. Nor had the principle of additionality been properly applied and EU funds had in part replaced local government funds.

They were told that 'so long as difficulties of this sort subsist, Sicily will have great difficulty in increasing its GDP. It will stay a depressed and poor region of Europe'.

To put Sicily's condition in perspective one might consider that during the Great Depression of 1929 unemployment peaked at twenty-four per cent in the United States. Think of the songs, the novels, the photography, the films from that period, the terrible hardship graven on ordinary people during the late 1920s and most of the 1930s, the fearful frugality that afterwards constricted for the rest of their lives, almost two generations of capital and labour in the industrialised world. Yet Sicily's *normal* unemployment today is over twenty-five per cent, which translates into lifelong unemployment for the youth and the women who make up the bulk of the unemployed. Sicily is not Bangladesh or Mali. It's a well resourced part of a hugely wealthy nation that likes to cut a *bella figura* on the world stage.

Its appalling economic performance reflects a centuries old challenge by the regime to capitalism and the rise of the industrial middle classes, those traditional generators of Western prosperity.

At a meeting with the press, the delegation Chair explained that members had come to Sicily to talk to those responsible for implementing funds in Sicily, and to visit some of the projects that had been completed or were in the process of being completed. It was not a commission of enquiry nor was it the responsibility of the European Parliament's delegation to control the implementation of EU funds in member states. That was the responsibility of the European Commission. Sicily was to receive in the new period slightly less money than it did between 2000-2006, which sum had amounted to eight billion euros.

Among the projects the delegation viewed was an eighteen-hole international standard golf course and hotel complex costing fifty million euros. That golf course will draw on considerable water resources in a climate whose annual rainfall is very limited, as are its underground springs.

Once on the island of Lipari I lay awake all night, my head under the sheets, trying to block out the throb throb of an engine which I discovered next morning had sounded from the 'water ship' riding at anchor and pumping water from its holds into onshore conduits for distribution to local residents.

In the opening pages of *The Snack Thief*, a novel by the popular Sicilian writer, Andrea Camilleri, the heroic Inspector Montalbano, soaped all over in the shower and ready to rinse off, has the water suddenly dry up, obliging him to run to the kitchen to salvage a few drops from the sink and then from the wash-hand basin in the bathroom, an emergency even installing several water tanks has failed to avert. Scarcity, Montalbano notes with exasperation, is worsened by the irregularity of supply. But the police officer's discomfort is nothing to compare with the calamitous consequences of severe water deprivation joined to starvation and endured for decades by the hapless residents of Partinico, their miseries earlier recounted in these pages.

Few amenities could therefore be more inappropriate to Sicilian needs and resources than a golf course attached to a luxury hotel. 'Private' investment was allegedly contributing forty-two million euros to the extravaganza, boosting eight million euros from the EU. A second holiday resort was also listed as a major item – to comprise a large luxury hotel set in a park of 42,000 square metres with swimming pool and sea views.

'Other enterprises were the conversion of an eleventh century abbey into a restaurant for visitors to a bio-agricultural domain; a sweet factory, a euromedical company and a compost company. No mention was made of projects associated with research and development, new industries, shopping malls, department stores or infrastructural developments: roads and railways, education, hospitals or childcare facilities. Nor was any reference made to Ikea's protracted and aborted negotiations to open a department store in Catania. (Erected in mid-2010.)

It's safe to say that no private investment of fifty million euros or considerably less enters Sicily without mafia agreement and all that the word implies. The two large construction projects will offer the usual 'rents' required to be distributed to 'clients' and help launder the illicit drug fortunes whose legitimizing is a constant problem for the mafia, or will be at least till the collapsed Vatican Bank reinvents itself – a process already in train.

Now that the more couth and kempt elements of the socially upmarket 'white' mafiosi have been spotlighted in alliance with unscrupulous doctors to fleece the privatized health industry, one can't help regarding with skepticism the 'euromedical' company listed as a project, Cuffaro himself being a graduate in medicine and surgery.

One hesitates to ponder on the uses to which the mafia might put a compost company.

Before leaving Palermo, the delegation met with the Mayor and local authorities, including the Bishop. The Mayor, banality personified, stated that the region was steeped in history and culture. His perception, one shared with the Church and other participating parties in a fifteen-council collaboration program for the region, was that development had to be seen not only in the context of economic 'welfare', but in preserving and promoting cultural aspects of the community, 'for this has a direct effect on society'. He did not elaborate on the 'direct' character of the effect. Presumably economic development does not have a direct effect. He acknowledged that the region remained poor and therefore qualified for assistance but the authorities did not want the national government to intervene in the management of that assistance.

One may infer that the Mayor, a member of Sicily's privileged minority, echoed the Church when he dismissed economic development as 'welfare' ranking it below preserving 'cultural' aspects of the community, this in a rich country where so many people live in a condition of grinding poverty. As for preserving culture, puppet theatres, a still living, uniquely Sicilian cultural tradition, focused on social commentary and rooted in the people, with enormous possibilities of training and developing young Sicilian talent, are shabbily treated by the administration.

The Bishop emphasised the importance of the Church in small local communities, pointing out that it owned and was responsible for seventy-five per cent of the cultural heritage in the region. How seriously it takes that responsibility is subject to conjecture. Scaffolding often stands about as long as burnt-out buildings, recalling the EU delegation's description of Sicily's classical heritage as 'under enhanced.' Much of the funding for preserving the legacy comes from overseas, suggesting that it simply represents another source of 'rent' to the regime.

****

Sicily's absurd pre-capitalist condition forces an artificial poverty on people who deserve better. Its long term character is sufficient to indicate that the regime profits handsomely from the situation and is determined to maintain it.

Consider the quality of life the system generates for ordinary Sicilians: they live in a region that is dangerously close to being a subsistence-level economy where 'subsistence' means not dying directly from starvation but from associated things like malnutrition, untreated medical conditions especially mental disturbances and woefully inadequate public health systems. Intra-regional public transport is so poor as to effectively imprison people within their local communities while the impoverished character of other basic utilities minimizes opportunities for social and economic advancement.

When Sicilians walk out of their front doors they emerge into a world of power and privilege, where human rights are banned from the lexicon, where justice can be deferred till the afterlife, and where fragile self-esteem is relentlessly undermined. Securing the most trivial service taken for granted in other parts of the old EU requires the conscious and unflagging exercise of charm, courtesy and, in many cases, deference of the most elaborate sort, depending on the imbalance of power between the parties.

People try not to offend. They never know whom they may be insulting. They hope their relatives are being careful too. In

Sicily, retribution is visited on a clan, not just on an individual. If your cousin even unconsciously insults someone with connections, you yourself may be called to account. Nor are children exempt. The desire for vengeance on a mafioso who turned collaborator and went into hiding saw his twelve-year-old son abducted and tortured, kept prisoner for twenty-six months during which time evidence of his torture was conveyed to his family before the child was ultimately strangled and his body destroyed in an acid bath. Direct life-threatening violence can occur at any time, the Italian state, alone in the developed world, shamefully sharing its monopoly of violence with a rival power – the mafia. It's a fearful place, Sicily, and the fear is kept stoked.

People are low voiced in public, not wanting to draw attention to themselves. They murmur in bars. They are diffident, very polite, warm and smiling. Above all, docile. For many, underlying the smiles is the despair that they might never in their entire lives get a job, never have any money, nor a prospect of marrying. They don't know how it is that things are the way they are, because many can barely read and write. Not till 1961 was the school leaving age raised to fourteen. They are discouraged from seeing themselves as rational beings, able to think and understand. Life is a great mystery. Authority, substantially the Church, tells them what to believe, how to think, and confirms in them that they are persons of little worth, inhabitants of a place they know is despised by ignorant people outside, people who would like to be separated from them because they think of Sicilians as parasites. If they eventually get away, they keep their origins secret.

Some strive to be self-employed, offering services secretly through a screening process; they don't want the mafia calling for the *pizzo* or the financial police looking for unpaid taxes. They fume quietly but are tight-lipped and live in the shadows, day after day. Young and hopeless. Young and angry. To be young and keen and intelligent is a desperate plight, to know that no matter how hard they work, how well they do in their exams, getting a job might never happen. And if the job arrives it will most likely be as a favour, not something gained on merit. Payback may come at a time and in a form that makes their hearts sink. If no job is found, then they may have to depend on ageing parents whose pension is enough to support two persons with few wants but not adult or adolescent unemployed children at a needy stage of their lives.

A headline run by *The Sicilian* newspaper a year or so ago was snapped up by Reuters and flashed around the world, causing widespread mirth at what is an unmitigated tragedy: 'But Mamma, every other 61 year old gets pocket money.' The story was based on a police report of quarrelling between a mother and her elderly son.

Every modern government knows the danger to public stability of having masses of long term unemployed youth, especially males, wandering the streets, like 'the sons of Belial,' as Milton put it, 'flown with insolence and wine.' (The wine may be hard to come by.) Sicily's twenty-five per cent unemployment figure would cause political palpitations even in the North of Italy, not to mention in any Australian government, the US Congress or the French National Assembly.

****

Dutch anthropologist Anton Bloch describes today's Sicilian landowners – the Church the largest of them – as rentier capitalists, a term generally denoting a group that scorns work, especially manual labour, and lives off rents accruing to land and property. Unlike 'production' capitalists, rentiers risk no capital and start no new enterprises. They challenge the link between 'work' and 'reward'. Income is perceived to result not from labour but from chance or a situation. So far as the Church is concerned, its huge income and assets are associated with its claim to a divine mission. Bloch could hardly contain his wonder at hearing a forty-year-old Sicilian truck driver tell him:

'Caro Antonio, you should understand one thing: work is a necessity, not a pleasure. People have to work in order not to die. Blessed is he who does not need to work. The man who

lacks brains or luck has to work with his hands. He is a dizgraziato *who will never become rich or even respected. Manual work has been made by the Devil.'*

A rentier regime blocks off the development of a civil society and the progress of democratisation. It favours authoritarianism because the ruling class has no other objectives but to resist those who would overthrow it, or just as bad, swamp it, by increasing its numbers. Basically the regime seeks to protect its investments and ensure that a flexible, cheap labour force is always on hand.

In societies where the government is likely to be the major and ultimate employer, a bloated, inefficient bureaucracy effectively takes on the attributes of a rentier class. To navigate the bureaucratic labyrinth potential investors must form partnerships with local 'fixers' who will seek a share of their profits, this also another form of rent.

Public services are mercilessly plundered by the *provedores* who win government contracts. No matter who the provedore is or what part of Italy they are from, they will find the mafia bloating the costs of a project, adding a huge 'rent' to the bill.

In 1994, as part of the school legality project earlier referred to, a magistrate told an assembly of Catania high school students that on seeking to buy a hearing aid, he was quoted 5,000 lire by a *provedore* who informed him that the public health service would be charged 100,000 lire for the same product, and that the price difference would be paid out to others (rentiers) involved in the network of corruption. The magistrate said that the public debt in Italy, generally was so high, normal state revenues could not meet the interest payments. Most recently, economic reports have named Italy as one of four EU members whose stratospheric level of debt threatens the stability of the euro.

At the same session, another official, lamenting the high incidence of truancy in Catania, explained that the mafia often recruited school-age children by putting them on a retainer, collecting rents (the *pizzo*) at the low end of the scale. This was a smart move, because the payments being 'trivial' the victim would not offer resistance to the young bagman. Thus, he would be available to do a job for the mafia when called on – 'and this could include murder', the official said.

Not all the money in the EU will make a whit of difference to Sicily, except to strengthen rentierism unless other member countries take serious steps to deal with a regime that is long past its 'use-by' date.

37

Fortress Sicily

Sicily became a fortress when the Reformation and the advance of science and technology in Europe began posing a real challenge to the power and wealth of the Church of Rome, threatening to end its 500-year hegemony over Western Christendom. A growing entrepreneurial middle class, spurred by opportunities associated with New World explorations was already giving evidence of the transfer of power its members would be seeking when the agricultural and industrial revolutions got under way. Resisting this transfer, maintaining not only Sicily but the entire Italian peninsula as an agrarian society, a theocracy, became the Church's pre-eminent interest. Sicily would be refashioned as a fortress from whose embrasures the Vatican hierarchy could launch its salvoes on change, demolishing history.

But prospects had been vastly different when the clerics of Western Christendom first arrived in Sicily during the High Middle Ages, secure in the military cover given them by the Normans. Then their Church was a fully fledged legal institution already 700 years old, a multinational corporation administered by a 'black' aristocracy of Pope, prince/prelates and priests, all claimed to be quasi-divine and attended by numerous lower orders, its pomp, ceremonies and ever evolving rituals a public manifestation of wealth and power meant to cow kings and commons. And they did.

Medieval feudalism reached its apogee in the Norman period, legitimized by the doctrine of the Great Chain of Being which originated with Plato and Aristotle and dominated Western European concepts of the cosmos from the Middle Ages right through to the eighteenth century, pervading the writings of Spenser, Shakespeare, Donne, Milton, Marvell and

Pope. A stunning fantasy of cosmic stasis, the Great Chain had every single living and non-living thing down to the lowest insect and smallest pebble slotted into a hierarchy, its order and influence pre-determined by God, and the occupants meant to stay where put – unless they entered the priesthood or convent.

God of course was above everything. Below him angels, seraphim and cherubim shone in graduated splendour while on earth, the 'royal priesthood' took precedence over any emperor. The propagation of such a doctrine for centuries, in a closed society, goes a long way to induce docility in a people.

Perfect order in feudal societies could, however, be challenged by events beyond parish controls. Plague and other forms of pestilence – cholera and malaria the most deadly – often exacerbated the geological disasters that intermittently afflicted Sicily, driving thousands of rural workers and miners out of the region. Post-Renaissance advances in science and technology drew the most adventurous or desperate labourers to more prospering parts of mainland Europe and later to the New World.

Faced with such crises Sicily's big landowners took to shedding the reciprocal obligations that were the rationale of feudal order. By the time a British force occupying Sicily in 1812 persuaded the local nobility to 'voluntarily' renounce their feudal status, such action was superfluous. Feudalism as originally conceived had long since given way to the perverted form that blights Sicily today.

In other parts of Western Europe, feudalism's demise had been accelerated by the agricultural and industrial revolutions that began in Britain and spread to the United States, with Germany and northern Italy racing to catch up once liberated from foreign rule. In what became known after the Reformation as Protestant Europe, ideas of liberalism and parliamentary rule paralleled the growth of capitalism, whereas in countries still designated 'Catholic', politics focused on preserving joint sovereignty of church and state in an agrarian, pre-industrial society.

France, despite its comparatively long history as a nation state, despite the magnitude of its role in the Enlightenment, the fervour of its Revolutionaries and their occasional outbursts of murderous anti-clericalism, remained staunchly Catholic, taking to industrialization very slowly. Nonetheless the wealth drawn from its overseas colonies bolstered its economy and the rapid growth of a middle class that avidly eyed Church properties and coveted its power. Not till 1905, however, did French citizens break the political nexus between them and the Church, determinedly seizing control of education – a long-standing and, even today, an ongoing area of struggle between them.

Losing its status and many of its holdings in France – causing thousands of unemployed clerics to seek work for the first time in their lives, with the state conscripting many into the armed forces – intensified the Church's determination to retain its shared sovereignty in Italy where nationhood and a rudimentary state were bringing very few benefits to Sicilians.

Northern parliamentarians, preoccupied with locating Italy among the liberal democracies, had little interest in the South, being generally ignorant of the area and wary of its people. Sicilians, only six per cent of whom were literate in 1913, were hard put to tell the difference between earlier oppressors and the mounted police of northern Italy who came riding roughshod over them when summoned by the regime to suppress starving men, women and children petitioning for a living wage. The nightmare story of Partinico and Danilo Dolci illustrates how determinedly and successfully the regime converted Sicily into a fortress, viewing it as an invaluable power base from which the Church of Rome can gratify its continuing ambitions for global dominion.

38

Fortress Sicily has been shaped and sustained by achieving high levels of illiteracy, unemployment and poverty – all associated with repulsing productive investment and keeping the region pre-capitalist. Violence supersedes all other techniques employed to sustain a static agricultural society. The Church of Rome's divine purpose placing no limits on the means by which it achieves its ends, it does not shrink from violence in theory or practice, and its history, past and contemporary, offers innumerable precedents to the hierarchy if the pontifical will should falter.

The mafia, a loyal ally of the Church and the nobility, exercises a carefully calibrated reign of terror over the populace. Any voice raised in public against the regime can be stilled without a sound, without inquiry and without an eye blink or phone call from anyone, so enmeshed are the three institutions and so astute their appreciation of their common interests.

Among the earliest persons to record the origins of what became the mafia and its alarming integration with the civil power was Patrick Brydone, writing in 1770 to his friends, among them Fellows of the Royal Society, that Sicilian landowners unable to cope with banditry were recruiting bandits and putting them into livery, using them for defence against other bandits and to administer a crude kind of justice to peasants in dispute. The most sinister aspect of this development, according to Brydone, was that these liveried bandits had been observed 'to usurp the civil power.'

One villain in particular, he wrote, imprisoned for being among some who had dug up treasures buried during the plague – considered a heinous offence and always cruelly punished – had composed a letter to his prince arguing so powerfully in favour of the group, that the prince had its members set free.

'These bandits', said Brydone, 'are a horrid mixture of stubborn vice and virtue always "borrowing" money from the peasants, promising to repay it on a certain day and never failing to do so even if they have to kill and rob an innocent person to get the money. They call this "maintaining their honour".'

It was less the bandits' villainy that concerned Brydone, however, than their status in the community. 'They are universally feared and publicly protected... The magistrates have often been obliged to protect them and pay them court, for if provoked they can be determined, desperate and vindictive.'

In 1770 came slouching out of Sicily's interior a rival to whatever state should eventually evolve in Italy, a class of armed, aspiring, haughty peasants, pitiless though pious, greedy for power, thoroughly integrated with their community, their families supplying the Church with prelates, priests and nuns as well as enforcers and preparing the most beautiful of their daughters for marriage to the gentry.

That the mafia identifies itself with the Church and the gentry is evident in the adoption of 'don' by its leaders: Sicilians, themselves, even police and politicians make the connection, addressing all three, priests, nobles and mafia chiefs, as 'don'. Moreover, there's amazingly little difference between mafia and Church 'values', particularly when the Church sanitises mafia behaviour, referring to the organisation as a *malanno* meaning a minor irritation, mere 'sinners' like the rest of us. 'We all have mafia in us,' Sicilians will murmur hopelessly. 'What can we do?' Their confusion of crime with sin is fostered by the Church which has little interest in the concept of 'crime' as behaviour demanding punishment by a state especially now that members of the priesthood are being brought before the courts on charges of child sexual abuse.

The Church/mafia alliance became brazenly overt in the post-War period when Luigi Sturzo, a Sicilian aristocrat and priest-philosopher returned to Italy after sixteen years' exile abroad. In his writings he had urged the Church to become politically active, contribute to shaping the post-War constitution and participate in a modern Italian government. Sturzo had experienced living in multicultural, religiously-diverse Britain and the USA, discovering that although the USA was the most extreme example of liberal democracy in Christendom, more than half its population were Catholics who donated huge sums of money to the Church. If liberalism and prosperity could work to the Church's advantage in this way, in a country where church and state were constitutionally separated and where more money was spent on pure science than in any other country – might the Church not rethink its position on liberty and risk-taking, on the role of discovery and the benefits of rising to the challenges in life? Ingenuous, to say the least, was Sturzo, beatified but, as I write, still waiting to be canonised.

In Sturzo's version of Catholic 'liberal democracy', an oxymoron if ever there was one, laity, not clerics should stand for Parliament, because politicians must not be 'directly' responsible to the Vatican. Catholic laity, however, should seek to implement Catholic values in government. That left wide open the question of a role for an opposition, an alternative government in waiting, especially if the alternative should include elected members of the Communist Party who presumably did not espouse all Catholic values.

To resolve this problem, the mafia, its authority grandly legitimised by the American occupation forces who had seen fit to install its 'dons' as mayors in western Sicily, menaced or bribed Sicilians into voting for the Church party, the Christian Democrats. While victory was never total, for fifty years, thanks to the Sicilian vote in the national elections, Italy became a one-party state. Nor was the mafia slow to remind the Church that without its support the Christian Democrats would lose not only in Sicily but in the entire South. And who would counter the communist vote in the North? With its continuous re-election thus guaranteed, the Church party became prey to corruption of such magnitude as to cause its implosion, ultimately forcing the Church to dissociate itself from its own creation.

If the historically close alliance between Church and mafia should seem far-fetched David Yallop's amazing inquiry into the Vatican Bank scandal of the 1980s, published in his book, *The Power and the Glory*, casts further light on it. Yallop reveals that a suspect questioned by Italy's financial police evidenced that he had seen Bishop Paul Marcinkus, head of the Vatican Bank, take personal possession of bags of cash given him by a mafioso for deposit in the Bank, allegedly proceeds from drug trafficking. Four mafia clans, the suspect said, had accounts with the Church Bank. Italian courts ruled that the American prelate's Vatican passport gave him diplomatic immunity from charges to be laid against him and he returned to the United States. The significance of the event is that no mafioso would dream of approaching a Bishop of the Church with a bag of illicit cash if centuries of trust had not been forged between the two institutions.

To meet the enormous financial loss incurred by the Vatican Bank, in 1984 the Italian government imposed a compulsory income tax, the opt-out '*otto per mille*', 'eight euros in a thousand,' – of which many Italians are completely unaware – to restore the Bank's liquidity after the Church declared itself unable to pay clerical salaries. This tax alone transferred almost a billion euros to the Church in 2004, the last date revealed by the Ministry of Finance.

Not to be deterred by secular laws, the Vatican Bank – then headed by an Italian – was again being investigated for money laundering. On 21 September 2010, police reportedly responded to an alert from a division of the Bank of Italy that two major transactions involving the Vatican Bank were deemed suspicious.

Such scandals intensify the despair of many decent Italians, Sicilians especially. What can they do to change things? Why do they not speak out? Write letters to the paper? Form political clubs? They're too scared. Anyone living in Sicily would be scared. They don't raise their voices above a whisper because they live in a reign of terror that has been honed over three centuries. Troublemakers are so very, very easy to dispose of: high profile judges, senior military officers, rich and powerful bankers, journalists, prime ministers, police officers, even the rebel Pope, John Paul I – anyone who threatens the regime. Patrick Brydone foresaw it all.

39

Fear and Silence

The silence of street crowds and the quietude of individuals make a powerful impression on visitors to Sicily. People keep their voices low in bars, and conversations – even those conducted on cellphones – are off limits to eavesdroppers. Not once in almost a year did I hear anyone call out or speak loudly in public. Sicilians have been historically accustomed never to assist the authorities with inquiries. In the first instance these authorities were foreigners, but in contemporary times they are the alliance of mafia, church and gentry.

Apprehensions of being named as a witness will cause Sicilians to flee the scene of an incident for fear of being questioned. Even a busload of passengers who have watched a happening from their windows will claim to have been napping at the time. Within fortress Sicily citizens are entombed in silence generated by fear.

During a decade of investigations begun in the late 1970s into Vatican Bank machinations the following people were assassinated for assisting with the inquiry.

1. A Milan magistrate investigating the activities of Banco Ambrosiano wherein the Vatican was the major shareholder.
2. A journalist who first began publishing articles on the elite membership of P2, a group of freemasons involved with Vatican financial activities, subsequently declaring himself ready to spell out Prime Minister Giulio Andreotti's ties to the mafia.
3. A witness who gave testimony on connections between persons engaging in illegal financial practices and the head of the Vatican Bank.

4. The head of the Rome security service who was also investigating the Freemason group.
5. The head of Palermo's CID who was following a trail on the Vatican's money laundering activities.
6. A media director who had witnessed a threat made by a Vatican connection to someone later murdered.
7. The Director of Banco Ambrosiano.
8. A woman executive of Banco Ambrosiano, alleged to have fallen to her death from a window in the building.
9. A prison inmate involved in the banking scandal and suspected of complicity in two murders, that of Pope John Paul I and of a person prepared to assist the police inquiry into the Pope's murder. The imprisoned felon generated the apprehension that he would eventually speak out to secure a commutation of his sentence. He was administered a lethal dose of a poisoned espresso.

In addition, an official appointed to 'clean up' Banco Ambrosiano narrowly escaped assassination. Such terrorist acts are powerful forms of propaganda, inflating the mafia's apparent omniscience and omnipotence and strengthening the conviction that Church and laity are the mafia's silent partners in crime.

Giulio Andreotti, seven times Prime Minister of Italy, was widely rumoured to have 'given the nod' to the political murder of the former Prime Minister Aldo Moro. Evidence of his complicity with the mafia finally led to his arraignment on charges of being associated with the criminal organisation and of arranging the murder of a journalist. He attracted the nickname of 'Lavazza' because of his suspected role in the espresso poisoning of the imprisoned felon only just referred to.

After Andreotti was found guilty of the above charges and awaiting sentence, a cardinal writing in the Vatican *Observer* violently denounced the magistracy for having exceeded its constitutional remit. On appeal, Andreotti was acquitted of the journalist's murder. On the second charge, with being linked to the mafia, the Palermo court found that this leader of the Italian government who boasted of friendships with three United States' presidents was not only linked to the criminal organisation but had actually been a *member* of the mafia – 'pricked' as they say – and was assisted by the organisation in his political career until the late 1980s when he angered leaders by failing to get one of their group released from prison. The Court's finding, however, had subsequently to be set aside on statutory grounds.

Between the beginning of the 1970s and the early 1980s before the Vatican Bank inquiries had begun to gain momentum, an estimated 15,000-plus Italians were victims of terrorist bombings by both 'red' (communists) and 'black,' (neo-fascists) carried out in railway stations, banks, trains or wherever large numbers of people could be targeted. Numerous police officers were among the victims. At the funeral of one police officer a second bomb attack destroyed many of the mourners. The terror was largely funded by anti-communist groups inside and outside Italy and was intended as 'a stratagem of tension' meant to so unsettle the masses as to raise a call for a military coup and the restoration of authoritarian government.

In Sicily, parallel with all this violence on the peninsula, internecine street wars between mafia clans were being fought with hardly a respite – just a break or two to murder another journalist and then slaughter the famous anti-terrorist general of the Carabinieri, Alberto della Chiesa sent to Palermo to investigate that journalist's death. Seven journalists in fact were murdered over the decade.

If one combines the apprehensions generated by this out-of-control violence with the ever constant fear of losing one's job – think of Antonia's father, driven by his father's death in a work accident to scavenging for his own food in the fields in order to leave more for the family – the anxiety and silence that still engulf many ordinary Sicilians can be appreciated.

What role is there for intellectuals in such a society? They may not be familiar with the Great Chain of Being but its principles are embedded in their subconscious. Most academics, teachers, journalists, writers and other professionals steadfastly confine their interests and activities to family and friends. They travel, they entertain, they attend theatres and the cinema, they brood over finding positions for their children when they finish university, but they avoid public pronouncements and controversy. They try to accumulate property where they can, small holiday houses, or occasionally an agribusiness that might end up proving too difficult to maintain. While they would undoubtedly be better off in a free Sicily, they live in sufficient comfort to keep their opinions to themselves. As a class their development has been perverted by their small numbers and the absence of a literate public equivalent to that which developed in Protestant Europe.

When I first knew Rita she denied that the mafia existed in Catania. In her fifty-plus years, she assured me, she had never met a mafioso. That surprised me since I'm pretty sure I encountered one or two myself at functions. They're not exactly invisible. Silvana Cirrone, the philosophy professor, told me, 'we know their families.'

One teacher in a vocational high school professed to be so shocked by the manifestation of mafia-type behaviour among her male adolescent students that she could feel no cultural affinity with them. 'Who are Sicilians?' she asked. 'I don't know these people. We have nothing in common.' Another teacher involved with Catania's 'Legality Project' aimed at 'science' students in specialised high schools, said she had lost hope of getting her students involved in the project because 'their parents are all CDs [Christian Democrats]'.

That teacher, interestingly enough, seemed to have taken no account of two teenage rebels, now Sicilian icons, Peppino Impastato and Rita Atria, both in their mid-teens when they chose to revolt against their family/mafia culture and opt for a fairer, more law-abiding society.

In the year 2000 Catania Council produced a booklet reporting the findings of a 1997 inquiry into the murder of Giuseppe 'Peppino' Impastato in 1978, nineteen years earlier.

The booklet also recorded responses by middle-school students to a dramatisation of Impastato's revolt against the mafia culture he was born into. Few students appear to have known anything of his story until a screening of the film *I Cento Passi*, *The Hundred Steps*, became available. That could well be because for two decades Impastato's death was officially attributed to suicide and the political nature of his activities consequently trivialised.

Impastato was the adored, lively nephew of a major landowner and mafia chief based in Cinisi, a district of Palermo, relatively close to the city. He seems to have led the life of an indulged young prince until the age of fifteen when his uncle was car-bombed by a rival Mafioso; pieces of the uncle's body were later discovered stuck to lemon trees hundreds of meters from the bomb crater. The boy was heartbroken and revulsed by the betrayal implicit in the murder causing him to turn against the mafia and everything it stands for. At seventeen he produced a newsletter called *The Socialist Idea* later joining the Italian Socialist Party of Proletarian Unity under whose aegis he cooperated in organising student, peasant and worker uprisings.

At twenty-eight, the youth broke new ground as a social critic when he joined with other young people to self-fund a community radio station, Radio Aut, (*Out*) and used it to ridicule the mafia. Cinisi became the fictitious Mafiopoli ruled by Chief Sitting Bully, whom everyone knew to be Tano Badalamenti, the killer of Impastato's uncle. Not many comedians try raising a giggle out of the mafia but the film shows local *carabinieri* in their cars tuning into the program and doubling up with laughter. The satire, though often savage, was conveyed in an atmosphere of merriment, jokes and upbeat music.

It interested me that Leone Calambrogio, a priest and principal of a professedly state high school for science students authored the preface to the Catania booklet and was thanked by those who published the booklet for 'vetting' it. Was the priest a 'rebel' or a censor? Predictably he claimed Impastato as a 'martyr' but the teenager, after his uncle's murder, had in fact turned to a local communist artist for solace, trying unsuccessfully to persuade the artist to paint a portrait of his uncle. Later he appears to have seen himself as nothing more than a left-wing social reformer drawing on the tactics then being adopted by youth all over Europe to achieve political and economic change.

Impastato's father, a low-ranking mafioso who ran a grace-and-favour pizzeria owned by Badalamenti was strongly pressured to 'control' his son – something that proved impossible. So he did the unthinkable: kicked his son out of the house, in the face of his wife's tearful protests. However, he did journey to the United States to seek help from a powerful mafia relative who gave him a 'watch out' message to take back to Badalamenti. The latter derided the warning and not long afterwards Impastato senior met with an 'accident'.

Nothing now would deter Impastato from pursuing the path he had chosen. At thirty, he decided to stand for the Council and fight the corruption within it. When the election was only hours away mafia hit men picked him up, beat him to a pulp and then fastened him to a railway track before blowing his body up with dynamite. The police decided he had committed suicide (?) and no charges were laid. In 1997 the case was re-opened and Badalamenti was sentenced to life imprisonment for the murder.

Impastato's mother became the leader of an anti-mafia association. In an interview she revealed that when her husband was alive she was never ever allowed to leave the house except to accompany her husband when he visited the house of Badalamenti and his wife.

Rita Atria, four years old when Peppino Impastato died, was fifteen like him when she lost the most adored person in her little world, her father, a mafioso murdered by a rival. Seething with a desire for vengeance she was persuaded by her older brother, also a mafioso, to show patience. Their day would come. While awaiting that day Rita started keeping a diary recording everything that she observed and heard of mafia activity. Exactly why she took that decision is not made clear, but certainly she knew of the work being done by Falcone and Borsellino.

Two years later her brother was murdered. Grief and outrage drove the brother's wife to approach police working on the maxi-trials and offer to assist them with their inquiries. The wife became 'a witness for justice' a status given legislative standing ten years later in 2001. Rita, highly intelligent and spirited like Impastato, decided she also would break with *omertà* and volunteered an enormous contribution to the maxi-trial inquiry.

It's impossible to over-estimate the significance of that inquiry, prior to which no mafioso had ever been brought before a court. What made the maxi-trial possible was that Giovanni Falcone, one of the two Palermo judges working to bring the mafia to justice, finally succeeded in persuading a senior mafia chief to become an informer and provide conclusive evidence that the mafia was indeed an organisation with a defined corporate structure and a hierarchy of control, totally directed to pursuing criminal activity. This countered the Church's constant reiteration that the mafia did not exist, Ernesto Ruffini, once Archbishop of Palermo, having famously dismissed it as possibly a brand of soap-powder. The Church's current and pernicious endeavour is to convince Sicilians that 'mafia' is a mind-set characterising all Sicilians.

To demonstrate that it is an organisation dedicated to criminal objectives means that membership of the organisation is enough to convict a person and put them in gaol. Merely to associate with the organisation is a crime. On that basis Falcone and his fellow Palermitano, Paolo Borsellino, were able to prepare the maxi-trials that brought hundreds of mafia into the justice department for interrogation, with many divulging more and more information about the organisation's character and activities.

Inspired by her sister-in-law's action, Rita, so she later recorded, travelled to Rome carrying boxes filled with diaries and demanded to speak to Paolo Borsellino. She offered information in exchange for vengeance. Borsellino turned on her and brusquely expelled her from his office. It took some time before the girl could be brought to understand that justice, not revenge, was the true object of the mafia inquiries and that justice benefited the whole of society.

Borsellino was ecstatic when he eventually examined her meticulously kept records with their names, dates and events. However, the girl was horrified to learn that she would have no credibility with the court if she did not acknowledge her own father's mafia involvement and the murders he himself had committed. That would never happen, she said, but by then she had formed a dependency on Borsellino. The judge, himself the father of a teenage girl, admired Rita's feisty spirit and quick wit. He teased her, calling her 'the mafioso in a skirt'. At a crucial moment in the proceedings when it looked as if the trial was going to collapse and his work go for naught, Rita decided to speak up. She had finally realised that her father and brother were part of a system with no benefits to offer Sicilians, especially not the women. The most powerful mafia bosses in her district menaced her from the dock while she gave evidence involving them and her father. Along with many of their associates, they went to prison.

Rita's mother, a bitter woman who had tried to abort her daughter in the womb and was prevented by her husband, had always detested the girl. Steeped in mafia culture, on hearing Rita had given evidence in court she disowned her and cursed her, later smashing her tombstone to smithereens single-handedly with a hammer.

The teenager lived a solitary existence in Rome, with a new identity and a fictitious family history – she and her sister-in-law being in separate witness programs. Before the maxi-trials, *omertà* precluded any necessity for a 'witness for justice' or for the witness protection program that is now well developed. The legislation has spelled out levels of protection required – whether or not a fake identity must be maximally comprehensive or limited to only one or two documents. It also sets time limits on the protection offered – a maximum of five years before the program comes up for review. Mafia who are arraigned and seek plea bargaining, are criminals and can enter a 'collaborators' program' which organises protection inside and outside prison.

Rita and her sister-in-law were both fond of Borsellino, whom they called 'Zio', uncle. When he and six of his escort were car-bombed only two months after Giovanni Falcone, Italy was shocked but Rita was totally shattered. In her despair she contacted an old boyfriend, not knowing that he was rising rapidly within the mafia clan who had killed her relatives. He came to her 'safe house' in Rome and urged her to return to the village with him. He would marry her and guarantee her safety. All she had to do was retract everything she had told the courts and say that Borsellino had pressured her to lie.

But Rita knew what plans the mafia had for her. Writing in her diary to Borsellino, she mourned: 'you have died for what you believe in, but without you, I too am dead.' A week later, she climbed onto the balcony of her seventh floor flat and threw herself backwards into the street, leaving a note that said, 'Now there's no one to protect me. I'm scared and I can't take any more.'

Rita's sister-in-law, her daughter and a woman defector from another mafia family in the same district have since become prominent in the anti-mafia movement.

Neither Rita nor Peppino Impastato was seeking martyrdom. On the contrary. Each wanted to live, to help shape a decent society. Their actions show that moral resistance to the mafia is no longer unthinkable, while the anti-mafia associations generated by the teenagers' deaths are evidence that Sicilians are feeling their way towards a change in culture. Fear is still ever present in their lives, but silence is no longer total.

40

To become a lucky country

I'm imagining Sicily an open society where Church and State are now totally separate. CCTVs are prominently displayed at major intersections in Sicilian towns and cities. Shops and businesses have been subsidized to install and maintain CCTVs on their premises. Posters everywhere warn that extortion with menaces is a crime and conviction will attract severe penalties. Police are pounding the beat like the plods in those popular British or Danish crime shows that focus on routine policing. Traffic police and road patrols are highly visible.

Doctors and lawyers are coming under close scrutiny by the financial police and being deregistered if they fail to abandon their historic unlawful practices. Their names are appearing in the local press. Pharmacists are likewise losing their licences when they refuse to obey parliamentary legislation and supply all legal products. Non-prescription products are now sold freely in shops other than pharmacies.

The state has wrested control of the public health system away from the mafia and is making available scores of traineeships for nurses, midwives and community health specialists.

Since modernity is now pretty old, and because past experience cautions some modification of reformative practices, there will be no uncompensated expropriation of land and property from the Church, which has, however, been disestablished. It will now have to be totally self-funding. The $1 billion or more euros that go to it annually from the *otto per mille* levy has been retained by the state and used to purchase Church land and properties for redistribution as community service precincts, including libraries, public meeting rooms and sporting facilities. Land will be released for industry and for small but economically sustainable farms. Eventually the Church will no longer be a significant landowner in Sicily or a significant employer.

Productive capitalists, manufacturers and other business people are moving in freely. The economy in this new secular state is starting to rev. Exports are soaring as a top image-making firm promotes the contents of Etna's fabulous larder. The outside world can't get enough of its famous blood oranges and pistachio nuts. The *marrons glacés* from the volcano's 3,000-year-old chestnut trees have been taken up by cinema chains in China and are topping the list of moviegoer munchies. Mining companies seeking opportunities are surveying the mineral resources Etna keeps churning out. Modern technology may make it economic to reopen the sulphur mines.

The University of Pisa has set up a campus in Syracuse to oversee and implement modern school curricula but with a Sicilian emphasis. The value of a scientific education is being vigorously promoted to parents and teachers and vast sums of money are being spent on installing laboratories in high-schools, universities and teacher training institutes. Science teachers from overseas are being hired until a new generation of teachers is available to move into the classrooms. Literacy goals and a zero tolerance policy on school truancy are being promoted through the press and public meetings.

Jobs are popping up all over the place. Even high-school students are finding work after school. Capitalists and unionists are negotiating industry agreements. No more resorting to prayers in the piazza when a strike is called. Construction cranes, some boasting global names, are crowding the skyline and new, uniformed building inspectors by the score are scrambling over building sites to make sure safety regulations and building standards are being observed.

Of course, with the expansion of the Sicilian economy and removal of the massive constitutional privileges that have for so long sustained the temporal power of the Church, rival religions are becoming more visible and eager to publicly voice their interests. Communities of Muslims, Hindus, American Pentecostalists and Waldensians are all keen to build places of worship in Sicily and the land being no longer tied up by the Church of Rome, they are heavily involved in construction programs. Perhaps descendants of the ancient Jewish communities might even think of returning.

The advent of capitalism with the employment opportunities it opens up and its demand for a highly educated population will make it increasingly difficult for the Church and the mafia to recruit very young children to their cause.

Such a scenario may seem unduly optimistic given Sicily's current condition, forecast to worsen now that Milan's financial sector is being described as Italy's new Mafiopolis.

However, this may be just the crucial development required to prompt the major EU members to act on behalf of Sicilians, for the French, the Germans and the British, even the United States, must be aware that their institutions are not safely quarantined from the pernicious influences at work within Italy.

International human rights lawyers need to join with Sicilian activists to bring the Italian state before the European Court of Justice or the European Court of Human Rights and charge Italy with breaching either Article 4 of the Italian Constitution – its obligation to create facilities that will generate employment for all Italians able and willing to work, or Article 8 of the European Human Rights Convention for the Protection of Human Rights and Fundamental Freedoms wherein Article 8 focuses on the right to respect for private and family life.

The remedy will inevitably require the separation of Church and State and the complete expulsion of the Church from the temporal sector. Italians will no longer be *subjects* of the Church, but members, like other Catholics in such countries as Australia, Britain, France and the United States. The Church of Rome's long-standing and unrelenting resistance to modernity will finally be opened to European debate.

If a legal cause of this dimension seems fanciful, one need only advert to the Airey v. Ireland case, originating in 1973. The plaintiff was a middle-aged Irish shop assistant, mother of four children and separated by agreement from a husband who had subjected her for years to physical and mental abuse. Later, at the stage of being constantly drunken and unemployed, the husband was threatening to move back into the home. The Irish constitution forbade divorce, stating that "No law shall be enacted providing for the grant of a dissolution of marriage." Those able to afford legal representation could, however, obtain a judicially ordered separation. Airey's total income would have been insufficient for this and she had no access to legal aid. Finally, after refusals by several solicitors to represent her without payment, one practitioner decided to lodge an application on her behalf with the European Court of Justice. The woman's main complaint against Ireland was that the state had failed to protect her against physical and mental cruelty from her allegedly violent and alcoholic husband.

Ultimately the case became an important precedent for arguing that the right to legal aid is an integral part of human rights. It has also been cited to demonstrate that there are economic and social rights dimensions within civil and political rights and that states may have positive obligations with respect to civil and political rights.

Would anyone have imagined in 1973 that a poor Irish woman beaten up for years by an abusive husband, having no money and no social connections, could, with the help of a local solicitor bring her state before a judicial body and gain a decision whose international ramifications are still not fully worked out?

More recently books like Geoffrey Robertson's *The Case of the Pope: Vatican accountability for human rights abuse* reflect preparations now in train for class actions to bring Cardinal Ratzinger before the appropriate jurisdiction on a charge of ignoring numerous complaints of paedophilia among clerics, reported to him over twenty-five years by his bishops. His refusal to act, encouraged what Robertson says, by its scale, could be considered a human rights abuse equal to genocide.

Sicilians have 150 years of history weighing in as evidence of the appalling injustices they endure daily. Of course, claims cannot come before the European Court without the claimants' having had recourse to their domestic system of justice. But it can be strongly argued that no system of justice acceptable to other autonomous regions of the European Union has ever operated within Sicily since the Unification of Italy.

The opening up of Sicily and the demise of the Church-mafia alliance can only benefit all members of the European Union, especially those who contributed the eight billion euros to Sicily between 2000 and 2008 and are up for a similar amount in coming decades.

A thriving Sicilian economy functioning in a well-administered society means that visitors to the region need no longer try to conjure up the civilizing spirit of Greece and Rome from relics half-buried in the sand. With a bit of luck, that spirit will be everywhere in the air.

Bibliography

A selected bibliography associated with research into the writing of *Sicily, A Captive Land*. This formal reading was greatly augmented by many interviews with local citizens, attending concerts and public meetings and travelling widely in the region. MRL

Brancati, Vitaliano *Don Giovanni in Sicilia*, Bompiani, Milan, 1943. This edition published for L'Espresso, 1988.

Brydone, Patrick *Il grand tour:* a cura di Rosario Portale: Introduction, transcription, translation and notes. Agora, Lugano, 2011.

Brydone, Patrick *Viaggio in Sicilia e a Malta, 1770.* A cura di Rosario Portale. Agora, Lugano, 2005.

Camilleri, Andrea, *Il cane di terracotta,* Sellerio, Palermo, 2005.

Camilleri, Andrea *Il ladro di merendine*, Sellerio, Palermo 2005.

Camilleri, Andrea *La Vucciria Renato Guttuso*, Skira, Genevra/Milano 2011.

Camilleri, Andrea *August Heat* (trans. Stephen Sartarelli) Picador, London, 2,000.

Collura, Matteo *In Sicilia,* Longanesi, Milano, 2004.

Di Falcone, Giovanni *Cose di Cosa Nostra* (written in collaboration with Marcelle Padovani), Fabbri, Milano, 1994.

Di Lampedusa, Giuseppe Tomasi *The Siren & Selected Writings*, (trans. From the Italian by Archibald Colquhoun, David Gilmour and Waldman). Introductions by David Gilmour. Harvill, London, 1995.

Di Lampedusa, Giuseppe Tomasi , The Leopard, Vintage, London, 2005.

Di Lampedusa, Giuseppe Tomasi , *Letters from London and Europe, 1925-30.* Ed.by Giuseppe Tomasi di Lampedusa and Salvatore Nigro. (trans. J.G. Nichols). Alma Books, Richmond, 2011.

Dolci, Danilo *La forza della nonviolenza: bibliografia e profile biografico di Danilo Dolci*. (2nd ed. Expanded). Giorgio Barone. Nota di Norberto Bobbio. Libreria Dante& Descartes, Napoli, 2004.

Dolci, Danilo (documentary film). *Danilo Dolci, Memory and Utopi*a. Stone Theatre (production). Director, Alberto Castiglione. Palermo, 2004.

Dryden, John JR. *Un viaggio in Sicilia e a Malta nel 1770-1701*. A cura di Rosario Portale. Agora, Napoli, 1999.

Dumas, Alexandre *La Cappella gotica*. A cura di Giuseppe Merlino. Palermo, Sellerio, 1990.

Farrell, Joseph *Sicily, a cultural history*, Oxford, Signal, 2012.

Goethe, Johann Wolfgang *Italian Journey*. Translated, with an introduction by W.H. Auden and Elizabeth Mayer. Penguin Classics, London, 1970.

Granozzi Luciano e Signorelli Alfio, a cura. *Lo sguardo dei consoli: La Sicilia de meta ottocento nei dispacci degli agenti francesi.* Agora, Napoli, 2001.

Hack, Margherita *In Piena Liberta e Consapevolezza: vivere e morire da laici* (con Nicla Panciera) Baldini & Castoldi, Milano, 2013.

Jones, Tobias *The Dark Heart of Italy,* revised edition, Faber,London, 2003.

La Pira, Giorgio *Il grande lago di Tiberiade:* lettere di Giorgio La Pira per la pace nel Mediterraneo (1954-1977) Polistampa, Firenze, 2006.

Lewis, Norman *In Sicily*, Picador, London, 2000

Lo Bello, Nino *The Vatican Empire*, Trident Press, Cape Town, 1969.

Mack Smith, Denis. Modern Italy, A Political History, Yale University Press, London, 2003.

Maxwell, Gavin, *God Protect me from my Friends,* Longmans, Green, London 1957.

Maxwell, Gavin The ten pains of death: a vivid portrait of the people of modern Sicily, Dutton, New York, 1960.

Pirandello, Luigi, *Luigi Pirandello: sei personaggi in cerca d'autore, Ciascuno a suo modo e Questa sera si recito a soggetto.* La Biblioteca Editrice, Milan, 1995.

Radcliffe, Ann *A Sicilian Romance,* , The Folio Society, London, 1987.

Robb, Peter *Midnight in Sicily,* Duffy and Snellgrove, Sydney, 1996.

Robertson, Geoffrey QC *The case of the Pope: Vatican accountability for Human Rights Abuse* A Penguin Special, London, 2010.

Sciascia, Leonardo, *Il giorno della civetta,* Adelphi,Milano, 1993.

Sciascia, Leonardo, Equal Danger (trans. From Italian, Adrienne Foulke). Intro by Carlin Romano) NY Review of Books, New York, 2003.

Sciascia, Leonardo, *The Moro Affair* (intro. By Peter Robb) and *The Disappearance of Majorana* (trans. By Sacha Rabinovitch. NY Review of Books, New York, 2004.

Sciascia, Leonardo, *Il Contesto: una parodia.* Feltrinelli, Milano 2005.

Simone, Rita *La Citta di Messino tra norma e forma*, Gangemi, Roma, 1996.

Smecca, Paola Daniela *Representational Tactics in Travel Writing and Translation:* a focus on Sicily, Carocci, Roma,2005.

Sturzo, Luigi *La Vera Vita: Sociologia del soprannaturale.* Vivere In, Roma, 2006.

Swinburne, Henry *Viaggio nelle due Sicilie negli anni 1770-1780.* A cura di Maria Grazia Nicolosi. Agora, Catania, 2000.

Taylor, Richard *How to read a churc*h Rider, London,2004.

Verga, Giovanni *Tutte le novella: volume secondo.* Oscar Classici Mondadori, Milano, 2006.

Verga, Giovanni *I Malavoglia*, Brancato, Milano, 2003.

Verga, Giovanni *Little Novels of Sicily,* Penguin Modern Classics, Harmondsworth, 1973.

Vittorini, Elio *Conversazione in Sicilia,* Biblioteca Universale Rizzoli *(I Grandi Romanzi)* 2006.

Watson, Lorna *The Errant Pen:* (A bibliography). *Manuscript journals of British travelers to Italy, 16th to 20th centuries.*, Agora, La Spezia, 2000.

Yallop, David *In God's name: an investigation into the murder of Pope John Paul*Bantam, London, 1984.

Zavattiero, Carlotta *Le Lobby del Vaticano: I gruppi integralisti che frenano la rivoluzione di Papa Francesco.* Chiarelettere, Milano, 2013.

Institutional publications

Ettore Majorana: a cento anni della nascita, nei giorni dello scomparso. Produced by the Province of Catania's Department of Tourism. 2006.

Cattivi ragazzi Catanesi ed. Elio Camilleri Published for Sicilian high schools by Sicily's Department of education. Catania, 1999.

Catania e il suo monastero, S. Nicolo l'Arena 1846, Maimone, Catania, 2001.

(The) Historical Museum of (the) Military Landing in Sicily, summer 1943 Le Nuove Muse, Catania, 2004. For The Regional Province of Catania.

*The Houses of Lava: a historical outline and description of the traditional buildings of Et*na. Funded by the European Union and published under the auspices of the Regional Province of Catania, 2001.

Peppino Impastato Finalmente ed. Elio Camilleri Published for Sicilian high schools by Catania's Department of Culture. Catania, 2001.

Un progetto per Catania: Il recupero del Monastero di San Nicolo l'Arena per l'Universita degli studi Catania. Sagep, Genova, 1988.

Tesori Mafiosi confiscati ed. By Elio Camilleri. Published for Sicilian high schools by Sicily's Department of Education.

Viaggi d'autore (Le vie del mondo) An anthology of writings about Sicily, published for the Italian Touring Club and curated by Marco Ausenda and Gianni Guadalupi. Milan, November, 1999.